Exploiting knowledge in health services

Edited by
Graham Walton and Andrew Booth

facet publishing

Published by
Facet Publishing
7 Ridgmount Street
London WC1E 7AE

Facet Publishing (formerly Library Association Publishing) is wholly owned by CILIP: the Chartered Institute of Library and Information Professionals.

First published 2004

British Library Cataloguing in Publication Data
A catalogue record for this book is available from the British Library.

ISBN 1-85604-479-3

Typeset from editors' disks by Facet Publishing in 11/13 Elegant Garamond and Humanist 521.
Printed and made in Great Britain by MPG Books Ltd, Bodmin, Cornwall.

Contents

Contributors

The editors

Graham Walton PhD BSc(Hons) MA MBA MCLIP started his work in health information and libraries 25 years ago in the Highland Health Sciences Library in Inverness, Scotland. He moved to Northumbria University in 1980 where he has undertaken a variety of roles. There are two main aspects to his current work at Northumbria University. As Research Fellow in the School of Informatics he manages research projects and is involved in a range of dissemination activities. He also has a role in the Learning Resources department where he oversees a large campus library and the library and information service it delivers to over 7000 health students. His PhD was concerned with exploring both the pressures for flexibility as well as the impact of flexibility on higher-education libraries. He is currently managing the Health eXL research project identifying the barriers to e-learning in health and how to overcome them. Another recent research project he has overseen is the HENSAL study that explored the use of learning resources by health students on placement in the NHS. Along with a contributor to this book (Susan Childs), in 2003 he was awarded by the National Information Forum for the successful JUDGE project that developed guidelines for self-help groups to evaluate and produce web-based health information. He has also recently completed a national survey of further education college libraries for the Chartered Institute of Library and Information Professionals. During 2002 and 2003 he was seconded to the North East Museums and Archives Council (NEMLAC) as Library Strategy Adviser where he was involved in producing their regional development programme, Libraries Leading the Way.

From 2003, he has been the Editor of the *Health Information and Libraries Journal*, the official journal of the Health Libraries Group. In 2003 he gave papers at international conferences in Turkey, Germany and Scotland. He is a member of the University Health Sciences Libraries executive committee. He is also Secretary for the Continuing Professional Development and Workplace Learning (CPDWL) Section of the International Federation of Library Associations (IFLA). Along with Andrew Booth, Graham was the joint editor for the companion volume to this book, *Managing Knowledge in Health Services*.

Andrew Booth BA(Hons) MSc Dip Lib MCLIP has 20 years' experience as a health information professional, since 1994 at the School of Health and Related Research (ScHARR), University of Sheffield, as Director of Information Resources and Senior Lecturer in Evidence Based Healthcare Information. His current brief is to support evidence-based healthcare within the University of Sheffield and Trent Region. An experienced trainer of end-users and NHS librarians in literature searching and critical appraisal, Andrew has developed and delivered the ADEPT course on applying evidence-based principles to literature searching in six NHS regions. Having attended the first ever UK Workshop in Teaching Evidence Based Medicine in Oxford, Andrew has subsequently tutored at three Northern and Yorkshire Evidence Based Practice Workshops in Durham. Andrew recently piloted three e-learning courses for NHS librarians for the NeLH Librarian Development Programme under the banner of the Facilitated Online Learning Interactive Opportunity (FOLIO) Programme.

Andrew is on the editorial boards of *Evidence Based Healthcare* and the *Health Information and Libraries Journal* (formerly *Health Libraries Review*). He chairs the Health Libraries Group Research Working Party and, in this role, contributes the quarterly 'Using Research in Practice' column to the *Health Information and Libraries Journal (HILJ)*. Andrew has been involved in organizing both the first Evidence Based Librarianship Conference in Sheffield (September 2001) and the second Evidence Based Librarianship Conference in Edmonton, Canada (June 2003). A keen writer, he has co-edited *Managing Knowledge in Health Services* (2000, with Graham Walton), *Evidence-based Practice for information professionals: a handbook* (2003, with Anne Brice) and a special issue of *HILJ* on Evidence Based Health Information Practice (2003, with Jonathan Eldredge).

The contributors

Steve Ashwell graduated in librarianship and information studies from UCE Birmingham in 1992. He has worked as a health information professional for 11 years at local and regional level in the NHS and higher education. He has held the posts of Purchasing Intelligence Project Officer, Librarian, Health Informatics Projects Officer and Acting Assistant Director of Knowledge and Information Sciences for the Public Health Resource Unit in Oxford. Currently he is Information Specialist with the National electronic Library for Health, with a particular interest in resource management systems, the e-Government Metadata Standard and interoperability between public health organizations.

John Blenkinsopp is the Lead Librarian at North Tees and Hartlepool NHS Trust based in Stockton on Tees. He is also a trainer in critical appraisal and evidence-based healthcare and is currently a Tutor in Health Informatics. Previously, John was a business specialist with the *Financial Times* and the BBC. He then moved to healthcare librarianship as a subject specialist at Manchester Metropolitan University and the Robert Gordon University, Aberdeen. Current research interests include barriers to library services and training in critical appraisal.

Janette Boynton is the Senior Health Information Scientist at NHS Quality Improvement Scotland. A key responsibility of the post is the undertaking of systematic literature searches for health-technology assessments and other evidence-based products, to support the organization in its role of providing advice and guidance to NHS Scotland on effective clinical practice and service improvements. Previous posts include Faculty Team Librarian at the University of Leeds and Information Officer at the NHS Centre for Reviews and Dissemination.

Anne Brice has held a range of posts in university and NHS libraries, and is currently Head of Knowledge and Information Sciences at the Public Health Resource Unit, Oxford. She is seconded to the National electronic Library for Health, where she is responsible for the Specialist Libraries programme, building knowledge networks and communities of practice around specialist healthcare domains. Anne developed the CASP Funding the Evidence training programme for enhancing the teaching and learning skills of librarians, and has a long-held interest in continuing professional development. Other professional interests include knowledge communities, e-learning in evidence-based healthcare, and evidence-based information practice. She is on the editorial board of *Hypothesis*.

Susan Childs is a Research Associate at the Information Management Research Institute (IMRI), School of Informatics, Northumbria University. Her interests are health information; evidence-based practice, particularly systematic reviews; user needs; the needs of the public; ICT, information and critical/-

evaluative skills; public understanding of health; information planning. She has been involved in research for many years; her initiation was the Clinical Librarianship project at Guy's Hospital, London, in 1978/80. She is Editor of *He@lth Information on the Internet*, published by the Royal Society of Medicine.

Jo Cooke is the local co-ordinator and social-care lead for Trent Focus, a Primary Care Research Support Unit funded by the Department of Health. Jo initially trained as a nurse at the University of Manchester, and held a variety of clinical posts in primary care. She was the lead research nurse for Community Health Sheffield in the mid-1990s and became a Research Fellow at ScHARR (School for Health and Related Research) during this time. Subsequently she held the position of Associate Director for Research in Practice (an Association of Directors for Social Services initiative intended to develop evidence-based practice in social care), based at the Department of Sociological Studies, University of Sheffield, between 1998 and 2001. During her time with Trent Focus she has worked to promote knowledge management at the interface between health and social care organizations. She chairs the SCARE (Social Care Access to Research Evidence) group which is working with SCIE and other evidence-based practice organizations to utilize research evidence at the health and social care interface.

Sharon Dobbins is the Knowledge Services Manager at the County Durham and Tees Valley Workforce Development Confederation. She provides strategic leadership for NHS library and information services in the area, and works on projects to improve partnership working and seamless access to high-quality resources and services. Prior to this, she worked in the academic sector as well as with the British Council before she took up her first post in health libraries as Trust Librarian at City Hospitals Sunderland.

Maria J. Grant a has a background in information science and provides litera-ture-searching advice and support within the Salford Centre for Nursing, Midwifery and Collaborative Research (SCNMCR), University of Salford. This includes supporting systematic reviews into health and social care practice and policy. Her research interests include enhancing practice through the investigation of optimal database searching, particularly in relation to qualita-tive research evidence. Maria is Chair of IFM Healthcare, a charitable organi-zation committed to improving the provision of information in enhancing healthcare management and delivery.

Angela Gunn is Information Resources Manager at the Health Care Libraries, University of Oxford. Previous posts include Reader Services Librarian at UMDS

Guy's and St Thomas' Hospitals and Site Manager at the St Thomas' Campus, King's College London. She has worked in healthcare libraries for many years. Her main experience has been in literature searching, user education and developments in electronic resources for users.

Susannah Hanlon joined the School of Informatics at Northumbria University in September 2000 having taught for nine years at Newcastle College. Main subject areas lie in ICT, information storage and retrieval, and data law and ethics. Research interests include legislation and ethics surrounding the handling of information, electronic publishing and e-learning.

Sue Lacey Bryant is Knowledge Manager to the Vale of Aylesbury Primary Care Trust. She draws on wide experience of working with healthcare teams, both within the NHS as a health educator and as an independent information specialist working principally with general practices. Sue has a particular interest in professional development issues. Committed to enabling colleagues to put knowledge to use in the workplace, Sue is familiar to many UK doctors as The Online Librarian. She is now Medical Knowledge Manager for Doctors.net.uk.

Valerie Monaghan is currently Learning Environment Manager with South Yorkshire Workforce Development Confederation in Sheffield. This role includes the strategic development of NHS library and information services, and clinical skills centres across South Yorkshire. Prior to that Valerie led on training, education and development of library staff across the former Trent health region. Valerie's career in the NHS began in 1993 when she set up one of the first health authority library services in England. It was during this time that her work around supporting access to information for primary-care staff began. This has since developed into an interest in supporting those who work at the health and social care interface, and she is involved in the SCARE group (Social Care Access to Research Evidence). Valerie's career as a librarian, however, began in the private sector where she worked for BP Chemicals for six years. Following this Valerie took up a post at Strathclyde University Library, and then spent some time working in local government.

David Peacock has worked in libraries across the health, higher education and public sectors. He has a masters degree in business information systems from Northumbria University. He is currently Knowledge Services Manager in the NHS Northern Workforce Development Confederation. David previously worked in the Northern and Yorkshire NHS Regional Library Advisory Service. His specific expertise and interests are around the delivery of electronic learning resources to NHS staff and students.

Susan Roe has a postgraduate diploma in Health Informatics taken at Sheffield University, and has worked for the NHS for five years providing information services to colleagues within the North Wales area. Three years ago Sue was given the task of developing a new all-Wales service, providing up-to-the-minute health-intelligence monitoring, in particular relating to documents produced by the Welsh Assembly Government, to NHS organizations throughout Wales. The Welsh Assembly Health Information Monitoring Service (WAHIMS) has a website hosted by the Health of Wales Information Service (HOWIS) and provides daily electronic alerts, via e-mail, to designated people within the various NHS organizations within Wales: these are then cascaded down to relevant personnel.

Steve Rose has 15 years' experience working in academic libraries supporting health-service research, healthcare management and medicine. He is currently Head of Health Care Libraries at Oxford University. Steve is also a committee member of CILIP's Health Libraries Group (HLG). Steve directed the HLG's 2002 conference in Edinburgh and also has overall responsibility for the 2004 conference in Belfast. Steve is particularly interested in issues relating to continuing professional development, and in developing electronic access to resources for users.

David Stewart was appointed Director of Health Libraries North West in June 1999. Previous posts include Director of Information Services at the Royal Society of Medicine and Deputy Director of Health Libraries in the Oxford Region. David has a first degree in medieval and modern history from Birmingham University and qualified as a librarian in 1981 at Birmingham Polytechnic.

Alison Turner has worked in the health-library field since qualifying in 1994. Alison's current post, as Library Partnership Co-ordinator for the National electronic Library for Health, involves liaising with the health-library community, setting up partnership projects and promotional work. Previously, Alison worked at Gloucestershire Hospitals NHS Trust, the School of Health and Related Research (ScHARR) at the University of Sheffield, and the University of Wales College of Medicine.

Alison Winning is Clinical Effectiveness Information Specialist, Doncaster and Bassetlaw Hospitals NHS Trust, Doncaster. She began her career as Research Support Information Officer for the Trent Institute for Health Services Research at ScHARR, during which time she provided a research-funding information service to academic and NHS staff. Currently Alison is providing a clinical-effectiveness information service across the Doncaster and Bassetlaw health communities, in which her professional interests, such as the implementation of research in practice and clinical librarianship, are particularly relevant.

Alison Yeoman is Research Officer at the University of Wales, Aberystwyth. She moved into information research from the medical publishing industry and has worked on several health-related projects including two evaluations of the National electronic Library for Health. Alison combines her current post with studying for a PhD focusing on information needs during the menopause.

Introduction

Health has a high profile in everybody's life. An individual's prime concern is to ensure that the quality of their own health and that of friends and family continues to be of high standard. Health is used as the basis for entertainment on television with programmes such as *ER* and *Holby City*. Documentaries investigating the latest health scandal or medical breakthrough are also given a high profile. Every day, newspapers include health reporting both as front-page headlines and in the later pages. For example, a random copy of *The Times* selected in September 2003 covered such diverse areas as the lack of research into the treatment for infertility, the personalities and characteristics of doctors, the impact of number dyslexia on children, the increase in sexually transmitted diseases and the need for screening, and trade union discontent about the use of private funding for new hospital buildings.

In such a diverse and rapidly changing sector as health, the knowledge base is also continually altering and evolving. In 2000, the editors of this book assembled the multi-authored title, *Managing Knowledge in Health Services*. The purpose of that book was to define and investigate the context, principles and practical skills needed to effectively manage the knowledge base of healthcare. It is a reflection of the turbulent health sector that, within three years of this first book appearing, there has been a pressing need for a companion book. This book is specifically not a new edition of *Managing Knowledge in Health Services*. In the intervening period, health has been changed fundamentally across all spectrums – politically, technologically, sociologically and financially. Librarians have had to acquire new skills to deliver new services to meet these changes. This new book therefore fulfils the broad general purpose of *Managing Knowledge in Health Services*. This first title is out of print but is freely available at www.shef.ac.uk/~scharr/mkhs. The two titles are complementary and provide an overview and analysis of the skills and services needed in libraries serving health professionals.

The structure and approach demonstrated in *Managing Knowledge in Health Services* have been retained. The book is divided into three separate parts. Part 1 provides the contextual background to healthcare and health information services. This includes a chapter giving a broad overview of some of the current developments shaping healthcare. The blurring of the health and social interface is examined as well as the impact of clinical governance. Developments such as the National electronic Library for Health and virtual outreach services are explored. There are chapters devoted to the opportunities arising from such factors as knowledge management, clinical librarianship and the education and training of clinicians.

Part 2 focuses on the principles required for effective delivery of services in a health library or information unit. There are chapters on managing projects, collaborative working, change management and staff development. The final three chapters in this part consider delivering hybrid services, creating portals and gateways and managing intellectual property.

In Part 3 the information sources and skills needed to effectively exploit the healthcare knowledge base are examined. The first chapter in this part identifies the wide range of evidence in health. The skills needed to effectively appraise the literature are also considered. Techniques necessary for the creation of effective web pages are described. The remaining chapters in this part explore funding sources and the process of undertaking systematic reviews.

The final section in this book, 'Conclusion: new roles and new challenges' allows the editors the opportunity to forecast future potential developments for healthcare librarians and information workers. The intention has always been for this book, like its companion volume, to be of use to all library and information services providers and students in health. Many of the chapters are also relevant to those working or studying outside the health sector.

Acknowledgements

The editors would like to thank all authors for their enthusiasm, commitment and willingness to share their expertise in their writing. Rebecca Casey at Facet Publishing has always provided prompt and accurate advice when the editors have needed it. Finally, the patience, understanding and stoicism shown by our respective wives and children should be acknowledged.

Graham Walton and Andrew Booth

Part 1
The context of managing the knowledge base in health services

1

New structures and principles in health services

Graham Walton

Introduction

In the four years since the companion volume (Booth and Walton, 2000) to this title was first published, the fast rate of change in health has continued apace. The approach taken in Walton (2000) has again been applied in identifying broad sociological, technological, economic and political trends. This chapter provides a perspective on what is shaping the health sector in 2004; it is informed by a workshop (Herman, 2003) organized by the United Kingdom's Chartered Institute of Library and Information Professionals (CILIP). This workshop identified key issues facing health librarians.

Sociological
Patient empowerment

Probably the most significant recent trend has been the pressure for empowering patients, stimulated in the United Kingdom by publication of the Bristol inquiry report (Secretary of State for Health, 2001). This report reveals an 'organisational failure of foresight based on a series of systemic and communication failures which contributed to oversight of an incubating hazard which led to disaster' (Alaszewski, 2002). The report acknowledges a defining moment in health and social care (Smith, 1998) and its recommendations are intended to improve confidence by enhancing public involvement through empowerment. This requires both respect and honesty for users and carers. Direct involvement with the public is seen as a mechanism for breaking down a defensive and insular culture.

This trend to adopt a client-centred, patient-empowered approach is characterized by patients wanting to be better informed and better educated (White, 2002). Patients will have less free time to receive treatment, be less deferential, and want more control and choice. They expect treatment to be safe and of high quality. Active participation by patients is significant in achieving better care and greater satisfaction (NHS Executive, 1999). However, many clinicians continue to treat patients as 'passive recipients rather than as equal partners in their own treatment and care' (Kendall and Lissauer, 2003).

Within libraries, an emphasis on undertaking user needs' analyses is similarly aimed at ensuring that the customer is at the centre of service developments. Project teams working on developing new library and information services (LIS) gain added value from active library user involvement.

Health clinician roles and working practices

This shift in the role of the patient is mirrored by changes within the healthcare team. Political, environmental and professional pressures have, in the United Kingdom at least, included the reduction in junior doctors' working hours, recruitment and retention problems and government targets for health outcomes. The NHS Plan (Secretary of State for Health, 2000) emphasizes the need to review and develop the scope and levels of practice, thereby having a significant impact on the nursing profession (Jones, 2003; Daly and Carnwell, 2003). Job titles such as clinical nurse specialist, nurse practitioner, advanced nurse practitioner; higher-level practitioner and nurse consultant have been adopted, often with little understanding or consensus as to the nature of, or differences between, such roles. Related initiatives are exploring the role of a generic health worker who can undertake activities previously divided among different health professionals.

Changes in roles are accompanied by pressures for clinicians to develop different working practices. Multidisciplinary teamwork encourages nurses to work in partnership with domestic and support staff to improve the ward environment. This 'new professionalism' embraces care based on 'shared practice, knowledge and values rather than differences based on jealously guarded systems of regulation, education and pay' (Kendall and Lissauer, 2003). Different professional groups need to develop new ways of working together, including adopting roles as local change agents to influence and improve service provision (Wanless, 2001).

Librarians must keep abreast of such changes and revise and develop information services to accommodate these developments. It will become increasingly difficult to justify providing different services to different user groups. Libraries also need to stock materials around change management and related management areas.

Collaboration and partnership

In writing about the so-called 'Third Way' (an alternative to socialism and capitalism), Giddens (1998) identifies a duty to collaborate and to link quality and equity with efficiency and permanence (Macdonald and Smith, 2001). These challenges focus on partnership working. The pressure to work more collaboratively was enforced by the NHS Plan (Secretary of State for Health, 2000) which signalled the integration of primary health and social care services within one organization called a care trust. As primary care and social services sectors become more closely integrated LIS will have to adapt to reflect new partnerships with new working styles. For effective collaboration organizations and professionals need to have common, achievable goals (Rummery and Coleman, 2003).

The competitive ethos that pervaded the 1980s and early 1990s is slowly eroding. Partnership working is one way to bring in expertise and skills not currently present in an organization. Within health, collaborative work is going on between the NHS, the higher education sector, voluntary agencies, charities and the commercial sector. As Chapter 11 attests, collaboration and joint working have obvious implications for the development and delivery of future LIS.

Ageing population

Across the world, governments are ill prepared to cope with the growing ageing population. In Japan, by 2025, 26% of the population will be over 65 with the percentage of the national income spent on the elderly rising from 2.5% to 10%. Numbers of people aged 75 and over continue to increase at the highest rate (Hardey et al., 2001). By 2031 there will be an estimated 34,000 people in the United Kingdom over 100 (a 425% increase since 1994).

The same trends are common to many countries: people are healthier, live longer and demand better medical care. Diseases such as Alzheimer's, dementia and osteoarthritis will become more prevalent as the number of elderly people rises. The economic impact of these trends for governments includes a surge in numbers of people seeking surgery for advanced-stage osteoarthritis (such as hip and knee replacements). Governments need to meet the escalating costs of treating these diseases. Librarians will witness an increased demand for material on all aspects of care for the elderly as increasing numbers of clinicians become involved in geriatrics.

Globalization

Globalization is another factor which has impacted on health. Evans (2002) has explored different interpretations of the term 'globalization', placing the 'borderless world' at the centre of globalization where 'internationalization, interdependence and universilization' are key concepts. New global economic, financial, social, cultural and political links bring societies and nations into increasingly closer contact (Banta, 2001). With global travel growing from 25 million passengers in 1950 to 500 million in 1993, and estimated to reach 1 billion by 2010 (Rodriguez-Garcia, 2001), the spread of old, new and re-emerging infectious diseases will intensify. Globalization involves the creation of links among corporations, international organizations, governments, communities and families (Waters, 2001).

As a result of globalization, librarians will encounter an increasingly international health-worker population. Some will have limited English-language ability and will expect access to professional information in their own language. Libraries will require staff who can meet these needs. This adds a further imperative to the need for effective staff-development programmes.

Technological

Biological warfare

Although there is little evidence to indicate that biological warfare and bioterrorism are prevalent the terrorist attack on the United States in September 2001 has made the threat of biological warfare a predominant concern for most Western governments. Infectious diseases have been used as weapons for many years. Biological-warfare agents are cheap and easy to obtain and disperse – even a small volume of an agent can cause high morbidity and mortality. The resulting public panic and social disruption can multiply the impact. As Western governments try to establish the best approaches to possible bioterrorism attacks theoretical exercises have revealed logistic weaknesses and false assumptions in treatment and prevention strategies (Beeching, Dance and Miller, 2002). The challenge is for libraries to make information on such threats available to health professionals in a timely fashion, if and when needed.

Pandemics

In recent years pandemics have had a major impact on many aspects of life. The most recent of these was the severe acute respiratory syndrome (SARS) that originated in China and resulted in a death toll of 770. While this outbreak now seems to be contained (Spread of SARS Slows, 2003), pandemics, such as SARS and AIDS, have a devastating effect on many, especially in developing countries (Stephenson, 2003). As of the end of 2002, 42 million people worldwide were infected with HIV, the virus that causes AIDS. In many countries, the loss of farm workers to AIDS has caused food shortages and potential famines. New diseases can appear very quickly with wide-ranging implications for the world. Media involvement is increasingly influential on the nature and level of impact of such diseases.

In many ways, libraries are central to ensuring that health professionals and health-service users develop a realistic understanding of these pandemics. Information that is balanced, clearly presented and grounded in scientific evidence often needs to counterbalance information produced by the media.

Electronic patient records

There appear to be many advantages in moving to an electronic patient record. Computers can manage care co-ordination and documentation and electronic patient record systems can monitor care (Safran, 2001). This frees clinicians to concentrate on interpersonal interactions and the provision of healthcare. Progress can be updated collaboratively via the shared electronic patient record with such records allowing access from a range of locations. Morgan (2003) defines an electronic patient record as the 'universal or longitudinal integration of all historical patient medical data, such as test results or drug allergies, into a single, secure electric record available to care providers from hospital to GP surgeries to community care facilities'.

At a theoretical level, the electronic patient record should lead to greater operational efficiency, but a recent conference (Electronic Records Target Unlikely, 2003) predicted that the government would miss its target of giving each patient an electronic record by March 2005 (Secretary of State for Health, 2000). Problems abound in the wholesale introduction of the electronic record. For example, a state-of-the-art £1140 million electronic patient record project in the West of England to produce records for 11 million people was recently aborted (Rogers, 2003). Various cultural issues must be addressed when introducing electronic patient records. Clinicians need to be involved from conceptual design through to implementation and maintenance. Relevance to practice and tangible benefits must be established. The developed interface must be easy to use and have a very fast response time. Having a powerful champion and advocate is also beneficial. Morgan (2003) reports that acceptance can come from demonstrating that an electronic patient record allows the reduction of medical errors, improvement of patient care and the saving of time. It is possible that a combination of newly educated health professionals with computer skills and healthcare consumers who demand digitally enhanced quality will drive through the adoption of the technology (Safran, 2001).

Electronic patient records provide opportunities for library services. Using information and communication technologies (ICT), electronic library services can be delivered in tandem with the electronic record. Lessons learnt in moving to electronic delivery of the patient record also have parallels when developing electronic library services.

Health informatics and evidence based practice

Georgiou (2001) argues that health informatics is the very engine room driving evidence-based practice (EBP). Clinicians must have access to the best available evidence to reduce uncertainties associated with clinical decisions (Thompson, McCaughan and Callum, 2001). Without access to high-quality research knowledge, evidence-based decision making is not possible. EBP involves 'integration of individual clinical expertise with the best available external clinical evidence from systematic research' (Sackett et al., 1996). Practitioners perceive a lack of access to systematic research, often cited as a reason why some professional groups fail to use this material (Thompson, McCaughan and Callum, 2001).

Evidence-based practice needs robust clinical information systems to ensure its success. Health informatics is defined as a discipline that integrates biomedical sciences, computer sciences and healthcare policy, management and organization (Georgiou, 2001). Advances such as online databases, the world wide web, e-journals and e-books have improved communications and spurred the development of EBP. The delivery of the National electronic Library for Health (NeLH) is covered in depth elsewhere in this book. As Turner et al. (2002) state, a key function of NeLH is to provide fast and easy access to evidence-based information to assist decision making. The challenge for the future is to integrate the electronic patient record with access to evidence provided by NeLH. Providing the information is not enough: work is also needed to ensure health professionals have basic computer skills as well as specific knowledge of available resources (Griffiths and Riddington, 2001). Distinctions between the roles of the health informaticist and the LIS professional will become increasingly blurred.

A major development in the United Kingdom has been the provision of 'NHS Direct Online' (Jenkins and Gann, 2003). This service is intended to increase citizens' access to health information and care services. Straightforward health information needs are answered by this service and its development focus has targeted a personalized, individual service for users.

Economic

The costs of healthcare always raise considerable controversy. The two core issues (rationing and cost containment) are considered elsewhere (Walton, 2000), but recent high-profile economic issues have included cost effectiveness and public–private initiatives.

Cost effectiveness

Economic evaluation compares the costs and consequences of one treatment against the costs and consequences of at least one other. Classic cost effectiveness involves achieving the same results more cheaply. Information is needed on both the resource use (costs) and benefits (often health gains) that would result from alternative approaches. Richardson and Griffiths (2000) state that when measuring cost effectiveness it is important to consider reduced mortality, increased longevity and reduced complications. In health, cost effectiveness is often used to determine the least expensive way to achieve a given output, and to establish if the same output can be gained with less input and the best way to spend a budget for a given group of patients (Donaldson, Currie and Mitton, 2002).

Costs in an economic evaluation can be attributed within three sectors. Patients and carers have costs, including out-of-pocket spending and allowances for their time (including employees' salaries, overheads incurred and facilities used). Other provisions for care must also be costed because savings in healthcare can lead to the costs being transferred (e.g. residential care, home help, social work). Then there are direct costs incurred in the health sector (medication, GP visits, inpatient costs). Cost effectiveness cannot be applied where new treatments require more resources. Within this environment, libraries too must demonstrate the cost effectiveness of their services. Librarians need to apply local data to demonstrate the benefits that their services deliver. Published studies on the costs and benefits of health LIS need to be identified and used to support such a case.

Public–private funding

Private finance initiatives (PFI) have existed in the United Kingdom for the last decade. They were introduced primarily to reduce the cost of public-sector capital projects. Within the NHS the usual process is to set up a limited company, which enters into negotiations with an NHS trust to supply the building, 'bed space' and the non-clinical services. An annual payment is made by the trust for these services. These contracts can last between 30 and 50 years. After this period the hospital may (or may not) be owned by the trust. Over £7000 million has been committed to the development and management of major NHS assets by means of PFI (Dawson, 2001).

Proponents of PFI claim it will lead to more investment without increasing public-sector borrowing requirements. Value for money is seen to come from costs over the life of the project being lowered because of greater private-sector efficiency and by the private sector assuming the risks normally carried by the public sector (Pollock, Shaoul and Vickers, 2002). Debates are currently taking place about the actual benefits around private finance initiatives (Dawson, 2001; Pollock, Shaoul and Vickers, 2002). Opponents argue that using private finance to build hospitals is expensive, constrains services and limits future options. With resourcing constraints, funding from both the public and private sectors needs to be considered by librarians. Charities, national lotteries and commercial concerns might provide funding. Service-development projects could also be sponsored by external agencies.

Political
Organizational change

Health services continue to encounter increasing organizational change. Walshe (2003) demonstrates that such reform and restructuring have continued for two decades or longer with some organizational change taking place almost every year. He succinctly summarizes the cumulative effects of this change and upheaval:

- Benefits from the change are usually not realized because subsequent ideas are implemented before the previous ones are evaluated.
- Each reform introduces costs in financial and human terms.
- Very often changes take the NHS back to where it started.
- Short termism is encouraged where there is rapid, major change on a regular basis. Innovation is very difficult to promulgate in this culture. This is further emphasized by Fairey (2003) (the first Director of Information Technology of the NHS) who argues that the major obstacles to the widespread use of IT in the NHS are the negative impacts of this level and rate of change.

Health LIS are not immune to constraints resulting from organizational change. Services need to be developed to meet changing user needs but this is difficult when the library itself has to cope with fundamental changes to library structure, reporting lines and sources of funding.

Local accountability

Various political strategies have been implemented to make health services more accountable to their local populations. For example, the establishment of foundation trusts (Great Britain. Department of Health, 2002) is intended to create a wholly new type of public-interest organization (Lewis, 2003). Foundation hospitals will be freed from central control and be owned by members drawn from local residents, patients and staff. They are intended to hold greater freedom over pay, non-pay rewards and recruitment. Jobanputra and Buchan (2003) identify such advantages as increased localism, devolved decision making, improved morale and improved performance. A disadvantage is that a two-tier service could emerge.

Lifelong learning

Numerous political strategies in the United Kingdom promulgate lifelong learning (Audit Commission, 2001; Great Britain. Department of Health, 2000, 2001). This reflects an increasing acceptance that lifelong learning should continue throughout the working life of all healthcare professionals. The Government also acknowledges that there should be a culture of lifelong learning with all NHS trusts expected to be learning organizations. The infrastructure for this is being established through the creation of workforce development confederations and the NHS University (NHSU). Continuing professional development (CPD) is also explicitly identified in government strategies. By adopting CPD and lifelong learning, trusts can ensure that competent and educated healthcare professionals are at the forefront of care delivery. The importance of lifelong learning for health LIS is similarly intense. David Stewart explores these issues in more detail in Chapter 13.

Quality

The Commission for Health Improvement (CHI) (www.chi.nhs.uk/eng/about/ whatischi.shtml)was established to improve the quality of patient care by reviewing care provided by the NHS in England and Wales. (Scotland has its own regulatory body, NHS Quality Improvement Scotland.) Its statutory functions are to monitor patient care and to improve quality by carrying out clinical governance reviews. It also monitors and reviews how the NHS meets the recommendations of National Service Frameworks (NSF) and National Institute for Clinical Excellence (NICE) guidelines. CHI also investigates serious service failures in the NHS. CHI leads, reviews and assists NHS healthcare improvement, while aiming to collect and share notable practice.

Concern has been expressed that the pressure on the United Kingdom's public services to measure achievement may skew priorities and encourage short termism. The award and withdrawal of quality scores to different hospitals has provoked further controversy. Health LIS must similarly address how quality is measured and reviewed (Hewlett and Walton, 2001). The mechanisms and approaches developed by health LIS, must fit within the culture and ethos of their overarching organizations.

Extending access

In responding to pressure from consumers, health services seek to establish how to offer increased access to services within existing resources. As part of the UK Government's aims (NHS Executive, 1999) to modernize the NHS, walk-in centres have been created with long opening hours, no need for appointments and at convenient locations. They provide information and treatment for minor conditions and also serve a health-promotion purpose. Similar developments have occurred in Australia, South Africa and the United States, known variously as emergency centres, ambulatory care centres or urgent care centres. Evaluation has shown (Anderson et al., 2002) that they are successful in meeting user needs. Problems have revolved around negative attitudes of other health professionals to their being nurse-led. There have also been some computer-technology issues. Librarians who face similar demands from health professionals for extended access to LIS may learn from this experience. ICT provides the delivery mechanism for increased access but carries implications for service development.

Key points

- The key sociological developments impacting on health are patient empowerment, health clinicians' roles and working practices, collaboration and partnership, an ageing population, and globalization.
- Biological warfare, pandemics, electronic patient records and health informatics, and evidence-based practice are all significant technological drivers.
- At the economic level key developments are cost effectiveness and public/private funding.
- The political influences on health are organizational change, local accountability, lifelong learning, quality, and increased access.

References

Alaszewski, A. (2002) The Impact of the Bristol Royal Infirmary Disaster and Inquiry on Public Services in the UK, *Journal of Interprofessional Care*, **16** (4), 371–8.

Anderson, E. et al. (2002) NHS Walk-in Centres and the Expanding Role of Primary Care Nurses, *Nursing Times*, **98** (19), 36–7.

Audit Commission (2001) *Hidden Talents*, London, Audit Commission.

Banta, J. E. (2001) From International Health to Global Health, *Journal of Community Health*, **26** (2), 73–6.

Beeching, N. J., Dance, D. A. B. and Miller, A. R. O. (2002) Biological Warfare and Bioterrorism, *British Medical Journal*, **324**, 336–9.

Booth, A. and Walton, G. (2000) *Managing Knowledge in Health Services*, London, Library Association Publishing.

Daly, W. M. and Carnwell, R. (2003) Nursing Roles and Level of Practice, *Journal of Clinical Nursing*, **12**, 158–67.

Dawson, D. (2001) The Private Finance Initiative: a public finance illusion, *Health Economics*, **10**, 479–86.

Donaldson, C., Currie, G. and Mitton, C. (2002) Cost Effectiveness Analysis in Health Care: contraindications, *British Medical Journal*, **325**, 891–4.

Electronic Records Target Unlikely (2003) *Nursing Standard*, **17** (40), 7.

Evans, G. (2002) Editorial. Globalization: where you stand depends on where you sit, *Primary Health Care Research and Development*, **3** (1), 1–3.

Fairey, M. (2003) Barriers to the Success of Delivering 21st Century IT Support for the NHS, *British Journal of Healthcare Computing and Information Management*, **20** (3), 28–30.

Georgiou, A. (2001) Health Informatics and Evidence Based Medicine — More Than a Marriage of Convenience?, *Health Informatics Journal*, **7**, 127–30.

Giddens, H. (1998) *The Third Way: the renewal of social democracy*, Cambridge, Polity Press.

Great Britain. Department of Health (2000) *Health Service of All Talents: developing the NHS workforce*, London, Department of Health.

Great Britain. Department of Health (2001) *Working Together – Learning Together: a framework for lifelong learning in the NHS*, London, Department of Health.

Great Britain. Department of Health (2002) *NHS Foundation Trusts*, http://doh.gov.uk/nhsfoundationtrusts/index.htm.

Griffiths, P. and Riddington, L. (2001) Nurses' Use of Computer Databases to Identify Evidence for Practice: a cross-sectional questionnaire survey in U.K. hospitals, *Health Information and Libraries Journal*, **18** (1), 2–9.

Hardey, M. et al. (2001) Professional Territories and the Fragmented Landscape of Elderly Care, *Journal of the Royal Society for the Promotion of Health*, **121** (3), 159–64.

Herman, C. (2003) *The Example of Health – Prognosis for the Profession? A draft report on an exploratory workshop held by the Chartered Institute of Library and Information Professionals on May 8th 2003*, London, Chartered Institute of Library and Information Professionals.

Hewlett, J. and Walton, G. (2001) Assessing the Quality of Library and Information Services for United Kingdom Health Professionals and Students, *Performance Measurement and Metrics*, **2** (2), 81–96.

Jenkins, P. and Gann, B. (2003) NHS Direct Online in 2003, *British Journal of Healthcare Computing and Information Management*, **20** (6), 25–7.

Jobanputra, R. and Buchan, J. (2003) Power Sharing, *Health Services Journal*, (May), 26–7.

Jones, A. M. (2003) Changes in Practice at the Nurse–Doctor Interface, *Journal of Advanced Nursing*, **12**, 124–31.

Kendall, L. and Lissauer, R. (2003) *The Future Health Worker*, London, Institute for Public Policy Research.

Lewis, R. (2003) Foundation trusts – What Do They Mean for PCTS and Patients?, *Care Plan*, **9** (3), 11–13.

Macdonald, G. and Smith, P. (2001) Collaborative Working in Primary Care Groups: a case of incommensurable paradigms, *Critical Public Health*, **3** (11), 253–66.

Morgan, M. (2003) Prove the Medical Gains, *Computer Weekly*, (17 June), 29.

NHS Executive (1999) *Patient and Public Involvement in the New NHS*, London, Department of Health.

Pollock, A. M., Shaoul, J. and Vickes, N. (2002) Private Finance and 'Value for Money' in NHS Hospitals: a policy in search of a rationale, *British Medical Journal*, **324**, 1205–9.

Richardson, G. and Griffiths, P. (2000) The Costs of Care: economic evaluation of treatments, *Nursing Times*, **96** (44), 44.

Rodriguez-Garcia, R. (2001) The Health Development Link: travel as a public health issue, *Journal of Community Health*, **26** (2), 93–112.

Rogers, J. (2003) NHS Cans Local Patient Record Work, *Computer Weekly*, (27 May), 4.

Rummery, K. and Coleman, A. (2003) Primary Health and Social Care Services in the UK: progress towards partnership, *Social Science and Medicine*, **56** (8), 1773–82.

Sackett, D. L. et al. (1996) Evidence Based Medicine: what it is and what it isn't, *British Medical Journal*, **312**, 71–2.

Safran, C. (2001) Electronic Medical Records: a decade of experience, *JAMA*, **285** (13), 1766–80.

Secretary of State for Health (2000) *The NHS Plan*, Cm 4818, London, The Stationery Office.

Secretary of State for Health (2001) *Learning from Bristol: the report of the public inquiry into children's heart surgery at the Bristol Royal Infirmary 1984–1995* (2001), Cm 5207, London, The Stationery Office.

Smith, R. (1998) All Changed, Changed Utterly, *British Medical Journal*, **316**, 1917–8.

Spread of SARS Slows (2003) *British Medical Journal*, **326**, 1232.

Stephenson, J. (2003) Growing, Evolving HIV/AIDS Pandemic is Producing Social and Economic Fallout, *JAMA*, **289** (1), 31.

Thompson, C., McCaughan, D. and Callum, N. (2001) The Accessibility of Research-based Knowledge for Nurses in the United Kingdom Acute Care Settings, *Journal of Advanced Nursing*, **36** (1), 11–22.

Turner, A. et al. (2002) A First Class Knowledge Service; developing the National electronic Library for Health, *Health Information and Libraries Journal*, **19** (3), 133–45.

Walshe, K. (2003) Foundation Hospitals: a new direction for the NHS reform?, *Journal of the Royal Society for Health*, **96** (3), 106–10.

Walton, G. (2000) Health Services: a contemporary approach. In Booth, A. and Walton, G. (eds), *Managing Knowledge in Health Services*, London, Library Association Publishing.

Wanless, D. (2001) *Securing our Future Health: taking a long term view*, London, HM Treasury.

Waters, W. W. (2001) Globalisation, Socioeconomic Restructuring and Community Health, *Journal of Community Health*, **26** (2), 79–92.

White, F. (2002) A PCT Nurse's Perspective, *Primary Health Care*, **12** (3), 18–20.

2

The health and social care interface

Valerie Monaghan and Jo Cooke

Introduction

Government policy is driving forward holistic, joined-up care, with the individual placed at the centre. This chapter explores the policy context of working across the health and social care interface, identifying key client groups and practitioners. It explores and contrasts the nature of knowledge, the information infrastructure, and culture of evidence-based practice (EBP) within each sector. Finally, the chapter reviews the literature and recent experience of working with health and social care practitioners and managers, to point to the way ahead for *joined-up* information services at the health and social care interface.

Holistic care demands closer partnership working between health and social care providers, underpinned by joined-up information and knowledge services. The role of knowledge in developing high quality services is clearly stated in the *Information for Health* strategy (Great Britain. Department of Health, 1998a) and the *Quality Strategy for Social Care* (Great Britain. Department of Health, 2000a), and is a core function of the Social Care Institute of Excellence (SCIE) which coined the phrase 'better knowledge for better practice' (SCIE, 2002).

The interface

Many people who use health and social services have complex needs; needs which do not recognise organisational boundaries. People with mental illness, older people, disabled people, need the active support of more than just the NHS. Their needs cannot be pigeonholed by the classification applied to services provided: secondary or primary, medical or nursing, health or social.

(Great Britain. Department of Health, 1998b, 3)

Individuals with complex problems require packages of health and social care. These are aimed at enabling clients to maintain independence, while protecting vulnerable individuals from harm, and providing care for those unable to live independently. Use of the term 'client' rather than 'patient' reflects the diverse range of people who are in receipt of joint services, and suggests a more holistic health model underlying the philosophy of joint care provision.

Recent developments in health delivery and policy aim to deliver care as close to the patient's home as possible. Care packages are required to operate seamlessly at the interface between primary, secondary and social care to support individuals in, or returning to, their homes. Although the delivery of care in the primary care setting has always suggested a need for interface working, this requirement has been strengthened with the advent of the primary care-led NHS.

Those planning and providing care to clients at the interface include field and residential social workers, allied health professionals (particularly occupational therapists), nurses (health visitors, school nurses and community nurses) and foster carers. Additionally, some elements of care packages are provided by the voluntary sector (e.g. Age Concern, Alzheimer's Society) or by private companies monitored by social services.

Modernization and the move towards seamless services

Recent policy demands closer partnership working between services to meet the needs of clients, reflecting the development of seamless services as a core principle within the NHS Plan (Great Britian. Department of Health, 2000b). Policy reforms and changes in legislation have enabled greater integration between services, reflected in joint planning, pooled budgets, joint commissioning and integrated delivery of services. National Service Frameworks (NSFs) embody a national strategic approach to joint planning, with local implementation through Health Improvement Plans and interagency Local Implementation Teams. NSFs require close interagency working and focus on client groups at the centre of interface activity. Many practitioners use joint assessment procedures and frameworks. Knowledge management services are key in supporting the planning and implementation of NSFs and should include knowledge and evidence from both sectors (Blackburn, 2001).

The modernization agenda has also demanded changes in organizational structures, as in the development of primary care trusts, where promising results from joint working have been evidenced (Simic, 1997; Peckham, 2000). Further advances towards integration exist through the development of care trusts and children's trusts. Practitioners within these organizations have health and social care backgrounds, but are employed under the NHS umbrella. Library and information services need to tailor their services to meet new demands from both sectors.

Cultural variations

Successful collaboration (see Chapter 11) involves understanding the culture, ideologies and values of partners, and valuing the unique contribution each partner can bring to the collaboration (Hudson, 2000; Benaim, 2001). EBP heralds the need to understand the culture of practitioners in order to bring about change (NHS Centre for Reviews and Dissemination, 1999). If healthcare librarians are to work across the interface, it is important for them to understand social care debates in relation to knowledge.

There are historical, structural and epistemological (i.e. concerning the nature of knowledge, its presuppositions and foundations, and its extent and validity) differences in the nature and generation of knowledge between health and social care. In contrast to evidence-based healthcare, with its emphasis on randomized controlled trials, social care offers a more inclusive model of 'knowledge'. Many authors support this model (Berman, 1996; Streatfield, 2002), and this view is shared by the *Quality Strategy for Social Care* (Great Britain. Department of Health, 2000a):

> staff who deliver services are also a vital source of information about what works and what does not. Their evaluations, from what happens in practice, must be central to service improvements, to spreading good practice and to the developing knowledge base for social care.

This highlights clear differences between health and social care with regard to what constitutes evidence. Knowledge managers dealing with practitioners working across the interface should be mindful to include practice and user-led information that is so valued in social-care practice.

Notwithstanding the above, a common theme in social-care literature and policy is the need to identify and use *research*-derived knowledge for practice, with *Modernising Social Services* (Great Britain. Department of Health, 1998c) clearly acknowledging that research should inform practice. However, knowledge managers should be cautious in assuming that lessons from EBP in health could be applied to the social-care context.

Major differences in the generation of research knowledge are apparent between the two sectors. Healthcare has a clear infrastructure to support and encourage research activity at national and local levels, while social services departments (SSDs) lie within local authorities (LAs) that are governed by local councils and elected members who decide how money is spent. As a result, differences between SSDs exist, with little investment in research activity. A scoping exercise of SSDs within one NHS region (Cooke, Owen and Wilson, 2002) identified only one local authority with a research department, and little or no research infrastructure in other SSDs. This reflects pragmatic decisions made by LAs towards supporting benchmarking activities, with performance management positions often replacing research posts (Barnes, 1998).

This lack of research infrastructure and funding has implications for EBP in social care. Not only is the research evidence-base limited, but also the lack of a culture and experience of research implies limitations for supporting critical thinking in practice (Hughes et al., 2000).

EBP and the culture of social-care practitioners and organizations

Social care has long been a 'doing' rather than a 'reflective' occupation. Pressures of work, both in volume and in riskiness, inhibit the development of conditions that are conducive to evidence-based practice, such as time (and permission) to read, time to share and debate practice issues with colleagues.   (Macdonald, 2000)

Recent studies addressing the cultural context of EBP in social care identify many barriers (Tozer and Ray, 1999; Hughes et al., 2000; Booth, Booth and Falzon, 2002). Cultural and environmental factors also have a part to play. Information-seeking behaviour by social-care practitioners often favours 'person-based' approaches rather than seeking information through literature. The Social Care Information Outreach (SCIO) project (Booth, Booth and Falzon, 2002), a questionnaire survey of 132 social-care practitioners and managers in the Midlands, found that they accessed evidence from colleagues (85%), line managers (69%), and contacts within other organizations (76%). In contrast, evidence was obtained from literature-based sources in smaller proportions: research presentations (34%), research summaries (47%) and computer databases (48%). Although face-to-face contact and personal experience is valued, other factors may make this type of information seeking more likely. Poor access to information and communication technologies (ICTs) may influence information-seeking behaviour and determine the experience and skills base of those wishing to access the knowledge base.

Information inequity

Historical differences exist between the two sectors in terms of information skills, ICT access and use, and library and knowledge management infrastructure, with social care being seen as the poor relation. The health sector made early progress in information-skills support following the emergence of evidence-based medicine (EBM). As early as 1993, training programmes in critical appraisal (CASP) were made available to healthcare practitioners; organized access to library services has existed for many years. However, the introduction of *Information for Health* (Great Britain. Department of Health, 1998a) led to greater promotion of clinical effectiveness and evidence-based practice, emphasizing the need for simplified access to the knowledge base for all healthcare practitioners, and stressing the role of library services in achieving this.

Organizations and structures facilitating the use of research in health-service development and improvement were created, supported by initiatives such as the National Institute for Clinical Excellence (NICE) and the National electronic Library for Health (NeLH) (Carr, 2000).

In contrast, developments within social care are more recent and reflect a different view of knowledge, focusing on data collection within the very broad definition of knowledge rehearsed above. However, the role of knowledge management (KM) is acknowledged:

> knowledge is information and, if properly shared, can make a significant difference to the way we operate and the quality of service we provide. All too often, the problem is one of not knowing where to get hold of the right information or how to pass it on to others . . .   (Great Britain. Department of Health, 2000c)

The *Quality Strategy* (Great Britain. Department of Health, 2000a) led to the formation of SCIE with the remit to create a knowledge base for social care, making it freely accessible to all practitioners. This process has begun, but is hampered by the need for SCIE to wrestle with issues around what constitutes knowledge and to deal with tensions between stakeholders (Edwards, 2002).

A report from Information Management Associates (IMA, n.d.) examines variations in the speed of KM uptake within each sector, concluding that an inequality in resources is a clear issue between the two sectors. Other differences include:

- current spending on knowledge services
- number of librarians employed in the respective sectors
- national strategies supporting libraries' ICT infrastructure development
- National Adviser post for libraries
- networks of libraries co-ordinating resource and service access
- established tradition of research awareness and evidence-based practice
- widespread access to the internet.

These inequalities impact on everyday practice for patients. A recent needs assessment of social workers at a hospital in Leicestershire concludes 'whilst Social Services staff and NHS staff may be part of the same multi-disciplinary team providing care for the same client, their access to the knowledge base is vastly different' (Harrison, Hepworth and de Chazal, 2002).

One could conclude that access and use of information within the healthcare sector is 'sorted', and that it is only the infrastructure in the social-care sector that is poorly developed. However, areas of relatively poor information access exist in health, particularly within primary care and community-based services (IMA, n.d.) with a relatively low level of formal library provision and where many staff do not have easy access to a computer terminal. As these areas are where much interface working takes place the two sectors may not be so very far apart.

Approaches needed to provide library services across the divide

In the light of these inequalities, and the imperative for health KM services to meet the demands of modernization, the health sector is beginning to address access and use of the evidence at the health–social care interface. In the absence of a developed library infrastructure in social care, healthcare librarians are well placed to provide services at the interface (Booth, Booth and Falzon, 2002). However, rather than ignore the warning that 'one size does not fit all' (Booth, Booth and Falzon, 2002), social care staff need an 'identifiable service address-ing their particular needs, rather than being presented with an amorphous health-dominated service' (IMA, n.d., 4.7.4).

Key areas for action, identified within the literature, suggest a starting point for service development:

- access to resources – electronic and physical
- skills training – searching and critical appraisal
- funded information service providing dedicated support to match particular needs of staff working in this area.

Projects discovered when researching this area include:

- healthcare library services supporting access to library resources and ser-vices for social care staff, as in Hampshire and the Isle of Wight where an 'access map' has been produced
- joint health and social care library plans and planning groups, including the Shropshire and Staffordshire library plan that has resulted in social care being represented in all healthcare library planning processes; the SCARE

(Social Care Access to the Research Evidence) group in Trent that brings together social care practitioners, academics and health information specialists to resolve issues around access to the evidence base

- training initiatives aimed at health and social care practitioners, including the development and roll-out of critical appraisal skills training (Spittlehouse, Action and Enock, 2000) in the South West of England; an evidence-based practice programme for mental-health staff in Portsmouth; and staff working across the interface within the primary-care setting in Rotherham
- regionally funded joint access to electronic databases and full-text journals, now replicated within the NHS National Core Content knowledge base; while recognizing that making resources available does not necessarily make them accessible, this provides a starting point.

In addition, some hospital-based healthcare library services are provided under service-level agreement by local-authority-run public library services. These local authority–NHS partnerships offer opportunities to support the needs of staff across the interface, yet in most cases this is only offered on an informal basis. Social-care staff who are not employed by hospitals are not officially entitled to membership of the library or to use its services, leading to inequalities across the sectors and within teams (Harrison, Hepworth and de Chazal, 2002).

How might library and information services be delivered to interface workers?

A key message is that librarians working at the interface need a flexible, fluid and informed approach. Childs and Goundry (2002) assert that 'library services will need to be very proactive to meet the needs of frontline staff', a characteristic that could equally describe those delivering services within the primary-care setting, a natural springboard for interface service development. Such has been the case in Northumberland where work has been undertaken to identify how the existing primary-care library service can support the needs of the newly formed Care Trust. Childs and Goundry (2002) conclude that all staff within the Care Trust should have access (in person or electronically) to information services, and information should be delivered to their workplace or desktop on request.

What might interface library services look like?

The key components of a service supporting those working at the interface might include:

1   *Access to full library services physically and remotely* (phone, fax, e-mail, internet/intranet) – Several authors stress the need to ensure that both traditional library services and electronic resources are available (Childs and Goundry, 2002; IMA, n.d.). Social care practitioners need access to abstracting services backed up by photocopied articles (Booth, Booth and Falzon, 2002).

2   *Dedicated professional library staff* (Childs and Goundry, 2002; Harrison, Hepworth and de Chazal, 2002; IMA, n.d.) – IMA (n.d., 3.4.4) stresses the need to 'provide a mediated information service employing specialist information workers to help practitioners find their way to appropriate information, at least until confident and effective electronic seeking and use becomes the norm'.

3   *Synthesized summaries of evidence* (Sheldon, 1998; Carr, 2000; Streatfield, 2002) – and targeted current awareness bulletins that are current, factual, succinct and brief (Childs and Goundry, 2002; Harrison, Hepworth and de Chazal, 2002; Roper, 2002)

4   *Information searching and critical appraisal skills training* (Sheldon, 1998; Spittlehouse, Acton and Enock, 2000; Streatfield, 2002; Booth, Booth and Falzon, 2002) – These may be adapted from training materials developed for the healthcare field, because the main difference between the needs of the two sectors is 'not so much course content, but the way in which the information is contextualised and presented' (Booth, Booth and Falzon, 2002).

5   *Provision and promotion of appropriate knowledge resources* (Blackburn, 2001; IMA, n.d.) – The IMA scoping study highlights how a co-operative approach to electronic library provision could aid convergence by providing a common information base.

6   *Knowledge management structure (e.g. discussion lists; grey literature bases; good practice examples)* – to support the generation and transfer of new knowledge (Berman, 1995 and 1996; Sheldon, 1998; Streatfield, 2002; Edwards, 2002). Berman (1996) highlights that 'interactive communications over the internet support the method of knowledge attainment (participatory and interactive) of social workers and the type of information used in practicing the profession'.

7   *Partnerships* (Cawthra, 1999; Carr, 2000; Spittlehouse, Acton and Enock, 2000; Blackburn, 2001; Roper, 2002; IMA, n.d.; Booth, Booth and Falzon, 2002) – Strong partnership working across the health and social care interface is required so that each sector can learn from, and with, the other (Spittlehouse, Acton and Enock, 2000). Partnership working is also strongly supported in policy; the *Partnership in Action* (Great Britain. Department of Health, 1998d) report states that 'sharing information between agencies to help enhance integrated services to individuals will be essential'.

Conclusion

Clearly, close partnership working is required across the interface, with benefits to be gained for all, and knowledge managers are key players in this process. Such interface working needs to be based on an understanding of the nature and content of the knowledge and cultural contexts in each field, and the needs of practitioners operating therein. Library and information services need to be tailored to support these identified needs. Joined-up working is likely to be appreciated most where the library and information infrastructure is less well developed. Joint working can break down barriers that exist within practice and around ownership of knowledge and is, therefore, key to improving the situation for those clients who are more vulnerable in our society. Knowledge managers can play an important role in facilitating and supporting access to resources, training and supporting social care staff in pursuit of this goal.

Key points

Health library and information workers crossing the health and social care interface should:

- recognize cultural and infrastructure differences between sectors
- develop services that meet the identified needs of practitioners at the interface
- work in partnership
- be proactive and flexible in their approach
- share best practice solutions to interface working.

References

Barnes, M. (1998) Editorial, *Social Services Research,* **4**, i–ii.

Benaim, R. (2001) Getting to Grips with Social Services. In Meads, G. and Meads, T. (eds), *Trust in Experience*, Abingdon, Radcliffe Medical Press.

Berman, Y. (1995) Knowledge Transfer in Social Work: the role of grey documentation, *International Information and Library Review*, **27**, 143–54.

Berman, Y. (1996) Discussion Groups on the Internet as Sources of Information: the case of social work, *Aslib Proceedings*, **48** (2), 31–6.

Blackburn, N. (2001) Building Bridges: towards integrated library and information services for mental health and social care, *Health Information and Libraries Journal*, **18**, 203–12.

Booth, S., Booth, A. and Falzon, L. (2002) *The Information and Training Needs of Social Care Practitioners: a literature review and survey*, University of Sheffield

Trent Institute for Health Services Research.

Carr, S. (2000) www.research.org.uk: supporting social work practice for Scotland, *Assignation*, **17** (4), 7–10.

Cawthra, L. (1999) Older People's Health Information Needs, *Health Libraries Review*, **16**, 97–105.

Childs, S. and Goundry, P. (2002) *Information Needs of Social Care Staff – Informing a Care Trust: final report,* Northumbria University Information Management Research Institute.

Cooke, J., Owen, J. and Wilson, A. (2002) Research and Development at the Health and Social Care Interface in Primary Care: a scoping exercise in one NHS region, *Health and Social Care in the Community*, **10** (6), 435–44.

Edwards, A. (2002) What is 'Knowledge' in Social Care?, *MCC: Building Knowledge for Integrated Care*, **10** (1), 13–16.

Great Britain. Department of Health (1997) *The New NHS: modern dependable*, CM 3807, London, The Stationery Office.

Great Britain. Department of Health (1998a) *Information for Health: an information strategy for the modern NHS 1998–2005: a national strategy for local implementation*, London, Department of Health.

Great Britain. Department of Health (1998b) *Modernising Health and Social Services: national priorities guidance 1999–00/2001–02,* London, Department of Health.

Great Britain. Department of Health (1998c) *Modernising Social Services: promoting independence, improving protection, raising standards*, London, The Stationery Office.

Great Britain. Department of Health (1998d) *Partnership in Action (New Opportunities for Joint Working between Health and Social Services): a discussion document,* London, Department of Health.

Great Britain. Department of Health (2000a) *A Quality Strategy for Social Care*, London, Department of Health, consultation responses at www.doh.gov.uk/scg/qualitystrategy.htm.

Great Britain. Department of Health (2000b) *NHS Plan: a plan for investment, a plan for reform*, London, Department of Health.

Great Britain. Department of Health (2000c) *Information for Social Care: a framework for improving quality in social care through better use of information and information technology*, London, Department of Health.

Harrison, J., Hepworth, M. and de Chazal, P. (2002) *NHS and Social Care Library and Information Services Interface: a study of social workers' information needs*, Loughborough University, Department of Information Science.

Hudson, B. (2000) Social Services and Primary Care Groups: a window of collaborative opportunity?, *Health and Social Care in the Community*, **8** (4), 242–50.

Hughes, M. et al. (2000) *What Works? Making Connections: linking research and practice*, Essex, Barnardo's.

Information Management Associates (n.d.) *National electronic Library for Health – Electronic Library for Social Care: health and social care interface scoping study: report*, London. IMA.

Macdonald, G. (2000) Social Care: rhetoric and reality? In Davies, H., Nutley, S. M. and Smith, P. C. (eds), *What Works? Evidence based policy and practice in public services,* Bristol, Policy Press.

NHS Centre for Reviews and Dissemination (1999) Getting Evidence into Practice, *Effective Health Care*, **5** (1).

Peckham, S. (2000) Primary Care Groups: a new opportunity for collaboration and participation, *Research Policy and Planning*, **18** (1), 12–20.

Roper, F. (2002) 4 Nations Child Policy Network: a child policy web site, *Assignation*, **19** (4), 49–51.

Sheldon, B. (1998) Evidence Based Social Services: prospects and problems, *Research Policy and Planning,* **16** (2), 16–18.

Simic, P. (1997) Social Work, Primary Care and Organizational and Professional Change, *Research Policy and Planning*, **15** (1), 1–7.

Social Care Institute of Excellence (2002) *Listening Exercise: summary of findings,* London, SCIE, www.scie.org.uk.

Spittlehouse, C., Acton, M. and Enock, K. (2000) Introducing Critical Appraisal Skills Training in UK Social Services: another link between health and social care?, *Journal of Interprofessional Care*, **14** (4), 397–404.

Streatfield, D. (2002) Towards Evidence-based Library and Information Work?, *IRWI*, (October), 3–4.

Tozer, C. L. and Ray, S. (1999) 20 Questions: the research needs of children and family social workers, *Research Policy and Planning*, **17** (1), 7–15.

3

Clinical governance and National Service Frameworks

Andrew Booth

Introduction

The last decade has seen the quest for clinical quality become an international movement (Leape and Berwick, 2000). In the UK the Bristol inquiry into poorly performing paediatric cardiologists received extensive media coverage and has focused professional and public attention on patient safety (Secretary of State for Health, 2001). Similarly, in the United States the report *To Err is Human* (Institute of Medicine, 2000) received extraordinary media coverage and commanded a prompt response from the President and Congress. Other countries have pursued quality initiatives and in Australia and New Zealand clinical leadership is seen as essential to emerging clinical governance strategies (Wright et al., 2001). The international landscape of health quality assurance has witnessed dramatic change. Against this backdrop it is helpful to focus on a single national initiative to exemplify current issues in information provision.

This chapter looks at the development of clinical governance and National Service Frameworks within the UK health service. It then examines implications of such developments for information systems. After considering responses to the clinical governance agenda including the clinical librarian, the primary-care knowledge service and the evidence gateway, the chapter examines implications of future developments in clinical governance for library and information services.

Clinical governance

Clinical governance is:

a framework [or more accurately a system] through which NHS organisations are accountable for continuously improving the quality of their services and safeguarding high standards of care by creating an environment in which excellence will flourish. (Secretary of State for Health, 1997)

Three expressions merit special emphasis. First, 'accountable'; prior to the 1999 NHS Act quality assurance initiatives, dating back to 1989 and the promotion of clinical audit (Great Britain. Department of Health, 1989) and embodied in the Promoting Clinical Excellence initiative (NHS Executive, 1996), had sought to establish, albeit quasi-voluntarily, a mechanism for monitoring and controlling clinical care. Clinical governance brought recognition that such approaches lacked teeth. Clinical governance attempts to establish mechanisms analogous to corporate governance such that the chief executive of any NHS organization is held accountable not only for the financial management of the organization but also, more critically, for the quality of clinical care (Boggust et al., 2002).

Second, clinical governance seeks to promote an 'environment in which excellence will flourish'. Clinical excellence requires not locally prioritized targets, but a whole-system approach (Scally and Donaldson, 1998). To achieve such an ambitious organizational agenda requires both infrastructure and efficient information systems at local and national levels:

high quality information is essential for good clinical governance and effective performance management. (Secretary of State for Health, 1997)

Clinical governance needs good information to assess the quality and performance of services . . . Health professionals need knowledge from research to support their clinical decisions. (NHS Executive, 1999)

Finally, 'safeguarding high standards of care' acknowledges the need for explicit national standards against which local performance is measured. Previously national standards had been championed by individual professional organizations and royal colleges. The prevailing climate is now for multi-professional work within broad disease or population groupings. Thus an extensive portfolio of National Service Frameworks was born.

National Service Frameworks

National Service Frameworks establish national standards and define service needs for specific care groups (Secretary of State for Health, 1997). These standards are disseminated through such channels as the National electronic Library for Health (NeLH). They are implemented through clinical governance and supported by professional self-regulation and lifelong learning (Secretary of State for Health, 1997). By early 2003, six National Service Frameworks had been published covering:

- mental health
- coronary heart disease
- cancer
- diabetes
- paediatric intensive care
- older people.

Further NSFs are scheduled in:

- children's services
- renal services
- long-term conditions.

While topics prioritized for National Service Frameworks were predictable their implications are markedly different. For example, Paediatric Intensive Care involves a circumscribed group of clinical staff working exclusively within an acute hospital setting. In contrast, Older People affects a broad spectrum of professionals working not only within healthcare but across a range of community and social service settings.

Having established the mechanism (clinical governance) and the means (NSFs), attention turns to monitoring. Conformity with national standards is monitored through the Commission for Health Improvement, the National Performance Assessment Framework and the National Survey of Patients (Secretary of State for Health, 1997). The Commission for Health Improvement (CHI) conducts scheduled visits to monitor trust performance against quantitative and qualitative measures. Data required for monitoring national clinical indicators is used by CHI prior to its visits. Recommendations are made in a report which is published and made freely available on the web.

Information requirements for clinical governance

Clinical governance requires a range of information responses only a few of which fall within the traditional domain inhabited by healthcare librarians:

> In order to deliver the clinical governance agenda, good quality, timely, accurate information is needed to establish baselines and to enable ongoing monitoring against standards and benchmarks.   (Roderick and Roderick, 2001)

Information systems were second only to 'dedicated time' in a survey of support required to conduct clinical governance (University of Leicester, 2000). Clinical governance includes evidence-based medicine (which places library-derived research literature at the centre), patient information (which requires a more hybrid informatics response) and risk management and clinical computing (which exist almost completely outside libraries). Such diffuse coverage is reflected in *e-Clinical Governance: a guide for primary care* (Simpson and Robinson, 2002). All requirements share challenges posed by the adoption and utilization of technology in supporting clinical governance objectives.

Responses to clinical governance

Clinical governance, a managerial manifestation of evidence-based practice, requires clinical practice to be based on reliable research, pursues quality-driven standards and focuses on continuous quality improvement in patient care. Underpinning this challenge is a literal battery of electronic resources such as the Cochrane Library, Best Evidence and Clinical Evidence. Indeed, the NeLH makes great play of its links with clinical governance (Turner et al., 2002). This wealth of information makes it imperative that skills in information retrieval and interpretation become commonplace among healthcare practitioners (Keeling and Lambert, 2000).

Clinical governance requires systematized approaches to organizational learning and knowledge management (Huntington, Gillam and Rosen, 2000; McColl and Roland, 2000). Both clinical governance and knowledge management, as discussed in Chapter 6, require 'A working environment which is open and participative, where ideas and good practice are shared, where education and research are valued . . . The challenge to the NHS is the active creation of such cultures in most hospitals and primary care groups of the future' (Scally and Donaldson, 1998). Arguably the library's greatest contribution to clinical governance is in helping to engender and sustain such a culture (Simpson and Robinson, 2002). However, this chapter focuses on more direct impacts within the clinical governance agenda.

Clinical governance requires:

- access to, and knowledge of, evidence-based information
- identification of information needed to support clinical governance
- skills in literature searching and critical appraisal
- methods of delivering information quickly
- dissemination of information
- identification of current research
- identification of guidelines.

Within this exacting menu, methods of delivery will depend on a healthcare organization's site, setting and available infrastructure. Examples explored below include clinical libraries, primary-care knowledge services and the evidence gateway.

Although the clinical librarian model is discussed more fully in Chapter 8 a main driver for its renaissance is the clinical-governance agenda. Barriers to the routine adoption of evidence-based practice (Secretary of State for Health, 1999), from the perspective of the individual clinician, include information overload, shortage of time, lack of knowledge of databases and limited access to IT facilities in a clinical setting (Pyne et al., 1999). Clinical librarian initiatives address such barriers through filtering the literature, thus saving clinicians' time, specialist database expertise and information services to clinical staff. The contribution of clinical librarianship to clinical governance is exemplified by initiatives at the University Hospitals of Leicester NHS Trust (Ward, Honeybourne and Harrison, 2001) and Barnet Primary Care NHS Trust (Reid, Ikkos and Hopkins, 2002).

Primary-care organizations are required to collect, collate and analyse information from primary, secondary and community care services, for several purposes including the implementation of clinical governance. Internal data requirements are complemented by a need for improved access to the research literature (Lacey Bryant, 1999). Several primary-care organizations have set up library services in response to this challenge. Typically these offer a package of electronic journals, deliver an enquiry service, loan books and provide information-skills training.

The 'evidence gateway' provides a single access point to information resources, either publicly via the web, on a subscription basis through password-protected packages, or, typically, both. Such a gateway, which may be part of a primary-care knowledge service as mentioned above, provides a 'local view' to complement national initiatives such as the NeLH. Probably the highest profile local evidence gateway is the Sheffield Evidence for Effectiveness and Knowledge (SEEK) project (see below).

Case study – city-wide approaches to clinical governance

The Disseminating Information for Clinical Effectiveness (DICE) project was initiated in Sheffield to anticipate concerns with clinical governance (Booth and Price, 2000). Three systems to support clinical governance were identified:

• an organizational information support system to service existing networks and committees charged with advancing local clinical audit, quality and clinical effectiveness

- a system to support clinical-effectiveness initiatives instigated by individuals
- a more proactive local system, requiring intensive support through filtering, synthesis, synopsis and analysis to support clinical governance at an organizational level.

A fourth associated need was for an information monitoring system to feed performance against agreed quality standards upward through each organization.

Two specific developments followed the appearance of the DICE report:

- **ShEBaNG** – a cross-city network for continuing development of clinical governance staff, facilitated by library staff, involving monthly critical appraisal activities
- **SEEK** – a city-wide evidence gateway (see below).

Sheffield Evidence for Effectiveness and Knowledge (SEEK)

Sheffield Evidence for Effectiveness and Knowledge (SEEK) supports the dissemination and uptake of information on clinical effectiveness for NHS staff across all health sectors in Sheffield. The principal target groups are:

1 those with an organizational responsibility for clinical effectiveness or clinical governance activities
2 clinical practitioners who require access to 'evidence' in patient-care decision making.

Information for Health charged each health community with providing 'every NHS professional with online access to the latest local guidance and national evidence on treatment' (NHS Executive, 1998). SEEK therefore sought to develop a mechanism to disseminate 'evidence' to support organizational clinical-governance needs and individual evidence-based practice, as well as to provide a content-rich resource to be exploited as an 'electronic library'. The chosen mechanism was a web 'gateway', bringing together local clinical guidelines and national information resources. The gateway provides access to:

- **the library** – a starting point for full-text materials (journals, books, reports), major databases and internet search engines and 'evidence digests'
- **local contacts** – links to local health-related web sites in Sheffield, trusts, health organizations, information providers, intranet links, etc.
- **learning tools** – tutorials and learning resources useful when updating skills in finding and appraising evidence

- **clinical topics** – major 'meta-sites' for each clinical speciality as a quality controlled jump-start to searching the internet
- **local clinical guidelines** – a single index to all clinical guidelines approved for city-wide implementation, supplemented by a listing of guidelines produced at a local trust level
- **national clinical guidelines** – approved by NICE, Prodigy, Royal Colleges, SIGN and other relevant organizations. This function is now commissioned nationally from the University of Sheffield by the National electronic Library for Health.
- **information skills** – training covering literature searching, evidence-based resources, internet navigation and critical appraisal skills.

SORTED! information requirements for clinical governance

The SEEK Project Board required the project to engage with clinical governance staff to identify current patterns of information use and to locate the project within broader information provision across the city. Whereas the initial DICE project had conducted interviews with clinical effectiveness staff across Sheffield (Booth and Price, 2000), it was decided to employ focus groups for this follow-up investigation. Focus groups are a qualitative technique useful for understanding people's perceptions of services and as a market-research tool when developing or implementing a service (St Leger and Walsworth-Bell, 1999). This method was appropriate in examining the perceptions of clinical-governance staff of the services SEEK provides and in further developing its services.

Two focus groups were held with 16 clinical-governance staff. Focus groups took place within a wider half-day programme of continuing professional development, badged under the title 'SORTED!' (Sheffield ORiented Techniques for Effective Dissemination). The focus group was accompanied by a didactic session updating developments in dissemination since the DICE project. This included findings from key reviews and a brief synthesis of clinical-governance reviews conducted by the Commission of Health Improvement.

A focus group protocol was devised, based on an article on the use of focus groups in a library setting (Crowley et al., 2002). It moved from general information behaviour to consider the possible role of the SEEK gateway. Finally, participants were asked to consider further marketing or promotion needs for SEEK services. 'NICE guidance' was the focus of discussion for each group, chosen because its mandatory nature requires formal organizational structures and processes. Participants were asked to think about what happens when NICE issues a new guideline or judgement on a new drug or procedure and their organization's response to receiving the guidance.

Generally, staff felt that the project has a role to play within the clinical governance agenda. However, it was seen as peripheral to existing activities, partly due to technical difficulties in bridging the service–academic (NHSNet–JANet) divide, requiring more work on gaining ownership by NHS staff and closer links with other sites and services to increase SEEK's centrality. These findings informed further development of the project.

Future developments in clinical governance

Significant time and effort has been invested in clinical-governance activities. It is almost unthinkable, therefore, that this legacy will not be around for many years to come, whatever the prevailing political climate. Future developments are likely to include the following:

1   Although clinical governance is envisaged as a whole systems approach (O'Connor and McDermott, 1997) this has rarely been achieved on an organization-wide basis. Clinical governance is likely to move increasingly from piecemeal achievements within clearly defined domains to become a process that allows for individual, group and organizational inventiveness and leadership from anywhere in the organization (Huntington, Gillam and Rosen, 2000). 'The wider organisational challenge is then to be able to convert an invention in one part of the system into innovation throughout it' (Huntington, 1996).

2   Closely linked to this is the 'learning organization'. Healthcare organizations must rapidly incorporate good practice into everyday work and employ innovation, enterprise and patient-centred approaches on an organization-wide basis. Within primary care this requires that a practice team assumes responsibility for reviewing its own care and making appropriate change. This may require protected time, periodic 'half-day closing' and away-days along with input from skilled tutors, workshop facilitators and even mentoring schemes.

3   Risk management will likely have an increasingly high profile (Wilson and Tingle, 1999). Concentrating clinical-governance resources on significant audit processes, for example, confirming that all clinical staff have been immunized against Hepatitis B, maximizes the impact of quality systems.

4   There is likely to become an increased movement towards routine data monitoring. For example, within primary healthcare organizations the collection of data on agreed topics across practices allows common approaches to reviewing and improving the quality of care (Newrick, Spencer and Jones, 1996; McColl et al., 1998). Data can be collected across all practices within a primary care trust to derive national performance indicators. *Information for*

Health envisages a patient-centred approach whereby clinical audit (and other aggregate) data is a by-product of information captured to support healthcare. Comparative data to support clinical governance in key clinical areas, and to monitor the NSFs, can be collected in a way that is consistent with *Information for Health* principles.

Conclusion

Clinical governance places a significant extra knowledge burden on those working in clinical care, particularly within primary care where information systems are less developed. However, many sources of information, both internal and external, are available. Clinical governance offers opportunities for those working in library and information services in healthcare to develop resources and services and to place themselves more centrally on the organizational agenda. The fact that clinical governance is a 'must do' not a 'nice to do' gives the library additional influence, provided it occupies this position of centrality. As every healthcare organization is required to become a learning organization (Nasir, Donaldson, Garcarz, Chambers and Ellis, 2003) this should add further credibility to an expanded role for library and information services. At the same time libraries will operate within a climate where the services that they provide are increasingly subject to 'governance' and accompanying concerns with risk management. With opportunity comes responsibility and local library managers will have to rise to this challenge if they are to fully exploit the knowledge required to support clinical governance and National Service Frameworks.

Key points

* Clinical governance is a system for ensuring accountability for clinical care and National Service Frameworks establish national standards and define service needs for specific care groups.
* Clinical governance requires significant information responses involving all types of data and information.
* Local responses to clinical governance include clinical librarians, primary-care knowledge services and evidence gateways.
* Future developments in clinical governance will likely see an increasingly whole-systems approach, development of learning organizations and a pre-occupation with risk management and routine data monitoring.
* Clinical governance should add to the credibility of library and information services as they occupy a more central role within health organizations.

References

Boggust, M. et al. (2002) Developing Strategic Leadership of Clinical Governance through a Programme for NHS Boards, *British Journal of Clinical Governance*, 7 (3), 215–9.

Booth, A. and Price, C. (2000) Models for Disseminating Information on Clinical Effectiveness in Health Organisations: lessons from the Sheffield DICE Project, *Journal of Clinical Excellence*, 1, 193–200.

Crowley, G. H. et al. (2002) User Perceptions of the Library's Web Pages: a focus group study at Texas AandM University, *Journal of Academic Librarianship*, 28 (4), 205–10.

Great Britain. Department of Health (1989) *Working for Patients*, London, HMSO.

Huntington, J. (1996) From Invention to Innovation. In Meads G. (ed.) *Future Options for General Practice*, Abingdon, Radcliffe Medical.

Huntington, J., Gillam, S. and Rosen, R. (2000) Clinical Governance in Primary Care: organisational development for clinical governance, *British Medical Journal*, 321 (7262), 679–82.

Institute of Medicine (2000) *To Err is Human: building a safer health system*, Washington DC, National Academies Press.

Keeling, C. and Lambert, S. (2000) Knowledge Management in the NHS: positioning the healthcare librarian at the knowledge intersection, *Health Libraries Review*, 17 (3), 136–43.

Lacey Bryant, S. (1999) Information Services for Primary Care: the organizational culture of general practice and the information needs of partnerships and primary care groups, *Health Libraries Review*, 16 (3), 157–65.

Leape, L. L. and Berwick, D. (2000) Safe Health Care: are we up to it?, *British Medical Journal*, 320, 725–6.

McColl, A. et al. (1998) Performance Indicators for Primary Care Groups: an evidence based approach, *British Medical Journal*, 317 (7169), 1354–60.

McColl, A. and Roland, M. (2000) Clinical Governance in Primary Care: knowledge and information for clinical governance, *British Medical Journal*, 321 (7265), 871–4.

Nasir, J., Donaldson, Sir L., Garcarz, W., Chambers, R. and Ellis, S. (2003) *Make your Healthcare Organisation a Learning Organisation*, Oxford, Radcliffe Medical Press.

Newrick, D. C., Spencer, J. A. and Jones, K. P. (1996) Collecting Data in General Practice: need for standardisation, *British Medical Journal*, 312, 33–4.

NHS Executive (1996) *Promoting Clinical Excellence: a framework for action in and through the NHS*, London, Department of Health, HMSO.

NHS Executive (1998) *Information for Health: an information strategy for the modern NHS 1998–2005: a national strategy for implementation*, Leeds, Department of Health.

NHS Executive (1999) *Clinical Governance: quality in the new NHS*, Leeds, NHS Executive, HSC 1999/065.

O'Connor, J. and McDermott, I. (1997) *The Art of Systems Thinking*, London, Thorsons.

Pyne, T. et al. (1999) Meeting the Information Needs of Clinicians for the Practice of Evidence-based Healthcare, *Health Libraries Review*, **16** (1), 3–14.

Reid, L., Ikkos, G. and Hopkins, W. (2002) Brief Communication. Clinical librarians at Barnet Primary Care NHS Trust: addressing the information requirements of clinical governance, *Health Information and Libraries Journal*, **19** (1), 52–5.

Roderick, N. and Roderick, A. (2001) The Myth of Accurate Clinical Information. In Lugon, M. and Secker-Walker, J. (eds), *Advancing Clinical Governance*, London, Royal Society of Medicine Press.

Scally, G. and Donaldson, L. J. (1998) Clinical Governance and the Drive for Quality Improvement in the New NHS in England, *British Medical Journal*, **317**, 61–5.

Secretary of State for Health (1997) *A First Class Service: quality in the new NHS*, Cmnd 3807, London, Department of Health.

Secretary of State for Health (1999) *Clinical Governance*, London, Department of Health.

Secretary of State for Health (2001) *Learning from Bristol: the report of the public inquiry into children's heart surgery at the Bristol Royal Infirmary 1984–1995*, CM 5207, London, Department of Health.

Simpson, L. and Robinson, P. (eds) (2002) *e-Clinical Governance: a guide for primary care*, Oxford, Radcliffe.

St Leger, A. S. and Walsworth-Bell, J. P. (1999) *Change-promoting Research for Health Services*, Buckingham, Open University Press.

Turner, A. et al. (2002) A First Class Knowledge Service: developing the National electronic Library for Health, *Health Information and Libraries Journal*, **19** (3), 133–45.

University of Leicester (2000) Survey of the Development of Clinical Governance in England and Wales, Leicester, University of Leicester.

Ward, L. M., Honeybourne, C. J. and Harrison, J. (2001) A Clinical Librarian Can Support Clinical Governance, *British Journal of Clinical Governance*, **6** (4), 248–51.

Wilson, J. and Tingle, J. (1999) *Clinical Risk Management and Modification: a route to clinical governance*, London, Butterworth-Heinemann.

Wright, L. et al. (2001) *Clinical Leadership and Clinical Governance: a review of developments in New Zealand and internationally*. Report commissioned for the Clinical Leaders Association of New Zealand for the Ministry of Health, www.moh.govt.nz/moh.nsf/c7ad5e032528c34c4c2566690076db9b/38dd32b7a22ca1 97cc256bb20081a301/$FILE/CLANZlitreviewfinal.pdf.

4

Virtual outreach services

Alison Yeoman

Introduction

It has long been acknowledged that certain groups of healthcare professionals have had limited access to hospital-based library resources. Early outreach services were launched in an attempt to improve access for these groups. Recently it has become clear that all health professionals, not just hospital specialists, are expected to make full use of research evidence, and the need for outreach services has become urgent. Not all patients come to their GP waving internet printouts but the fact that this can happen is changing attitudes towards access to the evidence in community and primary healthcare.

This chapter considers how virtual outreach library services have developed to support all healthcare professionals while ensuring that they meet the needs of those who have traditionally been marginalized. It then discusses factors that can contribute to the successful development of a virtual outreach service and how to ensure the long-term sustainability of such a service.

Access to health library services

The problem of ensuring adequate access to health library services for all healthcare practitioners is not new (Pifalo, 1994; Self, Wright and Waugh, 1998) but it has recently become both more prominent and more pressing. Concerns have traditionally focused on practitioners in rural locations, and in both the UK and USA there have been attempts to 'replicate the "information-rich" environment of a large academic health sciences center within the community setting' (Holtrum and Zollo, 1998). Access to information remains a problem for community-based healthcare practitioners, particularly those who are peripatetic (Rose, 1998; Yeoman et al., 2001), but levers such as evidence-based practice, clinical governance, continuing professional development (CPD) and the increased importance of applying research to practice have highlighted the need to provide effective library services to all health service staff.

Early outreach initiatives such as circuit librarians in the USA (Pifalo, 1994) involved a librarian travelling to each participating institution to provide a reference service, delivering materials and collecting requests for information. Such services were the forerunners of the wide range of outreach services available today, including clinical librarians, peripatetic librarians, primary-care knowledge officers, training programmes, websites, provision of electronic databases/directories and alerting systems (Yeoman et al., 2001; Booth et al., 2002). 'Outreach services', then, can cover a variety of activities and can serve users whether they are community-based or not. 'Virtual outreach services' can typically be thought of as using technology to reach their users, but a broader definition could include any services that provide access to information without the user needing to visit the library (e.g. a hardcopy bulletin posted to primary-care practices).

Recent years have seen successful projects bringing library services into primary-care practices through the development of practice resource centres and the work of peripatetic librarians (Downing, Higgins and Smith, 1999; Lacey Bryant, 2000; Pearson and Rossall, 2001). However, in the UK, as in the USA, provision of services and equipment to community-based doctors has sometimes been superior to that received by other members of practice staff such as nurses (Richwine and McGowan, 2001; Yeoman et al., 2001). Current outreach projects are often tailored to ensure that all community-based staff are given improved access to resources. Other groups likely to benefit from such services include students and those following CPD programmes who may struggle to find time to visit the library within opening hours, especially if they have family commitments. Initiatives may also be aimed at staff who are only just becoming aware of the requirement to apply research to practice in the context of their work and who may have previously unrecognized training needs (Ashworth, 1998; Urquhart et al., 1999a).

The need for virtual outreach services is clear and will continue to grow as practitioners' work patterns change and the demands made on them in terms of quality and audit of patient care increase. The ability to access and appraise information in order to improve decision making lies at the heart of government health strategy (Plaice, 2000), and the health library service has a key role to play in ensuring that all practitioners are equipped with the necessary skills and facilities to achieve this.

Factors contributing to the success of virtual outreach projects

Evidence from the literature and the Value and Impact of Virtual Outreach Services (VIVOS) project (Yeoman et al., 2001) has highlighted various key factors contributing to the successful set-up and running of these services.

Preparation

From the outset it is important to have a clear purpose. Although flexibility of approach is necessary to cope with the unpredictable nature of projects requiring participation from a number of stakeholders it is important to have an identifiable and attainable goal or vision. This vision must be communicated to all stakeholders and to the potential users themselves. Often a project champion will emerge, either from within the library staff or from one of the stakeholder groups (Banks et al., 1997). A committed project champion can achieve a lot and will communicate their enthusiasm to other team members and to the wider community, but it should be borne in mind that project champions may move on and the work they have started may falter. Furthermore, it is worth considering that the best person to start up a project with enthusiasm might not be the right one to ensure, carefully, its continuing success.

Collaboration

Effective collaboration, communication and co-operation (Urquhart et al., 1999b) must exist between all project managers, library and computing staff as well as with potential users. Full engagement of stakeholders is essential and roles and responsibilities must be clearly established with service-level agreements set up if appropriate. This may sound unnecessarily formal if the stakeholders are other departments within the same institution but it is easier to define responsibilities clearly at the start than to try to unravel misunderstandings at a later stage.

VIVOS project participants agreed that good communication with stakeholders such as IT departments was a key factor in the success of their projects but that it had not always been easy to achieve. Other writers agree on the importance of creating strong interdepartmental relationships (e.g. Grosman and Larson, 1996) and suggest that information professionals would benefit from finding ways of nurturing these relationships and creating an environment in which information and IT staff can work together and recognize each other's complementary skills (Plaice, 2000). Richwine and McGowan (2001) created an advisory board for their project (providing a virtual health library for

18 healthcare institutions and unaffiliated health professionals in rural Indiana). Board members included a physician, a nurse, a hospital administrator, a library representative from one of the smaller hospitals as well as library staff from the main hospital. The board was actively involved in the selection of resources and in plans for future service development.

However hard library staff work at building individual relationships, the value of a supportive institutional culture that encourages staff development and recognizes that the library contributes to education – in the fullest sense – cannot be underestimated. Lack of interest by hospital administration or concerns about financial commitment may preclude institutions from taking part in outreach activities (Richwine and McGowan, 2001).

Collaboration needs to be extended not just to project stakeholders but to the library and information community as a whole. The previous section stressed the need for thorough preparation before undertaking a new project; this should include learning from the experiences of colleagues who have faced similar challenges when setting up and running outreach projects (Lacey Bryant, 2000).

Training

Since most outreach initiatives contain an element of user training it is worth drawing out some of the main issues to consider.

Careful planning yet with flexibility

In line with recent trends linking information access to the appraisal skills necessary to apply that information effectively in practice, a 1996 exploratory study conducted for the NHS Executive by South Thames Research & Development Directorate recommends that educational providers should aim to develop integrated programmes that link the different research application process elements rather than training on specific skills sets (Ashworth, 1998). Such an approach may not be relevant for all outreach training programmes but when planning sessions it is important to consider all the needs of the users: it may not be sufficient to simply show them how to access a database if they do not know what to do with the information once they have located it.

Lack of practice following initial sessions can lead to skills loss

There are many reasons why trainees may not practise their skills even after enthusiastically attending a training session. Sometimes, frustratingly, these reflect the very barriers that prevented them accessing information in the first place. Reasons given by VIVOS interviewees include lack of confidence in their new skills, lack of time, continuing problems with availability of equipment, and perceived lack of need due to no participation in CPD activity since training. If time and resources permit, refresher sessions are often popular as is easy access to library staff (e.g. by phone) to ask for assistance (Royle et al., 2000; Yeoman et al., 2001). If a cascading technique has been used – training a group of practitioners and relying on them to pass on their skills to colleagues – there may be increased need for support to ensure that the process takes place as intended.

Training for library staff

Lastly, it is important not to overlook the needs of library staff who may themselves be unfamiliar with new services or be asked to take on a different role as part of the project.

Sustainability

'Outreach is not a short-term project, but rather a long-term commitment' (Dorsch and Landwirth, 1993). This is a daunting prospect since the commitment to long-term expenditure of resources and time in a rapidly changing environment should not be underestimated. However, it is important not to focus solely on the exciting challenge of launching a new service without considering the long-term implications of sustaining it and continuing to justify its existence to funding bodies and senior management.

For a start, however thorough the needs-assessment exercise carried out at the beginning of a project, simply providing access to information resources does not necessarily mean that people will use them (Urquhart and Hepworth, 1995; D'Alessandro et al., 1998a; Royle et al., 2000). A review of the information needs of rural healthcare practitioners in the USA suggests that librarians need to make sustained efforts to convince this group of the benefits of using information services and change their information behaviour (Dorsch, 2000).

Continued active promotion of services, rather than just a fanfare at the launch, and rolling training programmes can help ensure that users are kept informed and aware of the benefits of using the service. Several VIVOS interviewees felt that library services were not sufficiently promoted and claimed that they themselves had 'spread the gospel' among colleagues. Word-of-mouth recommendation from satisfied users may be very effective publicity but a more structured approach is needed too (Banks et al., 1997; Gosling and Westbrook, 2002).

Even with high levels of motivation among users and library staff in the early stages, maintaining momentum can be difficult. This is especially true when services are faced with challenges such as the delayed roll-out of IT equipment, uncertainties about future funding, lack of a culture that supports practitioners' research activities, or a perception among users that such activities are only appropriate if they are undertaking CPD (Urquhart and Davies, 1997; Newman, Papadopoulos and Sigsworth, 1998). Infrequent use of services means that skills gained in training sessions are easily forgotten, and disillusionment can set in.

Like users of other outreach services (e.g. Pearson and Rossall, 2001) those interviewed for the VIVOS project expressed a desire for continuous support and were in favour of post-training refresher sessions and easy access to help at the time problems occur – ideally along the lines of a 24-hour help-desk. Even though the service may be 'virtual' users like the personal touch (Self, Wright and Waugh, 1998) and the input of library staff does not stop with the finished website or the end of the training session. Consistent support for the library team at the home base, including those not directly involved in the project, should not be forgotten since their job roles may have changed and new skills may need developing.

Evaluation

Outreach services must remain in tune with the needs of their users, adding new components (Banks et al., 1997) and responding to feedback. A key element of this process is evaluation. It is easy to overlook or postpone evaluation activities, especially if library resources are stretched, but provision for evaluation should be integrated into the project from the start as part of an ongoing process of testing, evaluation, taking stock and moving on (Yeoman et al., 2001).

Evaluation can be carried out either by project staff or by external research teams. For external teams, who may be evaluating a number of outreach services, the challenge is to achieve consistency, e.g. in survey instruments, to allow common themes to be identified while remaining sensitive to the individual circumstances and requirements of each service. It is difficult to identify transferable principles across a range of projects with different objectives, working in different cultures and with different levels and sources of funding (Booth and Falzon, 2000; Booth et al., 2002, Yeoman et al., 2003).

Typical questions to be considered in an evaluation, especially if presenting the results to senior management, will focus on value for money and impact on patient care. Both are difficult to assess in a service of this type and the situation is not made any easier by the fact that a small percentage of users may be very enthusiastic and active which may skew database usage statistics (Urquhart et al., 2001; Yeoman et al., 2001). Even with other types of survey, results can be unrepresentative since, for example, many users dislike filling in online survey forms. Individual user identification can make this easier but can be a barrier to access (D'Alessandro et al., 1998b); indeed several VIVOS interviewees complained that they already had too many passwords to remember.

Booth et al. (2002) identify the following as key questions to be answered by an evaluation:

- What has the project's impact been on existing library services?
- Can the project demonstrate added value, over and above existing services?
- Is what we are doing value for money?
- How has the project affected information provision to the general public, either directly or indirectly?
- What has the project's impact been on direct patient care?

Enhancing the skills of the library team

Beyond the original challenge to the library team's project management, negotiation, communication and organizational skills inherent in setting up a new service, successfully sustaining an outreach service places increasing demands on librarians who may find themselves looked to as technical experts and trouble-shooters. Frequently job roles can expand from providing library services and database instruction as outlined in the project goals to encompass those of computer consultant or technician (Banks et al., 1997).

Rose (1998) gives a list of skills that information professionals need to face the challenges of getting evidence-based practice into the primary and community care settings:

- campaigner
- strategic planner
- outreach worker
- educator and trainer
- organizer and disseminator of secondary sources of information
- researcher (this includes evaluation skills identified by Booth et al. (2002) such as project management, questionnaire design, data collection, stakeholder analysis, web design, people skills)
- spoonfeeder (Rose himself queries this term but uses it in the sense of 'expert searcher')
- marketer.

A more recent study that includes analysis of job descriptions of information professionals in the health sector (Pearson and Urquhart, 2002) looks at the importance given to particular attributes and the frequency of their occurrence in job descriptions. The most frequently cited attributes are:

* communication and interpersonal skills (including customer focus and negotiating skills)
* teamworking
* personal organization skills
* logical and analytical thinking
* flexibility
* innovation and creativity.

Conclusion

'I believe that librarians can perform a more central role in introducing new users to the increasingly sophisticated information environment of health care and help encourage a wide range of practitioners to adopt evidence-based approaches to healthcare and decision-making.' This was Judith Palmer's vision in 1996. Current developments in virtual outreach services show that librarians are indeed at the fore in broadening the user-base of health information resources and developing the skills practitioners need to appraise this information and apply it to practice. It is vital that the momentum should not be lost and that projects remain as sustainable as they are innovative. Understanding and responding to the needs of users is, as always, a key factor in this process, but the value of understanding and learning from the needs and experiences of colleagues both from within the library community and from other participating departments/organizations should not be underestimated.

Key points

* The problem of ensuring adequate access to health library services for all healthcare practitioners has become more prominent and more pressing.
* Outreach programmes must serve all users who require access to evidence-based information at the point of care.
* A broad definition of 'virtual outreach service' could include any services providing access to information without the user having to visit the library.
* Online communities of practice can provide a wide range of services and are becoming increasingly popular.
* Factors identified as contributing to the success of virtual outreach projects are preparation, effective collaboration, training, sustainability, evaluation and library-staff development.

References

Ashworth, F. A. (1998) Training the Trainers: meeting the perceived learning needs of librarians who facilitate evidence based healthcare workshops in South Thames, University of Wales: unpublished dissertation.

Banks, R. A. et al. (1997) Outreach Services: issues and challenges, *Medical Reference Services Quarterly*, **16** (2), 1–10.

Booth, A and Falzon L. (2000). Evaluating Information Service Innovations in the Health Service: 'If I was planning on going there I wouldn't start from here'. In Eaglestone, B. and Dowd, C. (eds), *Proceedings of SHIMR 2000: 5th International Symposium on Health Information Management Research, Sheffield, June 2000*, Sheffield, University of Sheffield.

Booth, A. et al. (2002) Libraries without Walls Still Need Windows, *Health Information and Libraries Journal*, **19**, 181–4.

D'Alessandro, D. M. et al. (1998a) Barriers to Rural Physician Use of a Digital Health Sciences Library, *Bulletin of the Medical Library Association*, **86** (4), 583–93.

D'Alessandro, M. P. et al. (1998b) Evaluating Overall Usage of a Digital Health Sciences Library, *Bulletin of the Medical Library Association*, **86** (4), 602–9.

Dorsch, J. L. (2000) Information Needs of Rural Health Professionals: a review of the literature, *Bulletin of the Medical Library Association*, **88** (4), 346–54.

Dorsch, J. L. and Landwirth, T. K. (1993) Rural GRATEFUL MED Outreach: project results, impact and future needs, *Bulletin of the Medical Library Association*, **81** (4), 377–82.

Downing, L., Higgins, R. and Smith, T. (1999) *Peripatetic Library Service Project: assessing the value of a peripatetic library service for primary care in the Highlands, Final report*, Inverness, Peripatetic Library Service Project.

Gosling, S. and Westbrook, J. I. (2002) *The Influence of Professional and Organisational Factors on Health Professionals' Use of Online Evidence: an evaluation of the clinical information access program*, Sydney, University of NSW, www.ciap.health.nsw.gov.au/resources/research/index.html.

Grosman, J. and Larson, B. (1996) Team Building with Information System Departments: a hospital librarian's experience in coexisting, collaborating and cooperating, *Bulletin of the Medical Library Association*, **84** (2), 196–9.

Holtrum, E. and Zollo, S. A. (1998) The Healthnet Project: extending online information resources to end users in rural hospitals, *Bulletin of the Medical Library Association*, **86** (4), 569–75.

Lacey Bryant, S. (2000) The Information Needs and Information Seeking Behaviour of Family Doctors: a selective literature review, *Health Libraries Review*, **17** (2), 83–90.

Newman, M., Papadopoulos, I. and Sigsworth, J. (1998) Barriers to Evidence-based Practice, *Clinical Effectiveness in Nursing*, **2**, 11–20.

Palmer, J. (1996) Effectiveness and Efficiency: new roles and new skills for health librarians, *Aslib Proceedings*, **48** (10), 247–52.

Pearson, A. and Urquhart, C. (2002) Health Informatics Education: working across the professional boundaries. In Ashcroft, L. (ed.), *Continuity, Culture, Competition – the Future of Library and Information Studies Education? Proceedings of the 4th British Nordic Conference on Library and Information Studies, 21—23 March 2001, Dublin, Ireland*, Bradford, MCB University Press.

Pearson, D. and Rossall, H. (2001) Developing a General Practice Library: a collective project between a GP and librarian, *Health Information and Libraries Journal*, **18**, 192–202.

Pifalo, V. (1994) Circuit Librarianship: a twentieth anniversary appraisal, *Medical Reference Services Quarterly*, **13** (1), 19–33.

Plaice, C. (2000) Information for Health: opportunity to consolidate partnership working between librarian and other health information professionals, *Health Libraries Review*, **17** (2), 103–9.

Richwine, M. and McGowan, J. J. (2001) A Rural Virtual Health Sciences Library Project: research findings with implications for next generation library services, *Bulletin of the Medical Library Association*, **89** (1), 37–44.

Rose, S. (1998) Challenges and Strategies in Getting Evidence-based Practice into Primary Health Care: what role the information professional?, *Health Libraries Review*, **15**, 165–74.

Royle, J. A. et al. (2000) Evaluation of a System for Providing Information Resources to Nurses, *Health Informatics Journal*, **6**, 100–9.

Self, P. C., Wright, B. A. and Waugh, J. L. (1998) Remote Users of Health Sciences Libraries, *Library Trends*, **47** (1), 75–90.

Urquhart, C. et al. (1999a) *Getting Information to Vocational Trainees: report of the GIVTS project*, Library and Information Commission Research Report 26, London, Library and Information Commission.

Urquhart, C. J. et al. (1999b) Integrating Information Services with Vocational Training: the GIVTS project experience, *Health Informatics Journal*, **5** (4), 217–23.

Urquhart, C. et al. (2001) *NeLH Pilot Evaluation Project*, Final Report to NHS Information Authority, NeLH, Birmingham, NHSIA, www.nhsia.nhs.uk/nelh/pages/documents/aber.doc.

Urquhart, C. and Davies, R. (1997) EVINCE: the value of information in developing nursing knowledge and competence, *Health Libraries Review*, **14**, 61–72.

Urquhart, C. J. and Hepworth, J. B. (1995) *The Value to Clinical Decision Making of Information Supplied by NHS Library and Information Service*, British Library Research and Development Report 6205, London, British Library.

Yeoman, A. et al. (2001) *The Value and Impact of Virtual Outreach Services: report of the VIVOS project*, LIC 111, London, Resource: The Council for Museums,

Archives and Libraries.

Yeoman, A. J. et al. (2003) The Management of Health Library Outreach Services: evaluation and reflection on lessons learned on the VIVOS project, *Journal of the Medical Library Association*. In press.

5

The National electronic Library for Health

Alison Turner

Introduction

This chapter begins by charting the major milestones and achievements of the National electronic Library for Health (NeLH) since the launch of its pilot service. Lessons learnt along the way are shared. The NeLH is placed within the context of UK and international health-library developments. Key achievements of the NeLH offer an insight into the challenges of developing a national web-based service for health professionals.

Context

The NeLH is a digital library aimed predominantly at health professionals and managers in the National Health Service (NHS) although available on the internet to all. The NeLH is based around core evidence-based knowledge resources with links to commissioned specialized resources. Recent developments within the NHS reflect a new emphasis on knowledge management, for example:

- a focus on involving patients and public in decision making (see Chapter 1)
- a move towards 'joining up' health and social care (see Chapter 2)
- the development of National Service Frameworks for key health priorities (see Chapter 3)
- a renewed emphasis on lifelong learning (see Chapter 9)
- the launch of a National Programme for Information Technology (www.doh.gov.uk/ipu/programme/index.htm)
- the move towards a culture of learning from mistakes and service failures.

Health is a knowledge-rich sector and evidence-based practice has highlighted the importance of access to a sound knowledge base. Knowledge management is key (see Chapter 6), as evidenced by the development of the National Knowledge Service (www.nks.nhs.uk). The NeLH supports evidence-based decision making in healthcare, through the provision and delivery of a focused knowledge base in a format convenient to health professionals, at the time and place of need.

The NeLH complements existing libraries; concentrating on fast and easy electronic-only access to research evidence, clinical guidelines and critically appraised resources. Libraries across the health community offer access to the wider knowledge base, such as primary research, have a broader remit and offer face-to-face contact and localized services.

While the NeLH is funded specifically for England, comparable initiatives exist for Northern Ireland (www.honni.qub.ac.uk/), Scotland (www.elib.scot. nhs.uk/) and Wales (www.wales.nhs.uk). All offer access to the evidence base yet they differ in scope and remit. In England, the NeLH specifically supports evidence-based practice. Bibliographic databases (e.g. MEDLINE) and electronic journals remain the remit of NHS libraries, delivered via regional and local portals and intranets. In 2003, NHS libraries led the national procurement of a core collection of resources recognizing that the procurement of traditional library sources and the newer evidence-based resources have developed separately.

Health On the Net Northern Ireland (HONNI) is provided by Queen's University and provides a gateway to library services and the wider knowledge base for health and social care professionals in Northern Ireland. The e-library portal from NHS Scotland works alongside SHOW (Scotland's Health On the Web) to provide professionals, patients and librarians with links to databases, journals and evidence-based resources: 'Knowledge management to support the patient journey – one portal, one password, one pathway to learning' (NHS Education for Scotland, 2003). In Wales, the electronic library service is managed by the National Assembly of Wales, working in partnership with health libraries across the country. The aim of HOWIS (Health Of Wales Information Service) is to provide 'a seamless service bringing together information sources about the health and lifestyle of the population of Wales into a simple, electronic-based service' (Wenger, 2003). HOWIS has a broad remit, linking to health policy, bibliographic and evidence-based resources, library services and statistical information.

Electronic or virtual libraries are particularly appropriate where the user base is often large and distributed. Examples from around the world include the National Library of Medicine (www.nlm.nih.gov), while elsewhere in the United States portals are to be found, organized on a regional or local scale (Richwine and McGowan, 2001) or to meet specialist information needs

(Candler, Uijtdehaage and and Dennis, 2003). In Latin America and the Caribbean, the BIREME Virtual Library (www.bireme.org), led by the World Health Organization, is co-ordinating electronic library development. The Virtual Library brings together health information services to form a regional network, connected via the internet, with portals in Argentina, Brazil, Colombia, Cuba, Honduras and Mexico, linking to bibliographic and evidence-based resources. In Australia, the Clinical Information Access Program (CIAP) in New South Wales (www.clininfo.health.nsw.gov.au/) was implemented 'to provide clinicians . . . with access to knowledge resources at the point of care in public health care facilities and services' (Westbrook and Gosling, 2003). While emphasizing promotion of evidence-based resources, CIAP provides access to a wider knowledge base. Within Europe, electronic library initiatives include Germany (Korwitz, 2002), Denmark (Schneider, 2003) and Finland (Rajakiili, 2002). Much can be learnt from exploring this vast range of electronic libraries and examining similarities in information provision and variations in organization, funding and management. The above is merely a selection with many more examples to be found elsewhere in the literature.

Building an electronic library

In 1998 the Department of Health announced that 'there is now an opportunity to begin to develop from scratch an NHS accredited National Electronic Library for Health' (NHS Executive, 1998). Since then, the role of the NeLH has been recognized in several key documents (for example, Great Britain. Department of Health, 2002 and 2003a).

The NHS Information Authority (www.nhsia.nhs.uk) was commissioned to develop and deliver the Pilot NeLH, launched in November 2000. A small team of librarians, informatics experts, project managers and health professionals was formed to take forward the work. Individuals and organizations from different backgrounds and specialties have been involved in developing the library and this skill mix has been key to its success.

From the time of the launch of the NeLH, access has been the primary consideration. Initially, the NeLH consisted of a small selection of resources with access to licensed resources being restricted to the NHS private network (NHSnet) only. Within a few months access was enabled via the internet using the Athens access management system. This proved essential for the busy health professional, typically with limited internet connections in the workplace but now enjoying alternative access to the NeLH from home. The three years since the launch of the NeLH have seen its rapid growth with over 80 resources having been added, the vast majority being openly available to all. A few resources continue to be licensed specifically for NHS staff with authentication and authorization being managed using the Athens access management system.

With patient-centred care a priority for the UK health community, access to information has an important part to play and many advocate that patients and the public should share the same access as health professionals. Much of the NeLH is openly available to all. The NeLH also works closely with NHS Direct Online, a service geared entirely to the public, in facilitating access to information. During 2002, when England-wide access to the Cochrane Library and Clinical Evidence was launched, members of the public could, for the first time, access these two leading evidence-based resources.

For the first three years of the NeLH service, the priority was to organize knowledge, essentially developing a 24/7 one-stop source of knowledge. This was reflected in the early mission statement: 'to improve health and healthcare, clinical practice, patient choice and patient influence on the NHS by providing easy access to best current knowledge and information' (Gray and Toth, 2002). The strategy for 2003–6 updates this mission statement to supporting decision making by mobilizing knowledge.

Development of this one-stop shop involved gathering existing evidence-based resources and commissioning new products. Some existing resources were available free of charge on the internet while others were commercially available and were licensed on behalf of the NHS. Gaps still remained, hence the need to commission new resources, such as Hitting the Headlines, produced by the NHS Centre for Reviews and Dissemination. A detailed history of the development of the Pilot NeLH is outlined elsewhere (Toth, 1999; Toth et al., 2000; Turner and Vaughan, 2001; Turner et al., 2002). The pilot phase of the NeLH ended in Spring 2003. Following approval of the final business case and long-term funding, an open procurement exercise led to three-year contracts being agreed with suppliers.

Evaluation

During 2001, independent evaluations of the Pilot NeLH were conducted by the University of Wales Aberystwyth (UWA) and the National Computing Centre (NCC). The UWA evaluation included interviews with library and other NHS staff, a cost-benefit study and real-life case studies. Health professionals were largely satisfied suggesting that an electronic library can provide a 'climbing net' for subjects such as mental health and primary care, often difficult to reach through traditional library services. The cost-benefit study concluded that investment in the NeLH offered cost savings in terms of staff time: with estimates ranging from a conservative annual saving of £3 million to a more realistic annual saving of £12 million. The NCC study focused on technological aspects concluding that the NHS was technically ready for the NeLH. The NCC also found that clinicians looked to the NeLH to go beyond supporting patient care, particularly with regard to professional development and training. Further evaluative studies focused on specific aspects: communities of practice, access within public libraries and market research (see www.nhsia.nhs.uk/nelh/pages/background.asp).

Delivering an electronic library

The mission of the NeLH is to support evidence-based decision making in healthcare. It strives to achieve this by providing bibliographic databases, secondary publications and full-text publications. The NeLH tour (www.nelh.nhs.uk/tour) directs users through the generalist core collection via short summaries. See Table 5.1.

Table 5.1   The NeLH tour

Starting Out	NeLH search facility
	Specialist Libraries
Guidelines, Pathways and Protocols	NeLH Guidelines Finder
	NeLH Protocols and Pathways Library
	NeLH National Service Frameworks Zones
Evidence summaries	Clinical Evidence
	Cochrane Database of Systematic Reviews
	Bandolier
Clinical applications	Database of Abstracts of Reviews of Effects
	Hitting the Headlines
Individual studies	Cochrane Central Register of Controlled Trials
	NHS Economic Evaluations Database
	Bibliographic databases e.g. MEDLINE
Grey literature	Research Findings Register
	NHS Health Technology Assessments
Subject gateways	BIOME

This route, while not comprehensive, guides health professionals to answers for most clinical questions. However, the NeLH also provides access to a range of specialized resources such as:

- basic anatomy
- British National Formulary
- healthcare needs assessment
- medical dictionaries
- MIDIRS (midwifery resource)
- NHS cost and effectiveness reviews
- patient-centred care
- PRODIGY (primary care resource).

Serving specialist needs

Recognizing the needs of smaller sections of the user base, the NeLH commissioned 19 Specialist Libraries to pull together knowledge from research, data and experience within a particular specialty or profession (Brice and Gray, 2003). See Table 5.2.

Table 5.2   The 19 Specialist Libraries

Cancer
Child Health and Paediatrics
Communicable Diseases
Emergency Care (reported in Cooke, 2000)
ENT and Hearing Problems
Eyes and Visual Problems
Genetics
Cardiovascular Disease
Health Management (reported in Bell, 2002)
Patients and Public Involvement
Learning Disabilities
Mental Health (reported in Dearness and Tomlin, 2001)
Trauma, Orthopaedics and Musculoskeletal Disease
Nutrition and Metabolic
Oral Health
Respiratory
Skin Conditions
Health Problems in Old Age
Women's Health

In addition, the NeLH works with partner NHS organizations to develop Specialist Libraries in health informatics, knowledge management, public health and screening. Specialist Libraries build on the work undertaken by the pilot Virtual Branch Libraries. New Specialist Libraries will be developed for neurology, anaesthetics, palliative care and pathology.

Getting the message across

A market research study conducted during 2002 highlighted the need to raise awareness. Communications work is vital to the roll-out and uptake of a national service such as the NeLH. A sub-team is tasked with ensuring effective communication, publicity and public relations; raising awareness and ensuring users have the skills to get the best out of the NeLH are essential. The market research study targeted existing users and non-users via focus groups, interviews and an online questionnaire. Many users made repeat visits to the NeLH, quoting its emphasis on quality; the one-stop shop aspect; and its being quick and easy to use. Non-users were asked their reasons for not using the NeLH: they didn't know about it; they had poor access to computers; there were too few links from other sites; and they had limited access to training and support. The market research concluded that there was a definite and broad market need for NeLH but that a clear and simple strong message was required, using multiple communication routes. Such findings are pertinent to any electronic library service.

In responding to the market research, promotion is undertaken on two levels:

- directly to target user groups via conferences, mailings and presentations
- via health librarians, at the interface between national services and frontline health professionals.

Publicity materials, including posters, leaflets, bookmarks and pencils, have been developed (www.nelh.nhs.uk/publicity). The NeLH frequently works with NHS library services on joint publicity initiatives, maximizing impact and minimizing costs. To build and maintain relationships with key stakeholder groups, a newsletter (www.nelh.nhs.uk/update) and discussion list (www.mailbase.org.uk/lists/nelh) have been established. Ironically, the team uses significant amounts of paper to promote an electronic resource but there is still a need for paper-based promotion. Usage statistics at the time of major campaigns – for example, promotional inserts in journal issues – attest to the more successful approaches.

Usage statistics for June 2003 show around 100,000 unique users, and over 500,000 page views. NeLH is proving a durable and reliable resource for users, with around 40% returning to the site repeatedly. A feedback facility helps identify those features that are particularly useful or difficult, essential as users of an electronic library are remote, even invisible.

An awareness campaign has successfully raised the profile of the NeLH together with health libraries. An awareness week, coinciding with the anniversary of the launch, generated a 16% rise in use during November 2002. Market research suggests that word of mouth is a very strong medium; health professionals are likely to act more readily on the recommendations of colleagues than on generic publicity materials. Subsequent awareness campaigns have targeted 'champions' who will spread the word to their colleagues. A critical success factor has been uniting national and local events in a co-ordinated approach.

The overall challenge is to:

- raise awareness
- develop information skills in health professionals
- infiltrate daily working lives so that using library services and resources becomes 'natural'.

But this is not as simple as it sounds. Suppose we wanted 65% of NHS clinicians to be regularly using NeLH (assuming a ballpark figure of around 600,000 clinicians). To provide 1 hour of training every 3 years would require 20 trainers working 5 hours per day, 5 days per week. Add to this difficulties in reaching rurally based professionals and the task becomes insurmountable.

For this reason, the NeLH works in partnership with other library services, joining forces around marketing and training to unify and maximize communication efforts, promoting health libraries in general rather than the local services of each individual library. Such partnership working enables a wider reach for publicity campaigns and offers economies of scale. This is evident in the development of a Digital Libraries Network (www.nelh.nhs.uk/dlnet), to bring together library trainers to work in an integrated and co-ordinated way. Librarians benefit from the support and training to become digital library experts; they receive advance information together with tailored professional development. The approach offers co-ordination; recognition of the contributions of library staff; a valuable support structure; and opportunities to integrate national and local initiatives. A collaborative weblog (http://dlnet.blogspot.com) facilitates sharing of good practice. Building a network of trainers and offering resources and support centrally makes it possible to promote health libraries to the NHS workforce, currently 1.2 million (Great Britain. Department of Health, 2003b).

Partnership working

The NeLH team works closely with elements of the National Knowledge Service (www.nks.nhs.uk/), such as NHS Direct Online, nhs.uk, the electronic

Library for Social Care, as well as with local library services. It has worked with librarians on large and small projects, including site navigation, search-engine testing, and promotion. Librarians also lead such developments as Hitting the Headlines, Guidelines Finder, Document of the Week and the Specialist Libraries for Health Management and Heart Diseases.

Partnership with health librarians remains one of the highest priorities of the NeLH, which continues to have a dedicated librarian development programme and budget. The NeLH also works with such agencies as the National Institute of Clinical Excellence, the National Patient Safety Agency, NHS Direct Online and the Modernisation Agency.

Conclusion

This chapter has covered development of the NeLH from pilot to full service and the lessons learnt. The NeLH exists in a fast-changing environment and the team has developed flexible roadmaps to plan for the future. The specific role of the NeLH in supporting evidence-based decision making is now established within the UK health-library community. In tackling the challenges of developing a national web-based library for health, in partnership with NHS and other health librarians, the NeLH has carved a specialist niche and achieved a large user group. In moving from a focus, in its first three years, on drawing together the knowledge base the NeLH is now targeting the mobilization of knowledge, to make it a part of clinical and managerial decision making.

Key points

* The NeLH is aimed predominantly at health professionals and managers but the majority of content is openly available to all.
* Its mission is to promote evidence-based decision making by patients, clinicians, managers and commissioners through the organization and mobilization of best current knowledge.
* The NeLH sits within a larger health library community; whereas health libraries have a broad remit, the NeLH is focused on supporting evidence-based practice.
* Many similar initiatives exist within the UK and across the world; while there are many similarities in terms of content, the organization, management and funding of such services vary considerably.
* Partnership working is vital to the success of the NeLH; partnerships with health librarians remain an important part of the strategy.

- The NeLH has developed support mechanisms for librarians, in the form of a portal, a development programme and the Digital Libraries Network.

References

Bell, L. (2002) Guerrilla Tactics in Information Dissemination: developing a web-based resource for NHS managers, *Aslib Proceedings*, **54** (3), 158–65.

Brice, A. and Gray, M. (2003) Knowledge is the Enemy of Disease, *Library and Information Update*, **2** (3), 32–4.

Candler, C. S., Uijtdehaage, S. H. J. and Dennis, S. E. (2003) Introducing HEAL: the Health Education Assets Library, *Academic Medicine*, **78**, 249–53.

Cooke, M. (2000) National electronic Library for Health: emergency care, *Journal of Accident and Emergency Medicine*, Suppl. 3.

Dearness, K. L. and Tomlin, A. (2001) Development of the National Electronic Library for Mental Health: providing evidence-based information for all, *Health Information and Libraries Journal*, **18** (3), 167–74.

Gray, J. A. and Toth, B. (2002) A First Class Knowledge Service: developing the National electronic Library for Health, *Health Information & Libraries Journal*, **19**, 133–45.

Great Britain. Department of Health (2002) *Delivering 21st Century IT Support for the NHS: national strategic programme*, London, Department of Health, www.doh.gov.uk/ipu/whatnew/deliveringit/nhsitimpplan.pdf.

Great Britain. Department of Health (2003a) *Our Inheritance, Our Future: realising the potential of genetics in the NHS*, London, Department of Health, www.doh.gov.uk/genetics/whitepaper.htm.

Great Britain. Department of Health (2003b) *Staff in the NHS 2002,* London, Department of Health, www.doh.gov.uk/public/staff_in_the_nhs_leaflet_2002.pdf.

Korwitz, U. (2002) Building up the Virtual Medical Library in Germany, *Health Information and Libraries Journal*, **19**, 173–5.

NHS Education for Scotland (2003) *elibrary for NHS Scotland*, www.elib.scot.nhs.uk.

NHS Executive (1998) *Information for Health: an information strategy for the modern NHS 1998–2005, a national strategy for local implementation*, London, Department of Health, www.doh.gov.uk/ipu/strategy/.

Rajakiili, P. (2002) The National Electronic Library in Finland, FinELib, *Health Information and Libraries Journal*, **19**, 169–72.

Richwine, M. and McGowan, J. J. (2001) A Rural Virtual Health Sciences Library Project: research findings with implications for next generation library services, *Bulletin of the Medical Library Association*, **89** (1), 37–44.

Schneider, A. (2003) Denmark's Electronic Research Library, *EAHIL Newsletter*, **63**, 21–3, www.eahil.org/newsletter/63/May2003.pdf.

Toth, B. (1999) The National electronic Library for Health: the story so far, *He@lth Information on the Internet*, **9**, 9–11, www.hioti.org.

Toth, B. et al. (2000) National electronic Library for Health: progress and prospects, *Health Libraries Review*, **17**, 46–50.

Turner, A. et al. (2002) A First Class Knowledge Service: developing the National electronic Library for Health, *Health Information and Libraries Journal*, **19**, 133–45.

Turner, A. and Vaughan, P. (2001) The Pilot NeLH: progress and development, *He@lth Information on the Internet*, **23**, 4–6, www.hioti.org.

Wenger, P. (2003) Health of Wales Information Service: opening the gateway to health information for all, *He@lth Information on the Internet*, **32**, 8–9, www.hioti.org.

Westbrook, J. and Gosling, S. (2003) *Summary Report of the Results of the Evaluation of the Clinical Information Access Program (CIAP)*, Sydney, University of New South Wales.

6

Knowledge management

Andrew Booth and Anne Brice

Introduction

Internationally, knowledge management (KM) is having a significant impact on health services. In the past, developments have concentrated on private healthcare organizations but several countries are witnessing the emergence of KM concepts within the publicly funded health sector. This chapter looks at systematic approaches to KM within the UK's NHS Research and Development (R&D) programme and within the UK Government's Modernization agenda. It then exemplifies how library and information services (LIS) practitioners can implement the concept at a local, regional and national level. It concludes by addressing the future for KM within the health service of the twenty-first century.

What is knowledge management?

Margaret Haines, former Director of Research and Knowledge Management for the Department of Health's R&D Programme, has championed the following definition:

> The capabilities by which communities within an organization capture the knowledge that is critical to them, constantly improve it, and make it available in the most effective manner to those people who need it, so that they can exploit it creatively to add value as a normal part of their work.
>
> (Kelleher and Levene, 2001)

The sheer practicality of this definition counters a remoteness often experienced by health librarians when encountering such concepts as the 'National Knowledge Service'. KM employs techniques that can be exploited at a local, regional or national level:

> Knowledge management enables the skills, knowledge and processes of the organisation (its intellectual assets) to be used effectively, creatively and consistently to improve business performance and customer satisfaction. (TFPL Ltd, 1999)

Knowledge management in the health service

Healthcare systems are typically complex and bureaucratic and their organizational design often slows down decision making (Beveren, 2003). As health services are subject to high-profile organizational change it is unsurprising to see them become key players in adapting and validating KM practices from the public sector. The critical resource for any healthcare organization is neither money, nor estates nor facilities. The NHS has 1.2 million employees (Brice and Gray, 2003) and KM aims to 'leverage' the intellectual capital held in the skills, knowledge and expertise of these personnel. KM encompasses a broad collection of practices related to generating, disseminating and promoting knowledge sharing. It requires that the public sector adopt systematic approaches, currently employed by leading private-sector firms, and adapt management tools to systematically promote knowledge sharing. Within health services, understanding of KM is constrained by a 'focus on clinical knowledge and knowledge relating to evidence-based medicine' (NeLH 2001a). Clinical knowledge management is:

> concerned with the collection, processing, visualisation, storage, preservation and retrieval of health related data and information, whether it be on an individual or collection of subjects. (Wyatt, 2001)

More recently, health services have started to address other types of knowledge: about healthcare improvement; about 'customer service'; about management, leadership, change management; about new ways of working; and about organizational learning (NeLH, 2001a). KM also interlinks current healthcare thinking regarding evidence-based medicine, clinical governance and information and communication technologies (Plaice and Kitch, 2003).

Recent years have witnessed 'publication of a whole raft of health policy documents that have promoted reform towards a more patient-centered service, with direct implications for knowledge management' (NeLH, 2001a). *Learning from Bristol* (Great Britain. Department of Health, 2002), the Department of

Health's response to the public inquiry into the management of paediatric heart patients, outlines a 'programme of reform' to integrate NHS knowledge systems. NHS UK, NHS Direct Online, the National electronic Library for Health (NeLH), the electronic Library for Social Care (eLSC) and the NHS Modernisation Agency's Connections database were assembled under the wider umbrella of a National Knowledge Service (NKS) 'to support the delivery of high quality information for patients and staff'. The Department of Health already produces, procures and commissions knowledge for patients and staff based on research, data and experience (Brice and Gray, 2003). Yet such knowledge is unconnected and difficult to find. The NKS aims to develop common standards, mobilize a common core of knowledge (including the Cochrane Library and Clinical Evidence) and assure that resources are of consistent quality and content.

KM typically involves people, processes and systems and, despite inevitable overlap, each is targeted by a key national NHS player:

- people (NHS University) – equipping NHS staff with basic KM skills and imbuing them with recognition of the need to share information
- processes (NHS Modernisation Agency) – improving knowledge-sharing processes within, and between, organizations
- systems (NHS Information Authority) – developing a technical infrastructure to support KM.

See Table 6.1

Table 6.1   Major players in NHS knowledge management

NHS University	www.nhsu.nhs.uk/
National Knowledge Service	www.nks.nhs.uk/
National electronic Library for Health	www.nelh.nhs.uk/
National Electronic Library for Social Care	www.elsc.org.uk/
NHS UK	www.nhs.uk/
NHS Direct Online	www.nhsdirect.nhs.uk/
NHS Modernisation Agency	www.modernnhs.nhs.uk/
NHS Information Authority	www.nhsia.nhs.uk/
Department of Health Research and Development Directorate	www.doh.gov.uk/research

The role of knowledge management in R&D

KM has long been recognized within the NHS R&D Programme. The NHS Information Systems Strategy entrusted the UK Cochrane Centre and the NHS Centre for Reviews and Dissemination with better utilization of existing research (Sheldon and Chalmers, 1994). The R&D strategy has been a catalyst for KM (Rowland and Harris, 1998), aiming to create a knowledge-based organization within which all decisions are informed by scientific research. Unsurprisingly, the first Portfolio Director for KM was appointed within the Department of Health's R&D Directorate.

Paradoxically, even though an audit conducted for the R&D Programme identified £3.5 million of KM research projects, the role of research in developing KM is underexploited. Developmentally the R&D Directorate has made progress in managing 'explicit' knowledge – knowledge codified in books, reports or peer-reviewed journal articles and at the project stage via the National Research Register. However, 'tacit' knowledge – that knowledge not yet captured in written form – remains elusive. Outputs of 'tacit' KM are less advanced and less sophisticated than their 'explicit' counterparts.

Knowledge management and modernization

Following publication of the NHS Plan (Great Britain. Department of Health, 2000a), the health service embarked upon a programme of 'modernization' (Bate and Robert, 2002). Central to this vision, the Modernisation Agency provides 'a centre of excellence as to how knowledge and "know how" about best practice can be spread' (Great Britain. Department of Health, 2000b). Within the public sector, the NHS is influenced by the Office of the e-Envoy which aims 'to ensure that the country, its citizens and its businesses derive maximum benefit from the knowledge economy' (www.e-envoy.gov.uk/Home/Homepage/fs/en). The NHS Modernisation Agency (2003a) observes:

> We will know we have succeeded when knowledge about an improvement developed anywhere in the system rapidly becomes common knowledge and is actually used everywhere.

Singled out for particular attention is 'the breakthrough collaborative', a mechanism to 'help local clinicians and managers redesign local services around the needs and convenience of patients' (Great Britain. Department of Heath, 2000a). For example, the Orthopaedic Breakthrough Collaborative concentrates on improving care for patients requiring hip replacement surgery (Bate and Robert, 2002). The Modernisation Agency is committed to exploring 'healthcare improvement' in identifying robust methodologies and capturing and transferring this knowledge to other organizations.

The role of health libraries in KM

Keeling and Lambert (2000) identify opportunities for healthcare librarians 'at the knowledge intersection' by extending their role beyond provision of an information service to provide a KM service to the rest of the hospital community. This may trigger increased recognition for librarians' skills at board level, particularly among infrequent users, such as managers. Lopatin and Blagden (1997) advocate such librarian involvement:

It seems that both clinicians and managers have forgotten, or are unaware of, the skills of librarians. But we come equipped with critical appraisal skills and a great deal of knowledge of the new technology. Librarians are knowledge managers par excellence.

A report by TFPL (1999) agrees but cautions:

The knowledge management phenomenon presents the LIS profession with a unique opportunity . . . but to take advantage of that opportunity individual professionals need fully to understand the potential of those skills and the business objectives of the organizations that employ them.

KM and user education and training

While there is an obvious role for health librarians in designing information systems, creating classification systems and taxonomies, and implementing those systems, little attention has been paid to their contribution to user education and training (Koenig, 2001). A survey of KM systems implementations identifies that more than half of failures are attributable to inadequate user training and education (KPMG Consulting, 2000). Halliday (2001) highlights the opportunities that demand for information literacy skills might offer information professionals.

In developing and implementing KM within an organization an information professional requires such knowledge skills as an understanding of the context in which the health professional works; knowledge about the patient context; what type of information is relevant; how the professional works and how they would use the information once provided (Fennessy, 2001). The NHS University will likely include training in information and knowledge skills in the curriculum (Copper and Haines, 2002).

Communities of practice

'Communities of practice' (Kirkham, 2000) are 'groups of people who share a concern, a set of problems, or a passion about a topic, and who deepen their knowledge and expertise by interacting on an ongoing basis'. This focus on organizational learning highlights the potential contribution of the healthcare librarian. Communities of practice differ from teams and workgroups in that membership is usually voluntary. They tend to be more general, fluid and not tied into the delivery of tangible results. They have been identified as 'the killer knowledge management application' (Rumizen, 2002).

The Specialist Libraries of the National electronic Library for Health (NeLH) seek to develop and support communities of practice (Urquhart, Yeoman and Sharp, 2002). Health professionals have the opportunity to create online virtual communities that support communication, information exchange and dissemination as a powerful alternative to traditional personal networks. Research has identified four stages in the development of a community of practice: potential (connection), building (memory and context), engaged (access and learning) and active (collaboration) (Brice and Gray, 2003). Most of the Specialist Libraries were at the 'building' or 'engaged' stages of development, not having developed the active feedback and participation required to move to the active stage, characterized by collaborative working. Nevertheless this picture is changing. For example, the National electronic Library for Communicable Disease (www.nelh.nhs.uk/communicable) has been developing online communities of practice. Such communities are only of benefit if they support 'knowledge translation', developing multi-disciplinary information sources, facilitating active debate and influencing the production of new knowledge.

The role of technology

Internet-based technologies can stimulate organizational learning and foster 'virtual learning communities' (Booth, 2001). Groupware allows individuals to annotate existing documents to create and shape new knowledge. Bulletin boards provide a readily auditable trail of how ideas develop and evolve. Discussion lists and chatrooms yield opportunities for asynchronous (delayed) or synchronous (real-time) exchange of ideas. Action learning sets within a 'safe' virtual environment allow community problem solving.

At a personal level, intelligent agents allow users to personalize and customize searches, according to users' personal preferences, background and specialties, alerting them to postings in areas of interest. Nevertheless, the focus should be on the people and processes, not the enabling technologies:

If you're spending more than one third of your time on technologies for knowledge management, you're neglecting the content, organizational culture and motivational approaches that will make a knowledge management system actually useful.

(Davenport, 2002)

Getting started

Given that the KM agenda is potentially overwhelming and, indeed, that organization-wide approaches will likely be impractical if not undesirable, a local LIS practitioner may ask 'Where do I start?' Many practitioners counsel on the need to start small and to build with incremental steps. Booth (2001) suggests ten building blocks that can advance an organization towards KM (see Table 6.2).

Table 6.2   Ten building blocks of KM

Conducting a knowledge audit
Knowledge mapping
Providing a knowledge-sharing network
Compiling a database of expertise
Scanning the environment
Creating communities of practice
Measuring 'knowledge capital'
Organizing and classifying knowledge
Creating a chief knowledge officer
Conducting entry and exit debriefings

Davenport (1997) analyses four case studies and lists ten principles useful to LIS professionals in introducing KM within their organization.

1 Knowledge management is expensive (but so is stupidity!)
2 Effective management of knowledge requires hybrid solutions of people and technology
3 Knowledge management is highly political
4 Knowledge management requires knowledge managers
5 Knowledge management benefits more from maps than models, more from markets than from hierarchies
6 Sharing and using knowledge are often unnatural acts
7 Knowledge management means improving knowledge work processes
8 Knowledge access is only the beginning
9 Knowledge management never ends
10 Knowledge management requires a knowledge contract.

No 'one size fits all', so if one approach is unsuccessful one must return to the KM toolkit and try another.

Some commentators suggest that 'needs, problems and pains' can be explored using soft-systems methodology and action research (Fennessy, 2001). 'Quick wins' involve identifying problems and addressing them using KM principles. Big-bang approaches, involving organization-wide KM programmes, are rarely successful. Incremental approaches, employing one or two initiatives, do not require a formal strategy and allow pilot 'testing' on a small scale before rolling out on a larger scale.

KM extends good management practice required at all levels of an organization. As Gray (1998) states: 'We have managed money and buildings and people and energy. Now we need also to manage the most precious commodity of the twenty-first century knowledge and know how'.

Case studies
Department of Health

The Department of Health (DoH) is a member of the Government's Knowledge Network and its pragmatic approach to knowledge management focuses on:

- creating the knowledge base – both tangible and intangible
- making it available in a user-friendly form
- encouraging and skilling people to seek out, share and use knowledge (NeLH, 2001a).

The Department of Health's KM strategy covers leadership and accountability; people and change; content and processes; and information and technical infrastructure. It is built around people, processes and technology. The strategy embodies the importance of not overlooking existing 'pockets' of good practice within two simple concepts:

- *Recognizing existing examples of KM* – through use of e-mail, shared documents, desktop access to knowledge databases, an intranet, staff directories, meetings, seminars, informal chats at the coffee machine, etc.
- *Building on this by doing it better* – by improving access to information and 'joining up' information assets, providing training and guidance, piloting new ways to capture and share knowledge, etc.

Knowledge harvesting pilot project

NHS South East Regional Office carried out a knowledge harvesting pilot project in January–March 2002 (Andrews, 2002). *Shifting the Balance of Power* (*STBOP*) (Great Britain. Department of Health, 2001), the Government's attempt to devolve power and decision making to local NHS organizations, posed a considerable challenge to business continuity. Particularly at risk from losses of information, as people move to other jobs or retire, were Educational Commissioning and Business Case Approval. The Executive Team identified these as priority areas for knowledge harvesting and Directorate leads nominated lead staff with particular expertise where the 'baton' was to pass to a successor body.

Knowledge harvesting is used to elicit tacit knowledge from employees; it is appropriate for exit interviews and in helping new project teams to develop corporate memory. Hyperknowledge software was selected for organizing and presenting harvested knowledge. A short timescale made it essential to engage staff as quickly as possible. Following a briefing paper, prospective participants were contacted individually to arrange face-to-face meetings with the project manager.

The stages of knowledge harvesting were:

- an initial workshop where Hyperknowledge software was used to produce a high-level model, capturing the most important team objectives and activities, and testing their validity
- one-to-one interviews, typically two sessions of two hours' duration, between harvestee and harvester, observed by the Hyperknowledge consultant
- a consolidation workshop at which a single aggregated model was presented and further detail added before a final model was produced and agreed
- further detail to the model added by the consultants and project team; the captured knowledge formatted for publishing on the intranet.

Clearly, identifying individuals with the right skill set is central to its success. Such skills include:

- interviewing/questioning skills
- listening skills
- knowledge of specific task area
- knowledge of software
- business skills.

Participants reported that they benefited from articulating knowledge they possessed, particularly in group interviews, where more than one interviewee was present for knowledge gathering. However, they felt that explicit knowledge had been captured more effectively than tacit knowledge. Interviewers honed their interviewing skills and gained increased confidence. 'How and why' questioning helped to elicit more powerful information. However, the project was constrained by the uncertain backdrop of organizational change.

Sandwell Healthcare NHS Trust

At a local level, Sandwell Healthcare NHS Trust (2000) aimed to evaluate KM processes to support best practice in patient care, looking at knowledge flow across the Trust and within a local GP practice. The project included:

- KM infrastructure – information systems to support the management and transfer of information
- policies, processes and procedures to enable the sharing of information and its conversion into knowledge
- culture, attitudes and working practices of the staff involved.

Outcomes from the project included implementation of a KM strategy and development of an action plan.

Knowledge mobilization

Debate continues as to whether KM is the right term for 'more effective knowledge sharing' (Copper and Haines, 2002). Some commentators prefer KM to mean 'knowledge mobilization'. They feel that this concentrates on the mobilization of knowledge that has already been organized, consisting of 'all those actions required to deliver the knowledge wherever and when it is needed'. This includes not only making knowledge easily accessible to those searching for answers, but also incorporation 'into the electronic patient record to prompt and remind the decision maker and be available through a variety of dissemination channels' (National Knowledge Service, 2003).

Knowledge translation

Recent attention has focused on 'knowledge translation' (Davis et al., 2003), a term popularized by the Canadian Institutes of Health Research (CIHR) for 'the exchange, synthesis and ethically-sound application of researcher findings within a complex system of relationships among researchers and knowledge users' (Canadian Institutes of Health Research, 2002). Knowledge translation thus involves interaction between producers of new information and its translation into knowledge for users. It acknowledges the limitations of academic publication as a mechanism for dissemination and uses dynamic mechanisms to engage with decision makers. Systematic reviews represent specific examples of KT for a clinical audience and the challenge is to extend such methods to meet the needs of other potential users of knowledge.

Conclusion

The NHS has clearly made progress in implementing KM principles and practices. Such progress is piecemeal rather than organization-wide and reflects the absence of leadership. Confusion as to what KM is, and what it involves, requires that information professionals sell it, not as a textbook definition, but in terms of what it means for their organization. Tangible benefits of KM, as they specifically relate to an organization's specific goals, help to counter cynicism ('We haven't got time', 'What's in it for me?', 'Not another new initiative', 'Doesn't happen, doesn't spread, doesn't last', etc.) or, at the very least, inertia (NeLH, 2001a).

KM is undoubtedly useful in enabling the NHS to focus on exploiting information, promoting knowledge-sharing behaviours and leveraging investment in training, technology and resources (Haines, 2002). KM values the expertise and 'worth' of the health service's greatest asset and inevitably attracts players within human-resource management and information technology as well as library services. It must become 'so embedded in the way your organisation does things, so intrinsic in people's day-to-day ways of working, that nobody even talks about knowledge management any more – they just do it' (NeLH, 2001b). 'To survive and thrive' the NHS must become a 'learning organization' – skilled at creating, acquiring, interpreting and retaining knowledge, and then modifying its behaviour in the light of new knowledge and insights (Confessore, 1997; Cantle, 2000; De Burca, 2000).

Inevitably, 'knowledge facilitators' will become important in ensuring information harvesting, sharing and input from different stakeholders within the service, including patients and the public. Challenges facing KM in the NHS include the need to co-ordinate activities and provide standards, manage content, improve infrastructure, information and knowledge skills, encourage knowledge-sharing behaviours and support communities of practice (Haines, 2002). Challenges to be overcome include information overload, lack of protected time for learning, 'initiative-weary troops', lack of a robust evidence base and multiple agency networks. KM must become part of the strategic planning process for it will only succeed if it contributes to real improvements to patient services and impact on health: 'It is only by testing ideas, learning what works best and sharing our knowledge that we will really make things better for our patients' (NHS Modernisation Agency, 2003b).

Key points

- Knowledge management is significantly impacting on healthcare organizations.
- Within the NHS there are key national players with regard to people (NHS University), processes (NHS Modernisation Agency) and systems (the NHS Information Authority).
- Librarians have a major knowledge management role in connection with design of information systems, creating classification systems and user education and training.
- Most commentators advocate an incremental approach to knowledge management, building on existing good practice.
- Increasingly, emphasis is being placed upon such specific approaches as knowledge mobilization and knowledge translation.
- Knowledge management should be promoted in terms of benefits to the organization.

References

Andrews, S. (2002) *Late-harvested Knowledge*, (March),
www.sourceuk.net/articles/f02358.html.

Bate, S. P. and Robert, G. (2002) Knowledge Management and Communities of Practice in the Private Sector: lessons for modernizing the National Health Service in England and Wales, *Public Administration*, **80** (4), 643–63

Beveren, J. van (2003) Does Health Care for Knowledge Management?, *Journal of Knowledge Management*, **7** (1), 90–7.

Booth, A. (2001) Managing Knowledge for Clinical Excellence: ten building blocks, *Journal of Clinical Excellence*, **3** (4), 187–94.

Brice, A. and Gray, M. (2003) Knowledge is the Enemy of Disease, *Library and Information Update*, (March),
www.cilip.org.uk/update/issues/march03/article2mar.html.

Canadian Institutes of Health Research (2002) *Knowledge Translation Overview*,
www.cihr-irsc.gc.ca/7518.shtml.

Cantle, F. (2000) What is a 'Learning Organization' in General Practice?, *Health Services Management Research*, **13** (3), 152–5.

Confessore, S. J. (1997) Building a Learning Organization: communities of practice, self-directed learning and continuing medical education, *Journal of Continuing Education in the Health Professions*, **17** (1), 5–11.

Copper, A. and Haines, M. (2002) Small Steps and Big Leaps, *Library and Information Update*, (November), www.cilip.org.uk/update/issues/nov02/article3nov.html.

Davenport, T. (2002) Making Knowledge Work Productive and Effective, *Knowledge Management*, **6** (2), (November), www.kmmagazine.com/.

Davenport, T. H. (1997) Ten Principles of Knowledge Management and Four Case Studies, *Knowledge and Process Management*, **4** (3), 187–208.

Davis, D. et al. (2003) The Case for Knowledge Translation: shortening the journey from evidence to effect, *British Medical Journal*, **327** (7405), 33–5.

De Burca, S. (2000) The Learning Healthcare Organization, *International Journal for Quality in Healthcare*, **12** (6), 457–8.

Fennessy, G. (2001) Knowledge Management in Evidence-based Healthcare: issues raised when specialist information services search for the evidence, *Health Informatics Journal*, **7**, 4–7.

Gray, J. A. (1998) Where's the Chief Knowledge Officer? To manage the most precious resource of all, *British Medical Journal*, **317** (7162), 832.

Great Britain. Department of Health (2000a) *The NHS Plan: a plan for investment, a plan for reform*, London, Department of Health.

Great Britain. Department of Health (2000b) *The NHS Plan: implementing the performance improvement agenda. A policy position statement and consultation document*, London, Department of Health.

Great Britain. Department of Health (2001) *Shifting the Balance of Power*, London, Department of Health.

Great Britain. Department of Health (2002) *Learning from Bristol: the DH response to the report of the public inquiry into children's heart surgery at the Bristol Royal Infirmary 1984–85*, London, Department of Health.

Haines, M. (2002) Aslib Biosciences Group Lecture, Knowledge Management in the NHS, www.aslib.co.uk/sigs/biosciences/KMinNHS.html.

Halliday, L. (2001) An Unprecedented Opportunity, *Information World Review*, 18–19.

Keeling, C. and Lambert, S. (2000) Knowledge Management in the NHS: positioning the healthcare librarian at the knowledge intersection, *Health Libraries Review*, **17**, 136–43.

Kelleher, D. and Levene, S. (2001) *Knowledge Management: a guide to good practice*, PAS 2001, London, British Standards Institution.

Kirkham, S. (2000) Creating a Knowledge Community in the National Health Service of the United Kingdom, *Online Information 2000*, 249–53.

Koenig, M. E. D. (2001) *Knowledge Management, User Education and Librarianship*, 67th IFLA Council and General Conference, 16–25 August, www.ifla.org.sg/IV/ifla67/papers/085-99e.pdf.

KPMG Consulting (2000) *Knowledge Management Research Report*, London, Atos KPMG Consulting, www.kpmgconsulting.co.uk/research/othermedia/ wf_8519kmreport.pdf.

Lopatin, W. and Blagden, P. (1997) Knowledge is Power, *Health Service Journal*, (16 October), 28–31.

National electronic Library for Health (NeLH) (2001a, last updated 2003) *Knowledge Management in the NHS*, www.nelh.nhs.uk/knowledge_management/km1/nhs.asp.

National electronic Library for Health (2001b) *Getting Started*, www.nelh.nhs.uk/knowledge_management/km2/getting_started.asp.

National Knowledge Service (2003) *Mobilisation Workstream*, www.nks.nhs.uk/background_mobil.asp.

NHS Modernisation Agency (2003a) *Improvement Leader's Guide to Sustainability and Spread*, www.modern.nhs.uk/improvementguides/sustainability/.

NHS Modernisation Agency (2003b) *Improvement Leader's Guide to Managing the Human Dimensions of Change*, www.modern.nhs.uk/improvementguides/human/ fw.html.

Plaice, C. and Kitch, P. (2003) Embedding Knowledge Management in the NHS South-West: pragmatic first steps for a practical concept, *Health Information and Libraries Journal*, **20** (2), 75–85.

Rowland, H. and Harris, L. (1998) Doctor Know, *People Management*, **4** (5), 50–2.

Rumizen, M. C. (2002) *The Complete Idiot's Guide to Knowledge Management*, Madison WI, CWL Publishing Enterprises.

Sandwell Healthcare NHS Trust (2000) Developing Knowledge Management Processes to Support Best Practice in Patient Care: pilot project report, www.knowledgeboard.com/library/nhs_report.pdf.

Sheldon, T. and Chalmers, I. (1994) The UK Cochrane Centre and the NHS Centre for Reviews and Dissemination: respective roles within the Information Systems Strategy of the NHS R&D Programme, co-ordination and principles underlying collaboration, *Health Economics*, **3**, 201–3.

TFPL Ltd (1999) *Skills for Knowledge Management – Building a Knowledge Economy*, London, TFPL.

Urquhart, C., Yeoman, A. and Sharp, S. (2002) *NeLH Communities of Practice Evaluation Report*, Aberystwyth, University of Wales, www.nhsia.nhs.uk/nelh/pages/documents/cop.doc.

Wyatt, J. C. (2001) *Clinical Knowledge and Practice in the Information Age: a handbook for health professionals*, London, RSM Press.

7

Primary-care knowledge services

Sue Lacey Bryant

Introduction

During the 1990s, government policy within the United Kingdom (UK), as in other Western countries, has endeavoured to shift responsibility and funding for health services from the acute sector towards primary care. In the UK, significant organizational change has been instigated to accomplish this change, with the creation of new trusts to implement these policies in primary care. This chapter explores recent developments in providing knowledge services to a primary care-led NHS. The need to build an enduring infrastructure for sharing knowledge, integrating national and local initiatives to best effect, is considered. Examples are given of innovative knowledge services that are harnessing information technology, and of effective library services building on expertise in handling explicit knowledge to reach out to primary-care professionals. The important contribution of the National electronic Library for Primary Care Development Programme is discussed. Throughout, fresh opportunities and familiar challenges associated with establishing new knowledge services in a sector previously supported by relatively few information services are highlighted.

Developing knowledge services in primary care: the challenge

The challenge for those developing knowledge services in primary care is to build an enduring infrastructure for the transfer of knowledge through which to contribute to the transformation of healthcare in the twenty-first century. Alongside developing systems and services through which explicit knowledge can be captured and retrieved, there is a need to nurture communities of practice through which implicit knowledge can be articulated, shared and applied to problem solving (Bate and Robert, 2002).

The 'application of the knowledge we already possess has greater potential to improve the health of patients than any drug or technology likely to be developed in the next decade' (Brice and Gray, 2003). Not only do 'health professionals and policy makers have access to a large volume of research evidence and guidance relevant to clinical effectiveness' but there is also a growing body of literature on how to improve the implementation of research findings (Getting Evidence into Practice, 1999). Recognition of the importance of these knowledge assets, accompanied by purposeful and continuing investment in knowledge services tailored to meet the needs and preferences of staff based in the community, will be necessary if primary-care health services are to be able to realize the benefits of prior investment in research and in human resources.

A national knowledge base: strategic development

Primary-care knowledge services will benefit from greater strategic direction and investment in knowledge services across the National Health Service (NHS). The launch of an integrated National Knowledge Service (NKS) (www.nks.nhs.uk/), working with key partners including NHS Direct Online and the National electronic Library for Health (NeLH), is envisaged as 'a significant tool in delivering the NHS Plan' (Secretary of State for Health, 2002). This partnership of organizations that provide knowledge in the health and social care sectors will be instrumental in shaping the development of knowledge services for primary care.

Healthcare professionals, not least those based in the community, have been ill served by a lack of strategic development in the past. There are strong economic arguments in favour of national procurement and delivery of core content. Nevertheless, local innovation and investment are also required to improve the mobilization and utilization of knowledge at organizational level. Locating knowledge-management initiatives at the most effective level is an important strategic issue and it is vital to harmonize national and local developments (Lacey Bryant, 2001).

Learning from collaboratives and communities of practice

The experience of the NHS Collaboratives and of well established communities of practice, such as Doctors.net.uk, may offer insights into the tier at which different types of knowledge-sharing communities may function most effectively (for instance within a trust, across a health economy or at national level).

The explicit aim of the National Primary Care Collaborative, which has worked with more than 2000 practices serving approaching 11 million patients, is 'to support individuals and organisations to develop their capability to apply generic quality improvement skills and techniques to any clinical and organisational challenge' (National Primary Care Development Team, 2003).

A primary care-led NHS

Responsibility for the modernization of the NHS, for developing a service truly designed for patients, is entrusted to primary-care trusts (PCTs) (Great Britain. Department of Health, 2000). These young organizations take responsibility for delivering and commissioning care with the goal of achieving a modernized service from which the public may expect high-quality healthcare – consistently, quickly and conveniently (Secretary of State for Health, 2002). While it is too early to prejudge the outcome of the steps taken to shift the balance of power from hospital-based services to PCTs (Secretary of State for Health, 2002) many commentators are disappointed with its progress. One qualitative study across four urban health authorities illuminates the barriers and incentives encouraging the shift towards a primary care-led NHS. In summary, Craig, McGregor and Drummond (2002) conclude: 'The development of a primary care-led NHS needs to resolve a fundamental tension at the heart of the policy: those to whom power was devolved were neither equipped nor minded to engineer the strategic resource shifts necessary to underpin a more primary care-based NHS.'

Establishing knowledge services within primary care

In recent years, the primary-care context has served as a blank canvas on which innovative knowledge professionals might make their mark. A few knowledge managers and facilitators have been recruited directly into primary-care organizations. Many more information professionals have reached out to this clientele from the context of existing library services. Some have focused on technological knowledge management applications; others on information-skills training; the development of specialized information services (e.g. to support clinical effectiveness) forms a third strand of work.

All these knowledge workers find themselves engaging with large numbers of staff, from disparate disciplines, on many sites, over some miles. It may well be argued that providing access to effective knowledge services within this context is far more challenging and complex than delivering corresponding provision in a hospital setting.

Knowledge management: local policy

As yet, few trusts appear to have identified the benefits of investing in knowledge management. Consequently there is a real danger that knowledge is not being marshalled and managed. Work to deliver some commonplace requirements is sometimes duplicated, for example several statutory and voluntary organizations may be found to be maintaining separate directories of voluntary organizations in the health sector. Meanwhile, more complex developments, such as gathering and disseminating local clinical guidelines, cannot be addressed effectively without co-operation and co-ordination between clinical and information staff within different healthcare organizations. Furthermore, organizational change in primary care has led to a loss of 'corporate memory', as experienced personnel have moved into new trusts.

Knowledge workers will be sensitive to local opportunities, as well as to barriers to establishing effective and efficient knowledge services for primary care. In practice, they may find that they are able to take forward some knowledge-management initiatives within the broader context of health informatics, while developing others under the umbrella of clinical governance.

It may be productive to pay attention to helping managers recognize the diverse knowledge needs of staff and patients. Understanding the breadth of knowledge-related activities inherent in the daily work of trust staffs may help senior managers within PCTs to celebrate successes on which they can build. For, while 'knowledge management' itself is widely perceived as a transient vogue, trust managers readily recognize that 'Knowledge is every professional's concern' (Wyatt, 2001). Table 7.1 illustrates key activities through which healthcare staff within a trust may be found to be generating and managing knowledge. This framework might be used to reveal strengths, identify areas in which new approaches to KM might assist in meeting targets, and also to highlight projects on which a collaborative, multi-trust approach might prove most cost effective.

Table 7.1   Applying knowledge management within a primary care trust: one approach

KM 'drivers'	Key activities	Examples
Understanding what patients want to know	Public involvement	Patient satisfaction surveys
		Providing information on services, complaints procedures, etc.
		Providing patient information as leaflets, or as links to websites

Continued on next page

Table 7.1   *Continued*

KM 'drivers'	Key activities	Examples
Understanding what staff need to know to support their: • work • professional development • research	Ensuring access to: • services • skills • resources	Peripatetic knowledge management service Service-level agreements with library services, information management technology, etc. Support from colleagues with expertise in audit, research, information analysis Access to bibliographic databases
Using knowledge to inform healthcare policy	Managing the dissemination of evidence and guidelines Promoting best practice Exploiting Information management data	NICE Guidelines review group Desktop access to evidence Evidence-based commissioning Information management technology policy Audit cycle
Keeping up to date with changing policy, trends and clinical evidence	Updating services	Communications policy Print and e-newsletters Use of bulletin boards 'Alerting' services (e.g. ZETOC)
Developing an organizational 'memory'	Ensuring access to: • directories • databases • documents	Contacts lists, distribution labels Best practice database, HiMP resources catalogue E-access to PCT policy, protocols, referral guidelines
Embedding best evidence into practice	Collaborating with suppliers and other services Implementing guidelines and promoting best practice	Decision support: protocols and automatic reminders within computer systems Roving primary care development team
Making implicit knowledge explicit	Initiatives to share knowledge	Skills audit; expertise database Special interest groups, e-fora

Derived from Lacey Bryant, 2001

Since few PCTs have yet to consider knowledge as a strategic concern, the knowledge management policy documented by the Vale of Aylesbury PCT has attracted some interest. This represents one attempt to articulate the principles guiding this Trust's approach to knowledge in terms of commitment, culture, content, skills and use of information technology. (See Figure 7.1)

Vale of Aylesbury **NHS**
Primary Care Trust

Knowledge Management: policy

This policy aims to support the Primary Care Trust in achieving its main purpose of improving health, developing the best possible primary and community care and commissioning the best quality services.

1. Knowledge management
Knowledge management is concerned with mobilising the knowledge base of health care in a form that health professionals can use and apply. The aim is to enable Trust staff to access, understand and use knowledge derived from research, as well as from the body of experience of best practice.

2. Guiding Principles
The knowledge policy derives from guiding principles in relation to five main elements: Commitment, Culture, Content, Skills and Technology:

2.1. Commitment
Trust strategy, policy, service development and practice should be based on the best evidence available (from research and from practice). It is an explicit concern of the Trust to make information available to patients and staff.

2.2. Culture
By fostering the development of a learning organization, staff will be empowered to gain the knowledge and skills required to implement best practice.

2.3. Content
Access to high quality information is essential to achieving health improvements, to professional and organizational development and to research.

2.4. Skills
Members of staff need support to gain skills in finding and evaluating information, in using it to achieve change, and in keeping up-to-date.

Chairman
Chief Executive

Continued on next page

Figure 7.1   Knowledge Management Policy, Vale of Aylesbury NHS
Primary Care Trust

2.5. Technology
Information Technology will be used to improve access to corporate information and to available evidence of clinical effectiveness as well as to encourage staff to share their 'know-how' with colleagues.

3. Key objectives
The Knowledge Management service will work collaboratively with colleagues across the PCT to meet the following key objectives:

3.1. Developing a learning culture
To encourage the development of communities of common interest through which colleagues can question, learn and collaborate
To develop ways of sharing experience and promoting good practice.

3.2. Facilitating access to the knowledge base
To promote the use of high quality information, improving access to sources of preappraised evidence, clinical guidelines, bio-medical databases and the *National electronic Library for Health*
To facilitate equitable access to comprehensive library services.

3.3. Enabling staff to develop skills
To deliver peripatetic knowledge support and training to practices (with the aim of expanding provision to all staff, when resources allow)
To promote training in IM&T and information literacy (including critical appraisal).

3.4. Applying Information Technology
To develop an intranet as a virtual library and learning centre and as a corporate resource
To support the use of electronic communication as the preferred medium for written communication within the PCT
To create web links which facilitate access to high quality information for patients.

4. A collaborative approach
The knowledge strategy will be achieved through collaborative working, influencing and contributing to a range of initiatives across the PCT in Clinical governance, Education and Development, IM&T, Primary Care Development, Research and Development and Training.

5. Review
These objectives will be reviewed regularly; they are expected to pertain over a five year period.

Sue Lacey Bryant
Knowledge Manager
PCT Knowledge policy 05/12/01

Figure 7.1 *Continued*

Knowledge needs assessment

One tool that may serve as a catalyst for trusts to take ownership of their knowledge assets, and make a lasting commitment to proactive knowledge services, is a knowledge needs assessment. The Buckinghamshire and Milton Keynes NHS Knowledge Needs Assessment surveyed the needs of a sample of 1157 staff across all NHS organizations and general practices within the county. Key findings are that personnel are happy to use electronic communications and the majority have convenient access to the internet: 'Interest in information skills training is high, use of evidence-based resources is at times poor. Staff are eager for a managed system for accessing clinical guidelines and are willing to use decision support software.' Meanwhile, these respondents 'most frequently cite other people as their key source of information' (MacGuigan, 2002).

Harnessing information technology

One of the first electronic knowledge-management tools developed to combat information overload in primary care was the WAX Active Library. Although the early version lacked 'the transparency of information structure and fast access that GPs valued', this project demonstrated the potential applications of 'simple, fast information management tools' (O'Brien and Cambouropoulos, 2000). The advent of the internet, NHSNct and intranets has facilitated some exemplary knowledge-management initiatives from which valuable lessons may be learnt. Some examples are given below.

Capturing implicit knowledge

With a Clinical Knowledge Manager at the helm, St Helens and Knowsley Health Informatics Service is implementing an ambitious intranet development focused on capturing implicit knowledge, rather than merely documenting explicit knowledge. The flow of communications in and out of primary care was mapped from the perspective of the level of the general practice, the PCT and in relation to other trusts. Analysis of the dominant sources shaped the architecture of the intranet. The three essential components were identified as a directory of services (incorporating soft issues such as current projects and personal interests), a lessons learnt database (collating documents from all parts of the community) and web-based communities of practice.

Initial observations from this development are telling. While the web provides a framework through which any group might collaborate, this tool attracts most interest from communities that are either geographically dispersed or do not represent distinct organizational entities. It appears that it takes time for individuals to share their own work; initially it is departments and organizations that submit documents. 'It could be argued that explicit knowledge management must be in place for implicit KM to work, and that personal knowledge will be the hardest commodity to share' (Mimnagh, 2002).

Sharing explicit knowledge through web-based services

Primary Care Network Northamptonshire, a web-based service accessible via NHSnet, was launched to support family doctors and their colleagues within the primary healthcare team by providing rapid access to clinical protocols and guidelines, prescribing formularies and evidence-based information sources. Besides creating an information zone to update staff on local, regional and national initiatives, this network invested in a comprehensive training and awareness programme to accompany this technological development (www.healthcare-computing.co.uk/hitea/hitea2000winners.htm).

Knowledgeshare (www.knowledgeshare.nhs.uk/enquiries.htm) uses the internet to meet the information needs of healthcare professionals on evidence-based practice and clinical governance. Attached to the Library of the Sussex Postgraduate Medical Centre at Brighton, Knowledgeshare has a particular interest in addressing the challenge of improving knowledge flows within and between acute and primary care trusts. The overall approach is to maintain a central core of content, supplemented with local pages. The site facilitates an evidence-based practice discussion group and links to relevant online resources, including interactive pathways to resources that support quality assurance for local NHS staff.

The role of library and information services

Certainly, recent years have seen the emergence of more proactive library services, delivering both information and information-skills training into the complex environment of primary care. Knowledge workers are to be found in a number of guises. Whatever their remit, they face the common challenge of building effective partnerships with other knowledge-based services (embracing libraries, clinical effectiveness units, research and development services and more) within their own trust and with neighbouring institutions. Familiar challenges of attracting champions and funding pertain, yet the heightened role and purpose of PCTs have conferred a higher profile for knowledge services and generated new opportunities to serve an ever more demanding user base.

There is some indication that in some quarters the very term 'knowledge management', ill defined as it has been, has assisted library managers in relaunching their services and hence in attracting funding. Nevertheless, it appears that there is still some work to be done to establish equitable access and continuing funding for primary-care staffs to benefit from high-quality library services. The picture is a patchy one. There remain areas where library managers bemoan their inability to deliver even a basic library service to all their potential user groups, let alone to respond to aspirations to manage organizational knowledge. There is no shortage of examples of dynamic, well respected library services making a determined effort to overcome the barriers that primary-care professionals face (e.g. Aldridge, 2002).

Outreach services

Knowledge professionals continue to express concern at the level of information skills and awareness of information resources they observe in primary care. It is apparent that there is a massive training agenda, which must be closely related to more generic training in information literacy as well as basic computer skills.

Outreach services have become a familiar feature of knowledge services to primary care (see Chapter 4). Such work is both rewarding and demanding. A number of approaches are being used. An area-wide skills development programme in South Devon trained 1,300 staff in the first year alone. This programme reports that, rather than opt for sessions held in the practice, primary healthcare staffs 'still prefer to travel to a hospital where they can have two or more hours of dedicated, uninterrupted learning' (Martin, 2001). PCT staff in East London benefit from the support of a Training and Outreach Officer, whose work is being guided by a recent training needs analysis (www.thpct.nhs. uk/hiel/library/training/). St George's Hospital Medical School is among those libraries that maintain a website to support outreach (see infodiscovery, www.infodiscovery.org.uk).

The Practice Nurse Project in Leeds has forged a partnership approach between the NHS and Leeds Library and Information Services to meet the library and information needs of a decentralized local primary-health community (Walker and Thompson, 2003).

Delivering the potential for knowledge services in primary care

The NHS Plan calls for fundamental changes in thinking and practice, and knowledge management is the very stuff of organizational development. Yet many senior managers of PCTs have yet to be convinced of its benefits. As PCTs strive to meet government targets, and struggle to 'balance the books', those eager to promote knowledge services in primary care will be right to expect difficult times ahead.

Leaders of knowledge services for primary care may learn from research and experience in several areas. They will be keen to tap the rich reservoir of experience gained through the attempts of national and multi-regional NHS Collaboratives to spread good practice. After all, these Collaboratives are founded on faith in KM concepts: 'the importance of cross-boundary knowledge transactions, knowledge transmission and transfer, and communal exchange through both face-to-face and virtual means' (Bate and Robert, 2002). In addition, these developing services may benefit from a number of user studies and research projects on the knowledge needs and preferences of primary care staffs.

The National electronic Library for Primary Care Development Programme

Commissioned as a key part of the infrastructure required by a modern NHS (Burns, 1998), the National electronic Library for Health (NeLH) is working with NHS Libraries to develop a digital library for NHS staff, patients and the public. Usage figures are growing steadily (Turner, 2003).

The Primary Care Library was the first, largest and most used Virtual Branch Library of the NeLH project. Targeted at general practice, it aimed to promote clinical governance by making the evidence base available, 'enabling primary care professionals to find out what they need to know, whilst avoiding the pitfalls of information overload' (de Lusignan, Brown and Robinson, 2002). Reporting on this pilot development, de Lusignan et al. write: 'There is still an enormous skills gap in primary care, with many primary care professionals unable to use the resources already provided.' Indeed, they question 'whether a web-based interface can come close to answering the questions of its users – or if a librarian/informaticist/knowledge officer is required as an intermediary'. Equally fundamental is their conclusion that 'integration with primary care clinical systems as part of a broad approach to knowledge management within primary care' is critical if users are to be 'able to get the most relevant information in the shortest time' (Brown et al., 2002).

'The overall NeLH programme has adopted a prototyping approach' (Brice and Gray, 2003) and a new primary-care resource is being developed to contribute to that process of refining the solution until it meets the needs of users. This development is based on the premise that the whole of NeLH must focus on the vast knowledge needs of primary-care professionals. In practice, primary-care staff may require an understanding of the primary, secondary and self-care components of health problems, many of which are now managed through shared care. Beyond providing a common core of 'accredited clinical reference material' (Burns, 1998) a primary aim for NeLH is to nurture and involve users within specialized communities, to enable them to transfer knowledge and facilitate its mobilization, localization and application.

The National electronic Library for Primary Care Development Programme is focused on various key projects (Gray, 2003). The Common Core of Knowledge Project aims to produce a co-ordinated primary-care knowledge base. Another project (Knowledge Access and Delivery Project) is focused on ensuring that all the knowledge products funded centrally are interoperable. The last project (Outreach Librarian Support and Development Project) aims to identify and bring together outreach librarians, prioritize the knowledge needs of primary care and recommend a new partnership with NeLH. There is also an intention to develop a question-and-answering service for primary-care team members in England.

Conclusion

Primary-care knowledge services have many benefits to bring to health professionals, overwhelmed by demands upon their time and overloaded with information, and to those for whom they care.

While librarians, information specialists and knowledge managers each bring a different emphasis to their work, they share in common both the people skills and the understanding of technological applications that are required to project-manage effective knowledge solutions. However, there is a line of argument, yet to be fully debated, that the current relationship between health libraries themselves (whether in higher education or in the NHS), as between libraries and NeLH (and the NHS Information Authority of which it is part), tends to foster a widening divide between services and also between librarians and knowledge managers, to the detriment of primary-care users and patients. In years to come, will health librarians be remembered affectionately as a lost breed (like the leggers of the eighteenth century) or recalled as latter-day Telfords, responsible for constructing a sustainable twenty-first-century network through which knowledge flowed to the benefit of patients served by primary healthcare services?

Key points

• The focus of political attention and public aspirations for improving healthcare, primary care is a challenging environment in which to seek to develop knowledge services.

- Collaboration, co-operation and integration of knowledge initiatives and service developments are vital (nationally and within health economies).
- An exploration of collaborative ways of working and learning may offer opportunities to share implicit knowledge.
- Many managers of primary care trusts have yet to be persuaded to invest in knowledge services.
- A number of models of user-centred services, focused on addressing organizational priorities, are emerging and can be used to argue the case.
- The development of electronic information services, and specifically of NeLH, is transforming access to knowledge in primary care, day by day.

References

Aldridge, S. (2002) *Salford Teaching PCT Achievements since April*, www.doh.gov.uk/pricare/teachingpcts/oct-updates.htm.

Bate, S. P. and Robert, G. (2002) Knowledge Management and Communities of Practice in the Private Sector: lessons for modernizing the National Health Service in England and Wales, *Public Administration*, **80** (4), 643–63.

Brice, A and Gray, M. (2003) Knowledge is the Enemy of Disease, *Library and Information Update*, **2** (3), 23–34.

Brown, A. et al. (2002) The Primary Care Electronic Library for Health, *British Journal of Healthcare Computing and Information Management*, **19** (4), (May), 22–5.

Burns, F. (1998) *Information for Health: an information strategy for the modern NHS 1998–2005: executive summary*, London, Department of Health.

Craig, N., McGregor, S. and Drummond, N. (2002) Factors Affecting the Shift Towards a 'Primary Care-led' NHS: a qualitative study, *British Journal of General Practice*, **52** (484), 895–900.

de Lusignan, S., Brown, A. and Robinson, J. (2002) The Primary Care National electronic Library for Health (NeLH PC): a pilot of information-centred knowledge management for primary care, *Informatics in Primary Care*, **10**, 99–105.

Getting Evidence into Practice (1999) *Effective Health Care*, **5** (1), 1–16.

Gray, J. A. M. (2003) *The National electronic Library for Primary Care Development Programme*, NeLH.

Great Britain. Department of Health (2000) *The NHS Plan: a plan for investment, a plan for reform*, London, Department of Health.

Lacey Bryant, S. (2001) Putting the Knowledge Base to Work, *Clinical Governance Bulletin*, **2** (5), 14–16.

MacGuigan, D. (2002) *The Buckinghamshire and Milton Keynes NHS Knowledge Needs Assessment: final report*, www.qp-risib.org/quickplace/buckslis/Main.nsf/.

Martin, S. (2001) Teaching Healthcare Information Skills across the Community: an integrated approach, *British Journal of Healthcare Computing and Information Management*, 18 (3), 27–9.

Mimnagh, C. J. (2002) *Towards Capturing Implicit Knowledge: a practical application of intranet development*. Paper presented at Advances in Clinical Knowledge Management 5 on 22 April 2002.

National Primary Care Development Team: The National Primary Care Collaborative (2003) *The Collaborative Methodology*, www.npdt.org.uk.

O'Brien, C. and Cambouropoulos, P. (2000) Combating Information Overload: a six-month pilot evaluation of a knowledge management system in general practice, *British Journal of General Practice*, **50** (455), 489–90.

Secretary of State for Health (2002) *Delivering the NHS Plan: executive summary*, www.doh.gov.uk/deliveringthenhsplan/index.htm.

Turner, A. (2003) Update, *NeLH Update* (March), www.nelh.nhs.uk/update/sep03/default.asp.

Walker, C. and Thompson, H. (2003) The Practice Nurse Project: a partnership approach to information provision in Leeds, *Health Information and Libraries Journal*, **20** (1), 50–2.

Wyatt, J. C. (2001) Management of Explicit and Tacit Knowledge, *Journal of the Royal Society of Medicine*, **94** (1), 6–9.

8

Clinical librarianship

Susan Childs

Introduction

In the UK, the clinical librarianship (CL) role first emerged nearly 30 years ago. In recent years CL has experienced a renaissance. This chapter provides definitions of CL and outlines the tasks that clinical librarians undertake. The history of CL places current services in context. Recent systematic reviews and an early literature review provide the evidence for the effectiveness of CL. Discussion of the evaluation of the first UK CL project in 1978 explores further issues about evidence. Finally, competing future trends provide speculation on how the CL role might develop in the future.

The role of a clinical librarian

Definitions of clinical librarianship

The first CL programme at the University of Missouri Kansas City (UMKC) (http://research.med.umkc.edu/teams/cml/CMLhist.html) defines a clinical librarian as a 'health sciences librarian who provides special services in teaching hospitals by participating in rounds with assigned teams of students and faculty, noting clinical questions as they arise, and responding to the questions by providing backup literature on specific clinical conditions'. Cimpl (1985) gives the reasons for CL programmes as 'to provide information quickly to physicians and other members of the health care team; to influence the information seeking behaviour of clinicians and improve their library skills; and to establish the medical librarian's role as a valid member of the health care team'. The first UK Clinical Librarian Conference in 2002 (www.le.ac.uk/li/lgh/library/prog.htm)

gives the following definition: 'Clinical Librarianship is a proactive approach to supporting evidence-based medicine in the clinical setting by providing highly specific, quality filtered, patient centred information to clinicians.' Winning and Beverley (2003) state that clinical librarians 'provide quality-filtered information to health professionals at the point of need to support clinical decision-making'. More fully, CL:

> seeks to integrate information professionals into health care teams, mainly through their attendance at ward rounds and/or meetings in the clinical setting. CL programmes therefore aim to support clinical decision-making and/or education by providing timely, quality-filtered information to clinicians at the point of need. Such activities attempt to promote evidence-based health care, with the ultimate goal of improving patient care, as well as enhancing clinicians' use of research literature and knowledge of library information resources.

Wagner and Byrd (2004) give the purpose of CL services 'as a way to integrate health sciences library services and the literature searching expertise of medical librarians into the patient care setting'.

Tasks carried out by clinical librarians

Many tasks can be carried out by CL services: however, not all clinical librarians carry out all these tasks, and the details of how they implement the activities will also vary. Clinical librarians may:

* aim to support clinicians in clinical decision making, evidence-based practice (EBP), clinical governance, research, teaching, learning and continuing professional development (CPD)
* have a proactive approach, offering an outreach service
* be attached to clinical multi-disciplinary teams or clinical departments
* attend ward rounds and clinical meetings and other meetings such as journal clubs
* receive, or identify, information enquiries; search the literature for evidence; quality filter and evaluate this evidence; provide selected items to answer the query; aim to have a fast turnround of response
* train clinical staff to search and evaluate the literature
* provide a current-awareness service
* compile a database of clinical queries and answers
* provide the evidence for clinical tools such as guidelines and care pathways
* produce evidence summaries
* work in partnership with the standard health library services

(Lusher, 1998; Watson and Weist, 2000; Glassington, 2001; Reid, 2001; Ward, Honeybourne and Harrison, 2001; presentations from the first UK Clinical Librarian Conference in 2002 (www.le.ac.uk/li/lgh/library/ prog.htm) details of the Leicester CL project (www.le.ac.uk/li/lgh/library/clpii.htm; www.le.ac.uk/li/lgh/library/clpplan.htm); Harrison and Lewis (n.d.).

History of clinical librarianship to the present day

Beginnings in the USA

Gertrude Lamb established the first CL programme in the USA at the UMKC School of Medicine in 1971/2 (http://research.med.umkc.edu/teams/cml/CMLhist.html). This was in response to her realization that the medical literature was not being used effectively to support patient-care problems. She saw that there was a need both to provide a clinical enquiry service and to train clinicians in how to search the literature base. This new post was funded by a grant from the National Library of Medicine. A related concept was LATCH (Literature Attached to Charts) where a few relevant articles from the current literature that applied to the patient's condition were physically attached to their chart (notes) (Sowell, 1978). For coverage of the older literature see the UMKC Bibliography (http://research.med.umkc.edu/teams/cml/CMLbib.html) and Cimpl (1985). Lipscomb (2000) provides a brief editorial on this topic.

Beginnings in the UK

Jean Farmer initiated the idea of a CL service at Guy's Hospital Medical School, London. In partnership with Anne Wilkin she obtained funding from the British Library Research and Development Department for two 'guinea pig' clinical librarians, one in medicine and one in surgery, and an independent evaluation. The experimental service ran from 1978 to 1980. The clinical librarians reported their experiences (Childs, 1980; Moore, 1980) and there were evaluation reports (Wilkin, 1982; Wilkin and McColl, 1982).

Follow-on and resurgence

A number of CL services were started up in the USA following Gertrude Lamb's lead. As demonstrated by the publication record (Lipscomb, 2000) there was an expansion of interest in the idea until about the mid-1980s, when articles trailed off. Since the late 1990s interest in the idea has resurged again. Guise (1997) argues that CL is a key way of saving health-library services from disappearing under the threat of new technology. In the UK there was no CL service after the experimental Guy's service stopped in 1980 until CL came back into fashion in the late 1990s. The impetus behind this resurgence in the UK is that CL is seen as a way to support the busy clinician in meeting the requirements of initiatives such as EBP and clinical governance. A number of services have been set up (www.le.ac.uk/li/lgh/library/clcont.htm) and the first UK conference has been held (www.le.ac.uk/li/lgh/library/prog.htm).

Context

When the first CL services were set up in the 1970s the world wide web had not been invented: it was first available in 1991. E-mail was at its very beginnings and restricted to the computing community. Searching for medical literature required use of the printed indexing journal *Index Medicus*. MEDLINE was available but it was normally searched by librarians as intermediaries on behalf of the user. In the UK MEDLINE was accessible via teletype machines to the site in the USA. The service was only available in US office hours and was expensive. PCs and word processors were not available. The policy and cultural context was also different. The concept of EBP had not been thought of, nor information overload, nor critical appraisal of the literature. In the UK, it was before policies on clinical governance and clinical effectiveness. Of course in the 1970s people grappled with these issues and their problems and solutions. However they were not articulated in the formal way they are now, and were not covered in policy documents or created as 'movements'. CL, as set up by Lamb, can be seen as an attempt at a solution to what we would now call the problem of information overload and how to achieve EBP.

The effectiveness of clinical librarianship
The Guy's Hospital project

Wilkin (1982) undertook an independent evaluation of the CL service at Guy's Hospital. The aims of this project were modelled very closely on Lamb's service to allow for comparison. The findings from the evaluation challenged the underlying assumptions of CL services, and asked what was the evidence to support them. The evaluation found that the clinical librarians supported only a small number of clinicians who were mostly medics.

The Guy's project has been called a 'failed experiment'. More accurately, it is an experiment that produced negative results. The Guy's project was set up as an experiment to evaluate the CL hypothesis. It was not an evaluation of an existing CL service. Unfortunately people tend to think that negative findings mean failure rather than seeing them as contributing towards understanding of a phenomenon. See Greenhalgh et al. (2002) for an exploration of two different approaches to studying informaticist services. The Guy's project did fail in not disseminating widely its findings; a common problem with research. When new CL services were set up in the UK in the late 1990s the instigators were not aware of this literature and the useful messages it contained. The 'Diffusion of Innovations Model' (see Rogers and Scott (1997) for an overview) suggests a possible reason. Early adopters tend to accept innovations on faith, rather than concrete evidence. In general, most people would evaluate an innovation through the subjective opinions of adopters rather than on the basis of scientific research.

The early literature review

Cimpl (1985) carried out a standard literature review, covering the history of CL programmes, their purpose, approaches to CL services and additional CL roles. The types of evaluations looked at comprised surveys of recipients' views, e.g. by questionnaire, and cost considerations. However, none of these evaluations was objective or rigorous. In fact, Cimpl's findings were very similar to those of the recent systematic reviews below.

Recipients noted benefits from the CL services, such as enhanced patient care, education, and time saving. The library also noted benefits from increased visibility and enhanced CL knowledge. However, there were also negative opinions about the clinical librarians' medical knowledge and the fact that they produced irrelevant or unsolicited information. Library services also suffered as reference enquiries decreased. Some attempts were made to produce comparative costs, e.g. a favourable comparison of the costs of clinical medical librarianship (CML) services with standard laboratory tests or with other methods of providing problem-specific CPD. However, CL services were costly and could be seen as a luxury reference service.

The UK systematic review

Winning and Beverley (2003) carried out a systematic review of the literature from 1982 to 2001. The review aimed to identify studies that evaluated CL services; it included 16 unique evaluative studies and 33 descriptive studies. The majority of the services were based in US hospitals; there were only five UK studies. This is important to note because the organization and culture of healthcare and librarianship in the USA is different to that in the UK. The authors could not pool the results of the evaluative studies because of inadequate reporting and wide variations in methods used. They conclude that there is little evidence to support the view that CL services are effective, let alone cost effective. Further research by independent evaluation is needed:

- exploring the impact on patient care and identifying tangible success measures
- determining the preferred format of information provided to clinicians
- determining the extent to which clinical librarians should become part of the clinical team
- establishing the cost effectiveness of CL.

The US systematic review

Wagner and Byrd (2004) have also carried out a systematic review with the aim of finding evidence for the effectiveness of CL. They covered the period between 1974 and 2001 and 35 studies met their review criteria. They also produced a descriptive review of the wider CL literature. They conclude that 'The total amount of research evidence for CML program effectiveness is not great and most of it is descriptive, rather than comparative or analytically qualitative. Standards are needed to consistently evaluate CML or informationist programs in the future.' More research is required to address questions such as:

- What are the best clinical settings for CL services?
- What is the most effective way for clinical librarians to work?
- What is the best ratio of clinical librarians to clinicians?
- What training or skills do clinical librarians need to make them most effective?
- How effective are clinical librarians who anticipate information needs compared to those who just respond to direct requests?
- How best can CL services be evaluated, and be compared with other CL programmes?
- How do CL services compare with other methods of supporting evidence-based patient care?

The future

A number of service trends can be identified. Which of these will become successful is much harder to determine.

CL will remain a minority activity within the wider field of health librarianship

CL services are currently fashionable. However, this trend will probably die down again, as it did in the past, unless rigorous, objective, comparative evaluations are carried out. This research may say that CL is not cost effective. On the other hand, it may suggest ways that health libraries can support patient care more effectively. Davidoff and Florance (2000) note that though CL has been in existence for about 30 years the idea has not really taken off, except for its presence in a relatively small number of institutions. One explanation for this comes from the theory of diffusion of innovation (Plutchak, 2002). CL can be seen as still being at the 'early adopter' stage. Early adopters are willing to take the benefits on faith. Later adopters need more concrete proof, which is still sparse.

The CL concept will be widened into a new profession, the 'informationist'

Davidoff and Florance (2000) and Plutchak (2000) call for a new information specialist to provide information for clinicians at the point of patient care, the 'informationist'. The idea of an informationist builds upon the work of clinical librarians. Informationists should receive accredited training, be employed as part of the clinical team and be paid for directly by clinical services. Informationists would need understanding of both information science and the basics of clinical work, and could start off as either librarians or clinical staff. Their accredited training would cover principles of medicine and epidemiology, statistics, critical appraisal and information management. Their role would be to supply evidence summaries to answer patient-care problems. Additionally, by recording the gaps between questions asked and the evidence available they could drive the research agenda. They could also improve existing information-retrieval systems and develop new ones. In 2002 a conference was held at the National Library of Medicine to explore the concept of an 'informationist' (conference website www.mlanet.org/research/informationist/; Plutchak, 2002; Shipman et al., 2002).

CL will be replaced by other types of services

A wide range of evidence-based clinical services and resources is now available, providing summary information direct to the clinician, usually via ICT. Many of these services do not involve librarians. Here are some examples. A clinical informaticist service is one where clinicians submit questions to a specialist by phone, fax, e-mail or post. They then receive a summarized response based on a thorough search and critical appraisal of the relevant literature. This contrasts to the CL or informationist approach because there is no personal contact. See Greenhalgh et al. (2002) for a study of two service models. ATTRACT (www.attract.wales.nhs.uk/) (Brassey et al., 2001) is another example of such a service. The National electronic Library for Health (NeLH) (www.nelh.nhs.uk) is a digital library providing a wide range of evidence sources to support patient care, e.g. free access to the Cochrane Library, guidelines, protocols and care pathway databases. It also links to resources such as PRODIGY and Evidence Based on Call. PRODIGY (www.prodigy.nhs.uk/) provides clinical management information for GPs dealing with specific patients. PRODIGY can be incorporated into the surgery's clinical computer system. Evidence Based on Call (www.nelh.nhs.uk/eboc.asp) is aimed at young doctors faced with making clinical decisions when other sources of help are not available, e.g. in the middle of the night. Sackett and Strauss (1998) describe a small preliminary study of the use of an 'evidence cart'. The cart contained a computer, CD-ROM and hardcopy information resources. It was used on ward rounds to help with patient-care decisions. Nowadays technology such as personal digital assistants and portable computers with wireless networks can provide such resources in a far more convenient form.

Conclusion

The idea of CL has been around since the early 1970s. Except for the use of electronic information resources, the principles and tasks of CL are little different now than they were at the beginning. Similarly, rigorous, objective, comparative evidence for the effectiveness of CL services is still sparse. If CL is to have a unique identity which separates it from normal health librarianship then it must prove that clinical librarians integrate into healthcare teams, gain specific knowledge and skills from such integration, provide quality-filtered, summarized evidence, and improve patient care. Though evidence for this might be forthcoming, it will probably be linked to evidence that shows such services are very expensive, particularly if they are made available to all clinical staff. The principles behind CL might be better served if health librarians become involved with clinicians in producing the digital evidence summary resources and services and train clinicians and students in how to use them effectively.

Key points

- CL aims to support clinical decision making at the point of need and enable evidence-based patient care.
- Clinical librarians attend ward rounds and clinical meetings and provide quality-filtered, summarized information to answer clinicians' information needs and enquiries.

- However, the rigorous, objective, comparative evidence for the effectiveness of CL services is sparse.
- A new information specialist, an informationist, has been proposed; specifically trained and accredited, the informationist will be employed as part of the clinical team and be paid for directly by clinical services.
- The future of CL is under threat by the wide range of evidence-based clinical services and resources now available providing summary information direct to the clinician, usually via ICT.

References

Brassey, J. et al. (2001) Just In Time Information for Clinicians: a questionnaire evaluation of the ATTRACT project, *British Medical Journal*, **322**, 529–30.

Childs, S. M. (1980) *The Experiences of a Clinical Librarian in Medicine: final report for the period July 1978 to June 1980,* British Library Research and Development Report 5687, London, Guy's Hospital Medical School.

Cimpl, K. (1985) Clinical Medical Librarianship: a review of the literature, *Bulletin of the Medical Library Association*, **73** (1), 21–8.

Davidoff, F. and Florance, V. (2000) The Informationist: a new health profession?, *Annals of Internal Medicine,* **132** (12), 996–8.

Glassington, L. (2001) *The Library and Information Support for Clinical Effectiveness (LISCE) Project – Eight Months On*, www.ucl.ac.uk/kmc/kmc2/News/ACKM/ackm4/glassingotn.html.

Greenhalgh, T. et al. (2002) A Comparative Case Study of Two Models of a Clinical Informaticist Service, *British Medical Journal*, **324** (7336), 524–9.

Guise, N. B. (1997) Editorial. Advancing the Practice of Clinical Medical Librarianship, *Bulletin of the Medical Library Association*, **85** (4), 437–8.

Harrison, J. and Lewis, S. (n.d.) *Does Doctor know best?: a discussion of clinical librarianship*, ACKM2 abstract, www.ucl.ac.uk/kmc/ackm/ackm2/greenhalgh.htm.

Lipscomb, C. E. (2000) Clinical Librarianship, *Bulletin of the Medical Library Association,* **88** (4), 393–6.

Lusher, A. (1998) Getting Evidence to the Bedside: the role of the clinical librarian. In Bakker, S. (ed.) *Libraries without Limits: changing needs – changing roles: proceedings of the 6th European Conference of Medical and Health Libraries*, Utrecht 22–27 June 1998, Dordrecht, Kluwer Academic Publishers, 66–70.

Moore, A. (1980) *The Clinical Librarian in the Department of Surgery: a report of two years' experience*, British Library Research and Development Department Report 5686 , London, Guy's Hospital Medical School.

Plutchak, T. S. (2000) Editorial. Informationists and Librarians, *Bulletin of the Medical Library Association*, **88** (4), 391–2.

Plutchak, T. S. (2002) Editorial. The Informationist – Two Years Later, *Journal of the*

Medical Library Association, **90** (4), 367–9.

Reid, L. (2001) The Impact of Clinical Governance on the Library and Information Service: clinical librarian case study, *IFMH Inform Newsletter*, **12** (1), 1–3.

Rogers, E. M. and Scott, K. L. (1997) *The Diffusion of Innovations Model and Outreach from the National Network of Libraries of Medicine to Native American Communities*, www.nnlm.gov/pnr/eval/rogers.html.

Sackett, D. L. and Strauss, S. E. (1998) Finding and Applying Evidence during Clinical Rounds: the 'evidence cart', *Journal of the American Medical Association*, **280** (15), 1336–7.

Shipman, J. P. et al. (2002) The Informationist Conference: report, *Journal of the Medical Library Association*, **90** (4), 458–64.

Sowell, S. L. (1978) LATCH at the Washington Hospital Center, 1967–1975, *Bulletin of the Medical Library Association*, **66** (2), 218–22.

Wagner, K. C. and Byrd, G. D. (2004) Evaluating the Effectiveness of Clinical Medical Librarianship (CML) Programs: a systematic review of the literature, *Journal of the Medical Library Association*, submitted for publication (authors' communication).

Ward, L. M., Honeybourne, C. J. and Harrison, J. A. (2001) A Clinical Librarian can Support Clinical Governance, *British Journal of Clinical Governance*, **6** (4), 248–51.

Watson, J. A. and Weist, A. (2000) The Forest Healthcare Clinical Support Librarian: 6 months on, *Health Libraries Review*, **17** (4), 219–21.

Wilkin, A. (1982) *The Evaluation of a Clinical Librarian Experiment: final report for the period July 1978–February 1981*, British Library Research and Development Report 5731, London, Department of Surgery, Guy's Hospital Medical School.

Wilkin, A. and McColl, I. (1982) *Clinicians' Use of the Medical Literature: selected themes from a clinical librarian experiment and its evaluation in the UK*, London, Department of Surgery, Guy's Hospital.

Winning, M. A. and Beverley, C. A. (2003) Clinical Librarianship: a systematic review of the literature, *Health Information and Libraries Journal*, **20** (Suppl. 1), 10–21.

9

The role of LIS in supporting learning

*David Peacock, Graham Walton
and Andrew Booth*

Introduction

Healthcare library and information services (LIS) professionals have always supported students and those undertaking continuing professional development (CPD). Increasingly, they support statutory periodic refreshment and form collaborative partnerships with public and academic libraries. This chapter explores changes impacting on libraries as they evolve to accommodate emerging learning needs. It discusses problem-based learning, enquiry-based learning and 'clinical placements' before outlining a case study that typifies such changes. It concludes with the implications of these developments for the role of healthcare librarians.

Lifelong learning

The knowledge society and the accelerating development of information and communication technologies (ICTs) are driving lifelong learning (Roes, 2001). Consumers are demanding greater flexibility with regard to learning pathways, qualifications and accreditation for learning. Cross-sectoral developments include the National Grid for Learning, a network for schools, connecting public and national libraries, further and higher education institutions and the workplace, and the University for Industry, which provides an infrastructure to enable workers to identify learning pathways and providers who meet their needs (Great Britain. Department for Education and Employment, 1998). Key players include LearnDirect (www.learndirect.co.uk/) and the People's Network (www. peoplesnetwork.gov.uk/).

Other sociological and technological demands are reshaping pedagogic models (Twigg and Miloff, 1998):

• continual increases in student numbers
• widening participation to women, older students and students from ethnic minorities
• increasing work-based learning requiring flexible delivery
• emphasis on 'learning to learn' to combat obsolescence, and enable periodic 'refreshment', of knowledge
• budgetary pressures for more efficient and effective education.

Twigg and Miloff (1998) identify the role of ICTs in meeting such challenges:

• course materials offered independently of time and place, with modularization offering flexible learning routes
• increasing availability of the internet at home, on campus or in halls of residence
• more information via the web, either free or under institutional access agreements.

Increasing competition, across geographical boundaries, is already challenging the monopoly of institutional information services (Hughes, 2000). The learning environment of the future will be more student-centred, interactive and dynamic allowing group work on real-world problems with students determining their own learning routes (Twigg and Miloff, 1998). With increasing emphasis on information literacy to support lifelong learning (Brahmi et al., 1999) students will take more responsibility for their learning goals (Roes, 2001). Such changes are mirrored within healthcare where, for example, *Making a Difference* (Great Britain. Department of Health, 1999a) requires increased access to ICTs, more flexibility with part-time study and step-on, step-off study modes, longer placements, lifelong learning, continuing professional development and evidence-based practice (Gannon-Leary, Wakeham and Walton, 2003). Approaches to this agenda are discussed below.

Continuing professional development

Continuing professional development (CPD) ensures that 'health professionals keep updated to meet the needs of patients, the health service, and their own professional development. It includes the continuous acquisition of new knowledge, skills, and attitudes to enable competent practice' (Peck et al., 2000). The NHS recognizes work-based learning as a way to deliver lifelong learning for its workforce (Anon, 2002) and several documents are shaping the CPD agenda (see Table 9.1).

Table 9.1   CPD literature

Year	Title	Summary
1997	The New NHS – Modern – Dependable	Began modernization in the NHS and proposed 'clinical governance' to be reflected by all professional development programmes
1998	A First Class Service: quality in the new NHS	Proposed 'culture that values lifelong learning' in which CPD programmes identify and meet the learning needs of individual health professionals
1999	Continuing Professional Development: quality in the new NHS	Need for a locally managed, systematic approach to CPD with criteria to guide local health organizations
1999	Making a Difference: strengthening the nursing, midwifery and health visiting contribution to health and healthcare	Need for commitment to CPD and lifelong learning by individuals and organizations; continuing professional development programmes to meet local service needs as well as patient needs and the personal and professional needs of practitioners
1999	The NHS Plan: a plan for investment, a plan for reform	Commitment to support CPD for professional staff, and an expectation that staff should receive support to fulfil requirements of clinical governance and revalidation; emphasis on accredited workplace-based systems of learning
2000	Meeting the Challenge: a strategy for the allied health professions	How the government wants allied health professions supported in delivering the NHS Plan
2000	A Health Service of All the Talents: developing the NHS workforce	Importance of postgraduate education and lifelong learning and of ensuring that skills of all professionals are deployed appropriately
2001	Working Together – Learning Together: a framework for lifelong learning for the NHS	Proposes co-ordinated approach to lifelong learning supported by NHS University, covering continuing personal and professional development; outlines changes to the way the NHS's £2.5 billion yearly education and training budget is spent
2001	Making the Change: a strategy for the professions in healthcare science	Raises profile of 'professions in healthcare science' and outlines how they are to be supported in delivering the NHS Plan
2002	HR in the NHS Plan	Updates *Working Together, Learning Together* with respect to modernizing learning and development.

In addition, the Audit Commission's *Hidden Talents* report (Audit Commission, 2000) highlights inequalities in education, training and development for 600,000 NHS staff and looks at how trusts can obtain best value from training activities. Simultaneously, the National Audit Office's report *Educating and Training the Future Health Professional Workforce for England* (National Audit Office and Audit Commission, 2001), reviews arrangements for educating pre-registration health students.

The role of library services

Many government documents recognize the role of LIS in supporting learning throughout life. Library services are 'the bedrock' of education and training, and increased emphasis on continual, self-directed learning poses a considerable challenge to NHS libraries:

> library and IT strategies should provide a framework for ensuring equal access for all staff groups to the learning resources which support work based learning.
> (Great Britain. Department of Health, 1999b)

Developments such as modernization and clinical governance ensure that challenges facing health libraries are even more acute than those in other sectors. CPD should be purposeful and patient centred, participative, educationally effective, cross-boundary, should build on previous knowledge and skills, and be part of a wider organizational development plan (Great Britain. Department of Health, 1999b).

Skills escalator

In setting out its vision of modernized services, redesigned around the patient's journey, the NHS Plan identifies an imperative to develop its workforce. Such thinking underpins the ambitious agenda of the NHS University (NHSU) (Fryer, 2002) to not only meet the needs of the existing workforce but also to build, reward and support the NHS workforce of the future. The resultant strategy is the 'skills escalator', whereby staff pursue lifelong learning, constantly renewing and extending their skills and knowledge, enabling them to move up the escalator. At the same time roles, work and responsibilities are delegated down the escalator where appropriate.

Problem-based learning

Problem-based learning (PBL) 'uses carefully constructed clinical problems as a context for students to learn problem-solving skills and acquire knowledge about the basic and clinical sciences' (Albanese and Mitchell, 1993; Bligh, 1995; Kanter, 1998). Interest in PBL (Connolly and Donovan, 2002) now extends beyond medical education where a didactic 'chalk and talk' model had held sway (Johnson and Finucane, 2000).

PBL is claimed to improve student satisfaction as the focus shifts from *what* they learn to *how* they learn. The workload is heavy and many students find PBL time-consuming and exhausting. However, its added perceived relevance seems to justify the heavier workload. Several UK medical schools have accompanied a move to PBL with fast-track graduate entry programmes (GEP) to attract mature adult students with generic problem-solving skills. GEP students make heavier use of library facilities than traditional entry undergraduates (e.g. more use of journals, e-journals, photocopiers, printers, the library catalogue and databases) (Martin, 2003). In addition, there is increased pressure as students search for information on the same clinical problem at the same time. Increases in short-loan collections and textbooks, computer-assisted learning and provision of web resources (Myers, Saunders and Rogers, 2002) to answer clinical problems are also required (Rankin, 1992, 1993, 1996). Such demands may be countered by developing e-journals, e-books, database access and PCs in student halls of residence, yet planning physical resources remains important (Rashbass, 2000). Requirements include adequate tutorial rooms, access to multiple copies of textbooks, adequate photocopying facilities and economic costs for copying journal articles, computers and other technologies (Feuerman and Handel, 1998).

E-learning

E-learning figures prominently within the Government's education (Great Britain. Department for Education and Employment, 1998; Cabinet Office, 2000; Dawes and Hanscomb, 2002) and health service (NHS Executive, 1998; Burns, 1998) agendas. The NHS's framework for lifelong learning (Great Britain. Department of Health, 2001) is underpinned by an e-learning strategy, which includes the NHS University (www.nhsu.nhs.uk/). E-learning enhances learning by delivering content via the internet, intranet, video and audio-conferencing, e-mail, electronic discussion groups and CD-ROM (Roberts, 1999; Bargellini and Bordoni, 2001; Joch, 2003). Just because the future is digital does not mean that less physical space is needed. Students and staff demand hard-copy resources and access to facilities, services, staff and the learning culture of a physical library (Haldane, 2003). Access to electronic resources may reduce students' dependence on the physical library yet enquiry-based learning (learning in which learners engage with a self-determined process of enquiry, accommodating divergent thinking about problems and exploring different views of the world (Price, 2003)) requires increased resources and groupwork, increasing likely demands for support from professional librarians. On-site students typically access the library in self-service mode whereas providing documents to remote locations involves staff in retrieval and shipping. Staff and students require 'start-up' training and ongoing support and maintenance (Banwell, Rowley and Urquhart, 2003). Local collections, electronic reserve systems, document delivery software and bandwidth to support image and graphical applications incur additional costs. Electronic information resources demand copyright clearance and attention to security and authorization procedures. Geographical inequities pose additional challenges. Librarians are experienced in providing access to remote electronic resources but must now support newer mechanisms for e-learning (MLANET, n.d.), such as personal digital assistants (PDAs) (Whitsed, 2003a).

Clinical placements

Healthcare libraries must provide access to remote resources and negotiate services for their students at partnering institutions in distant locations. Although librarians have strong traditions of networking and outreach, meeting the resource needs of students who split their time between higher education and placements, clinical or otherwise, is a considerable challenge. Healthcare and academic library providers must ensure an optimal mix of physical and electronic services (Gannon-Leary, Wakeham and Walton, 2003). Such partnerships are also key to the success of the NHSU, since as many NHS staff work in the community as work in hospital.

Blended learning

Delivering learning electronically offers advantages in terms of speed, cost and scale (Beagle, 2000). However, electronic methods are only effective as part of an overall blend. 'Blended learning' describes the increasingly common combination of asynchronous self-study with traditional classroom, face-to-face activity (Whitsed, 2003b). Education has employed such models for hundreds of years with 'live' lectures supplemented with asynchronous homework and further reading. Blended learning addresses concerns of learners who feel that the social side of learning is lost in an online environment (Quinsee, 2001; Kazmer, 2002). Thus the NHSU, recognizing that everyone learns in different ways, will deliver learning to the classroom, workplace or online as appropriate (Fryer, 2002). Not all identified training needs are best met by e-learning, making it important to match a blended approach to preferred learning styles (Drury and Smith, 1999).

Blended learning requires blended services, exemplified by the 'hybrid library' where electronic and paper-based information sources exist alongside each other. End-user resource discovery and use is encouraged, irrespective of format and source (Pinfield et al., 1998). The hybrid library brings 'technologies from different sources together in the context of a working library, and also [begins] to explore integrated systems and services in both the electronic and print environments' (Rusbridge, 1998). It is not the sterile compromise that its name suggests but an innovative approach to delivering services irrespective of physical environment.

Case study

Flexibility in learning, support for learning, hybrid learning resources and inequities in the learning experience are addressed by the Health and Education Northumbria Students Access to Learning resources (HENSAL) project, which examined these issues in relation to their impact upon NHS students on placements and their use of university and NHS library services and resources (Middleton, Rowell and Walton, 2002).

Northumbria University health students undertake considerable periods of learning within the NHS; those on pre-registration courses spend up to 50% of their time on clinical placement. Significant numbers of NHS nurses and allied health professionals undertake part-time courses at Northumbria University for continuing professional development. Northumbria has also introduced problem-based learning for several courses. Hence, it was considered important to investigate students' experiences of accessing learning resources while away from the campus on clinical placement.

The Dearing report (NCIHE, 1997) notes a proliferation of flexible study methods, such as distance learning and e-learning, with increasing numbers of students unable to physically access their place of study. Provision of course materials and library and IT services via the internet has increasingly addressed this, and Northumbria University has responded with a hybrid library service of broad-based print resources alongside innovative electronic resources. For example, the Hylife for Health gateway offers print and electronic services for students on health-related courses, supplemented by traditional services, such as books and journal articles, delivered via a postal service. However, no research had examined use of these services by students on placement.

Data collection involved a questionnaire, to elicit students' views and perceptions, and two focus groups to seek the views of health students and practice placement facilitators (PPFs). PPFs are experienced nurses and midwives who liaise between the University and the host NHS trust to ensure that placements are of sufficient quality and quantity to sustain the commissioned numbers of pre-registration students. Out of a total number of 1990 health students, 415 completed their questionnaires.

Theme 1: flexibility of learning

92% of students felt that access to learning resources was either 'important' or 'very important' to their studies while on placement. 89% of students used the University library as their main library and 55% also used their NHS placement library. Public libraries were used by 28% of respondents. The University was used on a weekly basis by 45% of health students and the NHS placement library was used weekly by 27%.

30% of health students used the hybrid Hylife for Health and part-time and distance learning services. 25% of students used the Blackboard Virtual Learning Environment, an electronic environment for online learning comprising resources, course materials and information. Access to the internet is fundamental to students on placement, facilitating direct access to such services as Hylife for Health and Blackboard in whatever limited time students have available.

Theme 2: level of sophisticated use

When compared with other students who focus on teaching materials, health students are very sophisticated users of learning resources. They recognize the importance of e-journals and databases, reflected in their use of databases such as MEDLINE and CINAHL and full-text e-journals.

Theme 3: problems and support

Health students face a number of problems accessing and using the learning resources available to them on placement. Over 30% of health students reported difficulties accessing learning resources including:

* *Accessing study space* – Although study space was available to 59% of health students at their placement venue, 31% had problems accessing it. This problem was also identified by PPFs.
* *Physical access* – Opening hours proved problematic for 17% and the location of the library for 16% of health students.

- *Type of placement venue* – Typically those on placement in community/primary care or in nursing homes and hospices were disadvantaged compared with colleagues in hospital/acute settings.
- *Awareness of resources and services* – Over 50% of health students had either 'never heard of' or had 'never used' distance-learning services. A similar figure had never used Blackboard.

Such problems are exacerbated by health students' self-reliance in accessing learning resources. They do not seek or use available support from academic, library and IT staff in understanding and accessing learning resources. Workplace mentors were most likely to obtain support and information about accessing learning resources (32% of students consulted their mentor on a weekly basis for support about learning resources). The mentor is responsible for helping the student to achieve the intended outcomes of the placement and works the majority of the time with the student. Mentors are not necessarily the most appropriate staff group to support students in this area. The movement of pre-registration health education into the higher education sector has meant the separation of learning resources for students and working practitioners. Although mentoring staff may be familiar with learning resources accessible through the NHS they will not necessarily be familiar with services available to University students. PPFs were more appropriate for supporting and guiding students on learning resources.

Theme 4: inequities of access

Health students were based in a variety of types of placement including hospital/acute (64% of respondents); nursing home/hospice (10%); learning disability (8%); mental health (8%); and community/primary care (7%). The research compared and contrasted experiences of accessing learning resources, examining specific facilities at the placement venue.

- The local library/resource centre was accessible to 54% of health students at their placement venue but 31% reported difficulties in accessing it. Whereas 74% of students at the main hospitals reported a library/learning resources centre for their use on site, over 80% of those in community/primary care and over 70% of those in nursing homes/hospices had no access to a library/learning resources centre.
- Most students in hospital placements were able to access the internet while those based in nursing homes/hospices and the community reported greater difficulties. The study reported extensive use of home computers by many students for their studies, a significant finding when coupled with the

problems many students experienced in accessing a computer at their placement venue.

Access to learning resources is clearly not equitable for all students, with those owning a home computer holding a clear advantage. Students without access to a placement/resource centre (largely those in the community and nursing homes/hospices) are clearly disadvantaged and often have least opportunity to access a work-based computer with the internet.

The future role of health librarians in supporting teaching and learning

In the future, health librarians will likely have quite different roles and responsibilities in terms of information literacy teaching; course and curricula design and development; and supporting access to services and resources.

Information literacy teaching

Problem-based learning places great emphasis on information literacy. With PBL students being heavy LIS users, using the library earlier and more frequently and spending more time in the library than traditional students, there is a greater need for user education and for health librarian expertise to be harnessed in teaching information literacy. Librarians have a vital role in teaching users to identify, evaluate and use information efficiently and effectively, and to become self-supporting information seekers (Fridén, 1996).

The impact of such shifts in the role of health professionals on the largely reactive traditional role of health librarians, where users came to the library to seek assistance or to locate resources, cannot be underestimated. The role of the librarian as teacher requires that librarians seek out users proactively in a variety of settings, provide instruction about information resources and assist users in locating and evaluating information.

Involvement in course and curricula design and development

Librarian involvement in user education and information literacy training is frequently viewed by academic staff as 'useful if it can be fitted in but not essential'. Librarians are often seen as 'auxiliary staff' (Fridén, 1996). If information literacy training is to be integrated into formal education programmes, health librarians must be involved in developing and designing new curricula and courses (Gannon-Leary, Wakeham and Walton, 2003). Academic health librarians are increasingly being involved in curriculum planning, albeit to varying degrees. Librarians have an increasingly important role in supporting and advising academic staff as they explore electronic and print resources for the redesign of curricula and assess resources that may be required.

Supporting access to services and resources

Increasingly, not just secondary resources (such as bibliographic databases) but also primary resources (such as full text e-journals and e-books) are available electronically. Traditional library activities are changing to reflect these trends. The physical library collection is becoming less important, and the health librarian increasingly fulfils a gateway function, enabling the learner to access resources irrespective of physical location. The health librarian provides the appropriate navigational tools and ensures access to the appropriate resources, whether electronic or print. Yet the physical library environment remains essential to the learner. Future libraries or learning resources centres will have ubiquitous data connectivity (either wired or wireless) and be the focus for teaching, access and support of the virtual learning environment.

Conclusion

The above roles require the health librarian to develop partnerships, with educationalists and technologists and between health service librarians and academic health librarians. The recent procurement of the Dialog Datastar system by the NHS (a system not used extensively by higher education), exemplifies the need for co-ordinated information-literacy teaching by health service librarians and academic health librarians. Librarians are essential to the education and training of health professionals. Education providers, such as the NHSU, must 'recognise the potential for library staff to undertake other roles in the learning process, such as designing courses, developing learning materials, teaching information skills or acting as mentors' (CILIP, 2003).

Key points
- The concept of lifelong learning has had a major impact on health professionals.
- Government policy has highlighted continuing professional development for health staff as key.
- Problem-based learning and e-learning have implications for health libraries.
- There is a major demand for access to learning resources when a student is undertaking clinical experience.

- Librarians have a learning role around information-literacy teaching, course design and supporting access to services and resources.

References

Albanese, M. A. and Mitchell, S. (1993) Problem-based Learning: a review of literature on its outcomes and implementation issues, *Academic Medicine*, **68**, 52–81.

Anon (2002) Emphasis on Study for NHS, *Nursing Standard*, **16** (40), 17.

Audit Commission (2000) *Hidden Talents: education, training and development for healthcare staff in NHS Trusts*, London, HMSO.

Banwell, L., Rowley, J. and Urquhart, C. (2003) Is e-learning the Answer in FE?, *Library & Information Update*, **2** (4), 50–1.

Bargellini, M. L. and Bordoni, L. (2001) The Role of the Library in a New Learning Scenario, *Electronic Library*, **19** (3), 153–7.

Beagle, D. (2000) Web-based Learning Environments: do libraries matter?, *College & Research Libraries*, **61** (4), 367–79.

Bligh, J. (1995) Problem-based Learning in Medicine: an introduction, *Postgraduate Medical Journal*, **71**, 323–6.

Brahmi, F. A. et al. (1999) Teaching Lifelong Learning Skills in a Fourth-Year Medical Curriculum, *Medical Reference Services Quarterly*, **18** (2), 1–11.

Burns, F. (1998) *Information for Health: an information strategy for the modern NHS 1998–2005 – a national strategy for local implementation*, www.nhsia.nhs.uk/def/pages/info4health/contents.asp.

Cabinet Office (2000) *e-government: a strategic framework for public services in the information age*, www.e-envoy.gov.uk/EStrategy/EStrategy/fs/en.

CILIP (2003) *CILIP Praises Health University Vision: response calls for role of library and information professionals to be acknowledged*, www.cilip.org.uk/news/2003/030303.html.

Connolly, D. and Donovan, M. (2002) Introducing a Problem-based Learning Module into an Occupational Therapy Course, *Learning in Health and Social Care*, **1** (3), 150–7.

Dawes, D. and Hanscomb, A. (2002) Focus: a pilot study to assess the case for e-learning in the NHS, *NT Research*, **7** (6), 428–43.

Drury, A. and Smith, L. (1999) Trying to Make Professional Development Easier with New Technology Distributed Learning: a pilot project in healthcare, *British Journal of Healthcare Computing and Information Management*, **16** (9), 24–5.

Feuerman, F. and Handel, M. J. (1998) *Handbook on Problem Based Learning*, Lanham, MD, Scarecrow Press.

Fridén, K. (1996) The Librarian as a Teacher: experiences from a problem-based setting, *Health Libraries Review*, **13**, 3–7.

Fryer, B. (2002) Overview: NHS University, *Health Service Journal*, **112** (5793), Supplement 9, 11.

Gannon-Leary, P., Wakeham, M. and Walton, G. (2003). 'Making a Difference' to Nurse Education: the impact on HE libraries, *Journal of Librarianship and Information Science*, **35** (1), 33–48.

Great Britain. Department for Education and Employment (1998) *The Learning Age: University for Industry*, www.lifelonglearning.co.uk/greenpaper/index.htm.

Great Britain. Department of Health (1999a) *Making a Difference: strengthening the nursing, midwifery and health visiting contribution to health and healthcare*, London. HMSO.

Great Britain. Department of Health (1999b) *Continuing Professional Development: quality in the new NHS*, London, Department of Health, HSC 1999/154.

Great Britain. Department of Health (2001) Working Together – Learning Together: a framework for lifelong learning in the NHS, www.doh.gov.uk/lifelonglearning/.

Haldane, G. C. (2003) LISTENing to Healthcare Students: the impact of new library facilities on the quality of services, *Health Information and Libraries Journal*, **20**, (Suppl. 1), 59–68.

Hughes, C. A. (2000) Information Services for Higher Education: a new competitive space, *D-Lib Magazine*, (December), www.dlib.org/dlib/december00/hughes/12hughes.html.

Joch, A. (2003) Sites for Sore Eyes: e-learning tools make healthcare training available around the clock, *Healthcare Informatics*, **20** (4), 30–3.

Johnson, S. M. and Finucane, P. M. (2000) The Emergence of Problem-based Learning in Medical Education, *Journal of Evaluation in Clinical Practice*, **6** (3), 281–91.

Kanter, S. L. (1998) Fundamental Concepts of Problem-based Learning for the New Facilitator, *Bulletin of the Medical Library Association*, **86** (3), 391–5.

Kazmer, M. M (2002) Distance Education Students Speak to the Library: here's how you can help even more, *Electronic Library*, **20** (5), 395–400.

Martin, S. (2003) Impact of a Graduate Entry Programme on a Medical School Library Service, *Health Information and Libraries Journal*, **20** (1), 42–9.

Middleton, A., Rowell, G. and Walton, G. (2002) *Health and Education Northumbria Students Access to Learning Resources (HENSAL) Project: case studies of NHS pre-registration trainees and SCITT trainees*, Information Management Research Institute, Northumbria University.

MLANET (n.d.) *MLA Statement on Essential Library Support for Distance Education*, www.mlanet.org/government/positions/disteduc_2.htm.

Myers, G., Saunders, S. and Rogers, G. (2002) Beyond the Virtual Library: electronic curriculum web resources, *Electronic Library*, **20** (6), 473–80.

National Audit Office and Audit Commission (2001) *Educating and Training the*

Future Health Professional Workforce for England, London, HMSO, www.nao.gov.uk/pn/00-01/0001277.htm.

National Committee of Inquiry into Higher Education (1997) *Higher Education in the Learning Society: report of the National Committee*, London, NCIHE.

NHS Executive (1998*) Working Together with Health Information: a partnership strategy for educational and professional development to support Information for Health*, www.doh.gov.uk/ipu/develop/nip/together.htm.

Peck, C. et al. (2000) Continuing Medical Education and Continuing Professional Development: international comparisons, *British Medical Journal*, 320, 432–5.

Pinfield, S. et al. (1998) Realizing the Hybrid Library, *D-Lib Magazine*, (October), www.dlib.org/dlib/october98/10pinfield.html.

Price, B. (2003) *Studying Nursing Using Problem-based and enquiry-based Learning*, London, Palgrave.

Quinsee, S. (2001) Facilitating e-learning, *Library Association Record*, 103 (10), 616–7.

Rankin, J. A. (1992) Problem-based Medical Education: effect on library use, *Bulletin of the Medical Library Association*, 80, 36–43.

Rankin, J. A. (1993) Preparing Medical Libraries for Use by Students in PBL Curricula, *Academic Medicine,* 68, 205–6.

Rankin, J. A. (1996) Problem-based Learning and Libraries: a survey of the literature, *Health Libraries Review*, 13 (1), 33–42.

Rashbass, J. (2000) Will Technology Kill the Healthcare Library?, *Health Libraries Review*, 17, 51–5.

Roberts, R. (1999) Learning to Learn – Over the Internet: can cyberspace assist education in the health domain?, *British Journal of Healthcare Computing and Information Management*, 16 (9), 32–4.

Roes, H. (2001) Digital Libraries and Education Trends and Opportunities, *D-Lib Magazine*, (July/August), www.dlib.org/dlib/july01/roes/07roes.html.

Rusbridge, C. (1998) Towards the Hybrid Library, *D-Lib Magazine*, (July/August), www.dlib.org/dlib/july98/rusbridge/07rusbridge.html.

Twigg, C. and Miloff, M. (1998) The Global Learning Infrastructure. In Tapscott, D., Lowry, A. and Ticoll, D., *Blueprint to the Digital Economy*, New York, London, McGraw-Hill.

Whitsed, N. (2003a) Learning and Teaching, *Health Information and Libraries Journal,* 20 (2), 119–23.

Whitsed, N. (2003b) Learning and Teaching, *Health Information and Libraries Journal*, 20 (3), 189–91.

Part 2
Managing the knowledge base

10

Managing projects

Andrew Booth

Introduction

With their increasing involvement in project management, information professionals require a different skills set from that required for day-to-day management of a service (Moore, 1998; Thornley, 1998). This chapter covers the
practicalities of project management and briefly identifies such formal
approaches as PERT, Critical Path Analysis and the PRojects IN a Controlled
Environment (PRINCE II) methodology. The chapter concludes by considering software, both generic and specific to project management.

What is project management?

Project management (PM) is the 'planning, monitoring and control of all
aspects of a project and the motivation of all those involved in it to achieve the
project objectives on time and to the specified cost, quality and performance'
(British Standard BS 6079–1, 2000). Health librarians frequently encounter
PRINCE project methodology which further defines a project as 'a management environment that is created for the purpose of delivering one or more
business products according to a specified business case' (CCTA, 1996).

Modern PM emerged between the 1930s and the 1950s in the defence and
aviation industries. The quintessential project is the Apollo space project. That
project involved multiple manufacturers delivering to a common schedule and
utilizing a wide range of PM tools and techniques. Although information technology has improved communication, recent years have emphasized behavioural ('soft') PM techniques such as leadership, motivation and team working.

As library-related projects become increasingly complex and pressures to deliver become more critical, PM is considered a necessity. Projects that are completed quickly, to budget and that achieve their objectives are typically those where libraries have invested in PM. Although 'project *management*' implies that library managers have most to benefit from such techniques all team members gain from familiarity with project milestones and critical paths.

Case study: What does a project look like?

In 1998 a regional report called for improvements to access and resources for primary-care staff. Funding was provided to establish a project with anticipated benefits of 'providing a model of best practice in knowledge management and supporting evidence based practice, lifelong learning and Continuing Professional Development, research and audit amongst primary care staff'.

The project was initially funded over a timescale of two years. A project initiation document (PID) was produced with the objective of improving access to information resources for all primary-care staff. The PID defined key aspects as follows:

- to establish an enquiry service by e-mail/fax/phone/personal visit
- to exploit existing library resources
- to support lifelong learning
- to initiate a clinical-effectiveness current-awareness service
- to promote the National electronic Library for Health
- to offer training in accessing and appraising the evidence base
- to develop intranet access to national and local clinical guidelines
- to provide a referral point for staff providing accredited health information to patients
- to assist the evaluation, to be undertaken by a local academic unit.

A project board was established, including the project team and representatives from the Health Authority, the local NHS Trust, a regional library adviser and three Primary Care Groups. The project board was responsible for developing realistic plans, recruiting project staff, monitoring progress, delivering to budget and achieving sustainability. A project reference group consisted of the project team, library staff from the local NHS Trust, representatives from Health Promotion and IMT (Information Management and Technology) and a regional library adviser. This group initially met monthly, providing regular reports to the project board. Costs included expenditure on a knowledge manager and investment in an intranet.

Differences between project management and service delivery

A project comprises:

- *An objective* – an outcome that you want to achieve
- *Benefits* – what you expect to achieve by the project
- *A timescale* – when you want to achieve it by
- *Costs* – resources needed to achieve your objective and realize your benefits (MacLachlan, 1996).

Library projects will differ from library service delivery with respect to timescale, costs and benefits. Typically a project has a clearly defined timescale whereas service delivery is ongoing, around an annual cycle of delivery and evaluation. Similarly, while service costs are typically built into an annual budget cycle and handled as recurrent expenditure, a project involves one-off or capital expenditure. Finally benefits within a service are usually encapsulated in service-level agreements or contracts while benefits within a project usually target value added features.

Planning a project

The first task when planning a project is to clearly define the start and end dates. Within this overall timeframe you then outline the project's major stages. If the project is particularly complex you will find it helpful to subdivide it into subprojects. It is then possible to decide what resources you need for each stage or subproject. Some resources may already be in place (in the existing infrastructure or staffing complement) but you should compute any others within the project budget. Formally identifying resources, even for internal 'projects', allows you to quantify the actual 'cost' to the organization and to be explicit about opportunity costs. Budget estimates and product specification are 'iterative' – involving negotiations on cost and quality. If your project is to run smoothly you will need to highlight any weaknesses, together with contingencies, identify any barriers and subject them to formal risk analysis and define clear lines of control or authority.

Stages of project management

In managing a project you will require specific managerial attributes:

different types of projects require different approaches to the management process and different individual skills to cope with associated, specific levels of ambiguity and uncertainty in start-up and implementation phases . . . leaders need to be equipped with skills necessary to negotiate, manage and decrease uncertainty around objectives and methods definition in project start-up and implementation phases.

(Cicmil, 1999)

1 At the conceptual stage the project team has to be creative, envisaging different routes by which an objective might be attained.
2 At the definition stage, with a course of action already selected, goals and objectives are determined.
3 The planning stage requires that time is scheduled and resources identified.
4 Implementation is where mechanisms are put in place to manage and control resources.
5 Finally is completion, not simply in the formal sense of delivering the project outcomes but in celebrating the achievement and reflecting upon the journey travelled.

Why projects fail

Projects usually fail when they:

*   do not deliver on time
*   do not keep to the budget
*   do not meet the agreed quality.

Such failures are more common than one might think. No one overriding factor causes project failure. A single factor, or several factors in conjunction, may be involved. Examples include those listed in Table 10.1.

Table 10.1 Reasons why projects fail

Lack of user involvement
Long or unrealistic timescales
Absence of, or poorly defined, requirements
Scope creep (insidious growth in scale during the life of a project)
No facility to control the introduction of unanticipated changes
Poor prototyping or testing

All the factors listed in Table 10.1 involve management and training, rather than technical issues, and apply regardless of whether your project is heavily reliant on technology or possesses a 'low-tech' specification (Loo, 1996). Your project could be regarded as a failure even when you deliver everything to the quality, time and costs previously specified. For example, your project may covertly go over budget if staff members have to work at evenings and weekends to compensate for poor project planning or if you have to absorb extra costs elsewhere in the organization. If, for instance, in conducting a retrospective catalogue conversion, project staff are left burnt out and demotivated, despite delivering to time and cost, this might be construed a failure. You may regard a project as a failure if the deliverable fails to yield the benefits for which it was originally conceived. So an integrated cataloguing and circulation system may be installed on time and to budget but fail to yield improvements over previously separate modules. As Cicmil (1999) observes:

> Scholarly work and empirical evidence in recent years have illuminated a delicate issue of differentiating between project goals (the ultimate benefit or purpose of the project) and delivery objectives (the outcome or product of project effort according to the specification, and within time and cost constraints).

Although a project's success is not purely down to the project manager, this role is key and requires appropriate skills (Thornley, 1998). Research highlights the importance of communication, followed by leadership and motivation, organizational, planning and team-building skills (Taylor, 2000).

Minimizing the risk of project failure

Library managers should devise a risk-management plan to minimize the risk of project failure. This involves identifying each risk factor, estimating its impact, developing strategies to minimize the risk, and designing contingency plans. Of course each risk factor differs according to:

- its impact (serious problems disrupt more simple ones)
- its probability (common problems occur more often than unusual ones)
- its urgency (urgent problems must be dealt with more rapidly than non-urgent ones and command greater resources).

Most projects fail not because of technical concerns; the three principal causes of failure are 'people, people and people'. For a project to be successful, it must:

- satisfy stakeholder groups
- meet quality expectations/requirements
- be within cost
- be within deadline

- deliver sustained and actual benefits
- provide professional satisfaction and learning.

Clearly, if these criteria are applied, very few projects are successful. A library manager should have monitoring systems in place to spot where 'slippage' might occur. You should measure performance against the project's specification and scope, monitor cost through budget reports and track time through the project schedule. In addition, you should use 'softer' ongoing monitoring to monitor the morale of your team and the success with which junior members of your team are negotiating the learning curve.

Knowledge management for project management

Increasing interest in knowledge management has targeted knowledge from projects, notorious for not 'passing the baton' (Booth and Falzon, 2001; Falzon and Booth, 2001). While every project is different some similarities might be anticipated and errors avoided: 'Project information is rarely captured, retained, or indexed so that people external to the project can retrieve and apply it to future tasks" (Weiser and Morrison, 1998). Information professionals need to expand their role as custodian of the 'project archive' by exploiting explicit and tacit knowledge held by project staff. Knowledge-management techniques are even more critical within the concentrated timescale of a project (Disterer, 2002).

Tools and techniques

Most PM techniques exist to control or monitor time, cost or critical dependencies. (See Table 10.2.) If you plan and conclude a project on time and to the agreed cost you may consider that the actual tools chosen are largely irrelevant. An exception is where PM techniques are specified by the commissioners; as with NHS projects which require PRINCE II methodology. Even here there is variation in how strictly PRINCE II is applied. Many library managers claim that the framework is more valuable than the specific mechanisms it employs.

Table 10.2 Project management tools and techniques

1	Simple calendar
2	Timeline with intermediary targets
3	Work breakdown structure – a basic diagram that documents and describes all the work that must be done to complete the project
4	Task analysis – an observation-based technique that elicits knowledge from the users for whom a product is intended

Continued on next page

Table 10.2 *Continued*

5	Stakeholder analysis – listing all key stakeholders and assessing the likely impact each stakeholder or group of stakeholders might have on the project; this assessment is used to develop management strategies to secure the support necessary to allow the project to proceed
6	Gantt chart – provides a standard format for displaying project-schedule information by listing project activities and their corresponding start and finish dates
7	PERT (Performance Evaluation Review Technique) – a network analysis technique used to estimate project duration when there is a high degree of uncertainty about the individual activity duration estimates. PERT uses probabilistic time estimates based on optimistic, most likely, and pessimistic estimates of activity durations
8	CPM (Critical Path Method) – used to predict total project duration, the critical path is the longest path through a network diagram
9	Flowchart
10	Outline
11	Lists
12	Spreadsheets

PRINCE II

PRINCE (PRojects IN Controlled Environments) is a *de facto* standard for project management used extensively by the UK Government. PRINCE II is the latest incarnation of a methodology that has been used for many years and embodies the 'experience of scores of projects, project managers and project teams' (CCTA, 1996). PRINCE II is process-based so you can easily tailor it, and scale it down if necessary, for smaller projects. In fact, project managers frequently talk of using a 'cut-down' version of PRINCE.

As a generic tool PRINCE II incorporates a great deal of common sense. Many users consider that they could achieve a similar outcome without ploughing through a 400-page manual. Nevertheless its systematic approach minimizes the risk of your overlooking something important. An important feature of PRINCE II is its 'management by exception' which reduces unnecessary meetings.

Key roles within PRINCE II are the project manager (with 'responsibility to manage the project on a day-to-day basis to deliver the required products within the constraints agreed with the project board' (CCTA, 1996)) and the project board, chaired by the 'executive' who represents 'the customer and [is] owner of the business case'. Other project board members include a senior user, a senior supplier and the project manager. Despite being verbose and bureaucratic PRINCE II is widely used and readily available, being distributed by the Stationery Office.

Project management software

PM software automates the process of breaking a project into discrete tasks and estimating time and resources. Software can produce project plans and Gannt charts and can be used to allocate resources. However, project-planning software deals only with planning and scheduling. It does not manage the project and does not remove the need to define and control the project. Although you could use general-purpose software, such as a Microsoft Excel^{TM} spreadsheet, there are obvious advantages in using an integrated package where changes made are automatically computed for their impact on the budget and human resources.

Benefits of PM software are well summarized by NASA:

> project management tools can enhance our ability to continuously improve the way in which projects are managed. With increased access to project data, informed decisions can be made. . . . Potential project risks can be identified and mitigated in a timely fashion. Projects will be met on time and on budget.
>
> (Project Management World Today, 2001)

The current market leader, Microsoft Project^{TM}, is particularly strong at managing schedules and resources, communicating project status, and reporting project information. Most people who use Microsoft Project™, or indeed any PM software, are learning how to use the software *and* how to do project planning. Both involve a steep learning curve. Time spent on a training course may appear unwelcome, particularly at initiation of a project, but will reap dividends, particularly when you embark upon a subsequent project!

You do not need to use PM software for all stages of the project. You can use other software such as spreadsheets (e.g. Microsoft Excel™) and word processors (e.g. Microsoft Word™) for tracking activity and costs. For example, you could use Microsoft Excel™ to store project phases and invoicing milestones, as well as to manage cash flows.

As with any software, the PM software market changes continually. The US-based Project Management Institute (www.pmi.org) publishes an annual software survey. Increasingly, virtual working requires built-in web publishing (for sharing documents among the team), e-mail capabilities and a web interface (allowing team members to amend project documents remotely).

Strengths and weaknesses of a project management approach

A project-management approach, when appropriately applied, can enable a library manager to achieve a synergy, whereby a multidisciplinary team focuses on a common goal, making it easier for it to carry out its job. It promotes team building and provides opportunities for individual growth and development. However, it requires effective leadership to achieve goals successfully.

The increasing complexity of projects has led to recognition of the limitations of PM approaches. Early PM is characterized by intuitive approaches. Subsequent reliance on scientific approaches has gradually been supplanted by recognition that the 'human element' cannot be rationalized away with flow-charts and diagrams. You will need to take into account behavioural factors, characterized by 'judicious project management', where tools and methods become subservient to business goals and objectives (Computer Sciences Corporation, n.d.).

Conclusion

While many textbooks cover PM basics (Frame, 1994; Roberts and Ludvigsen, 1998; Martin, 2002), a library manager must recognize that success does not depend upon mechanistic application of Gantt charts and budgets. You must pay attention to holistic concerns with both staff and organization. Your success depends not merely on project deliverables but includes such intangibles as the feel-good factor and opportunities for personal development.

PM is thus one of many areas of management that requires interpersonal skills, not just technical ability. You should identify risks to the project, not merely from technical and logistic constraints but also from poor communication, low morale and dysfunctional teamwork. In this respect service delivery and project management have much in common.

Key points

- Project management requires a different skill set from that required for service delivery.
- Project management can be distinguished from service management with regard to costs, benefits and timescale.
- Different phases of a project require different skills of the project manager and different characteristics from team members.
- Project failures may occur even when project deliverables are delivered on time; soft as well as hard outcomes should be factored into the equation.

- Project management requires significant attention to aspects of knowledge management.
- Project-management techniques and software should support but not direct the course of a project.

References

Booth, A. and Falzon, L. (2001) Evaluating Information Service Innovations in the Health Service: 'If I was planning on going there I wouldn't start from here', *Health Informatics Journal*, **7** (1), 13–19.

British Standard (2000) BS 6079–1, *A Guide to Project Management*, London, BSI.

Central Computer and Telecommunications Agency (CCTA) (1996) *PRINCE II: project management for business*, London, Stationery Office.

Cicmil, S. (1999) An Insight into Management of Organisational Change Projects, *Journal of Workplace Learning*, **11** (1), 5–15.

Computer Sciences Corporation (n.d.) *Project Management in the 1990s*, PEP Paper 26, www.cscresearchservices.com/foundation/library/P026/RP16.asp.

Disterer, G. (2002) Management of Project Knowledge and Experiences, *Journal of Knowledge Management*, **6** (5), 512–20.

Falzon, L. and Booth, A. (2001) REALISE-ing their Potential?: implementing local library projects to support evidence-based health care, *Health Information Libraries Journal*, **18** (2), 65–74.

Frame, J. D. (1994) *The New Project Management*, San Francisco CA, Jossey Bass.

Loo, R. (1996) Training in Project Management: a powerful tool for improving individual and team performance, *Team Performance Management: an international journal*, **2** (3), 6–14.

MacLachlan, L. (1996) *Making Project Management Work for You*, London, Library Association.

Martin, V. (2002) *Managing Projects in Health and Social Care*, London, Routledge.

Moore, K. A. (1998) Project Management: can libraries benefit? *Bibliotheca Medica Canadiana*, **20** (2), 72–3.

Project Management World Today (2001) *NASA Selects PM Software*, www.pmforum.org/pmwt01/education01-11.htm.

Roberts, K. and Ludvigsen, C. (1998) *Project Management for Health Care Professionals*, Oxford, Butterworth-Heinemann.

Taylor, A. (2000) IT Projects: sink or swim, *The Computer Bulletin*, www.bcs.org.uk/publicat/ebull/jan2000/article1.htm.

Thornley, R. (1998) The Librarian as Project Manager, *Bibliotheca Medica Canadiana*, **20** (2), 70–1.

Weiser, M. and Morrison, J. (1998) Project Memory: information management for project teams, *Journal of Management Information Systems*, **14** (4), 149–66.

Working collaboratively

Sharon Dobbins

Introduction

Collaborative working has become the norm in health and social care (Skelton and Abell, 2001), and most health-library and information professionals are involved to some extent in working with others within organizations, across organizations and across sectors. While there are many benefits in using a collaborative approach to service planning and delivery, there are also a number of challenges that can jeopardize even the most straightforward of ventures. This chapter considers the main drivers and benefits relating to collaborative activity in the health-information sector and explores some of the challenges and barriers inherent in a joined-up approach. The many forms that collaboration can take are described and guidelines for the implementation of successful collaborative initiatives are proposed. The chapter concludes with a summary of the skills required for competent collaborative workers, leading to successful working across professional, organizational and sectoral boundaries. Recent examples of collaborative working are referred to throughout the chapter.

Collaboration

The *Collins English Dictionary* (2002) provides two definitions for 'collaborate': 'to work with another or others on a joint project' and 'to cooperate as a traitor, esp. with an enemy occupying one's own country'. In this chapter, we shall be focusing on the first definition! Collaboration and partnership working in the health sector present a complex picture (Wildridge, 2002). This is reflected in health libraries where a wide variety of types of collaboration exists, including contracts, consortia, alliances and service-level agreements (Childs and Banwell, 2001).

Key drivers

There are many reasons why collaborative working takes place. Melling and Little (2002) identify two types of drivers to collaborative working: self-motivation and external pressure or internal and external drivers. An examination of these reveals the context in which collaborative working takes place in the health information sector.

Internal drivers include the culture of collaboration, as collaborative working is part of the value system and organizational culture of library and knowledge services. This is demonstrated by the long history of partnership in the library sector (Melling and Little, 2002), for example in interlending schemes and collaborative cataloguing. It is recognized that there is a need for joined-up thinking to avoid duplication and reinventing the wheel, leading to many initiatives at national, regional and local level. Service improvement is significant as Moore and Carpenter (2002) maintain that the main driver for co-operation between libraries is 'a desire for mutual benefit, achieved by extending the range or quality offered by the libraries to their users'. As Twidale et al. (1997) comment, 'no one person can know everything', and it follows that no one library can provide for all needs.

Further internal drivers include the increasing scarcity of resources which is driving library managers to seek ways of achieving better value for money through collaborative working. One recent example of this is the national procurement of a core collection of databases and electronic journals (Gibbens, 2003). An opportunity to raise the profile and image of library services can be another driver. The People Flows project (Nankivell, Foster and Ellkin, 1999) identified that agreement at high levels is often required in co-operative work and 'libraries could benefit from this by gaining a higher profile with strategic organisational managers'. Many library managers are motivated by the increasing opportunities to utilize technology to join up services. Obvious examples of this are the internet, OPACs and the new OpenURL standard (NISO Committee AX, 2003), offering the facility to link to a number of data sources from different providers.

There is also a variety of external drivers. Within the public sector, the call to partnership, particularly working across boundaries, comes from central government (Great Britain. Department of Health, 1998). As Melling and Little (2002) state, 'The UK government expects to see a strategic approach to their provision with collaborative working and partnerships a keystone to the approach.' In addition, Moore and Carpenter (2002) identify regionalism, joined-up government and a willingness to finance change and development as three major political shifts which are stimulating increased co-operation in the public sector.

In the health and social care context, Pampling, Gordon and Pratt (2000) comment 'Partnership has become a legal, almost moral, imperative in the health and social care world in recent years.' In policy document after policy document the analysis is consistent and welcome. Top-level activity is also taking place between health and education, for example the Strategic Alliance for Health and Social Care between the Department of Health and Higher Education Funding Council (Crisp and Newby, 2002), and the development of Health and Education Strategic Partnerships (Normington and Crisp, 2003). The development of the NHSU will provide many opportunities for further collaborative working (Great Britain. Department of Health, 2002). Libraries, both physical and virtual, will be part of that partnership matrix to support the developing learning culture of the NHS.

Challenges and barriers to effective collaboration

A number of challenges and barriers have been drawn from the literature on partnership working (Hawkins and Malley, 1999; Childs and Banwell, 2001; Shaw, 2001; Banks, 2002; Melling and Little, 2002; Childs and Dobbins, 2003; Thornhill, 2003). These are summarized using Childs and Banwell's (2001) categories of barriers in *Partnerships for Health*.

Constraints that restrict the freedom of action of organizations, sections within organizations and individuals

Political, organizational and practical constraints affect effective collaborative working. Despite much effort to join up government and create alliances, significant barriers still exist between health and education, health and social care and also between health organizations themselves. Differences exist in organizational structures, decision-making processes, political or strategic interests.

Funding

Funding can be a barrier in a number of ways. First, the availability of recurrent funds is often the prerequisite for sustainable collaborative work. Second, an imbalance of existing resources or new funding can lead to conflicts within the team or limitations on the development of projects. Finally, the existence of different decision-making processes for different organizations makes bidding for funds difficult.

Information and communication technology (ICT)

Barriers in ICT are well documented, the principal issues being the licensing of electronic content, limitations of ICT infrastructures and interconnectivity problems between networks, for example JANET and NHSnet. International partnerships may face even more basic problems of difficult or non-existent internet or e-mail facilities.

Cultures

Cultural barriers can include management styles, expectations and language. Individuals or organizations may carry baggage from the past, which may affect future working. NHS organizations in particular have had to move from working in competition with each other to partnership working. This massive cultural change takes time. Finally, 'deep-resource sharing' initiatives require partners who are willing to surrender autonomy or control.

Change

The constant state of change in the NHS results in disrupted relationships and changes to policy, both of which may threaten initiatives. Collaborative ventures can also cause change, which may be resisted by colleagues and stakeholders. Achieving ownership and agreement on new ways of working throughout the organization is also a considerable challenge.

Complexity

The fragmented and confusing picture of activity in the health-information sector has already been alluded to. This causes confusion for those who are planning implementing and utilizing collaborative initiatives. There may also be complexities within collaborative ventures, for example through an unwieldy number of partners.

Types of collaborative working

Collaboration can take many forms. Moore and Carpenter (2002) identify improving access to library resources and collection development as being the two most popular forms. There are many examples of access agreements in health, through the development of service-level agreements between NHS and higher education (HE) organizations and also through the development of integrated services (Blackburn, 2001). There has also been activity in collaborative collection development – the subject of a literature review by Stutz (2002). Many other forms of collaboration exist, most of which were identified by Brophy (2001) and through the People Flows project (Nankivell, Foster and Ellkin, 1999):

- *Document delivery* – There are many examples of this on a national basis (The British Library), subject basis (Nursing Union List of Journals) and a local basis (the Health Libraries Network (HLN) operating in the North East of England.)
- *Networked reference and referral services* – Links have been established with South Australia health services, through the Chasing the Sun project, which aimed to pilot a round-the-clock enquiries service for clinicians seeking information for patient care when libraries are usually closed (Information and Library Service Development. NHS South West Workforce Development Confederations, 2002).
- *Union catalogues* – The Durham and Teesside Health Libraries Alliance is developing a union catalogue of NHS holdings in the County Durham and Tees Valley Workforce Development Confederation (WDC) patch. This is supported by a daily van service that facilitates the mobilization of materials between libraries.
- *Signposting and mapping services* – The provision of clear information of library and information services within WDC areas has improved the awareness of services available. A good example is the Three Confederations Electronic Library for Health and Social Care.
- *Strategic planning* – The London Health Libraries Strategy and Development Group, working across the five WDCs in London, has formulated a joint business plan (London Health Libraries Strategy and Development Group, 2003). Other examples are provided by Shemilt and Lockett (2002) and Lord (2002).
- *Service development* – Pearson and Rossall have reported on the development of a successful practice library resulting from collaboration between a GP and a librarian (2001).
- *Research and development* – NHS and HE collaboration is demonstrated in the Health and Education Northumbria Students Access to Learning resources (HENSAL) project, jointly funded by the Northern England WDC and School of Education, University of Northumbria. This project examined the availability of learning resources for students on placement (Middleton and Rowell, 2002).
- *Creating electronic content* – The Sheffield Evidence for Effectiveness and Knowledge (SEEK) website brings together partners in the NHS and HE to develop a one-stop shop for local clinical guidelines and national

information resources to support clinical governance and evidence-based practice.

* *Staff training and development* – Many joint training initiatives can be cited. The Nordic/Baltic health libraries provide an international example through their Transfer of Knowledge programme (Müller et al., 2002).
* *Lobbying* – One of the key functions of the North East Museums, Libraries and Archives Council (NEMLAC) is to act as an advocate for library services at a local, regional and national level. HELICON seeks to do this at a national level in the health-library and information field.

In her study of partnership between resource-rich and resource-poor countries, Shaw (2001) also mentions visits, provision of resources and provision of technical support for training.

Foundations of successful collaborative working

Guidelines, advice and models can be found in the literature to enable practitioners to achieve successful collaborative working (Hawkins and Malley, 1999; Nankivell, Foster and Ellkin, 1999; Childs and Banwell, 2001; Comptroller and Auditor General, 2001). Table 11.1 outlines a number of key factors which should be considered when embarking on any collaborative work.

Table 11.1 Success factors for collaborative activity

Factors relating to collaborative activities	Factors relating to collaborators
• Clear and transparent working arrangements and management structures	• Ability to look to the future and learn from the past, particularly where joint working has previously been problematic
• Evaluation and monitoring of collaborative activity	
• Flexibility in the use of resources	• Agreed need for partnership and for some 'deep-resource-sharing' ventures, a willingness to give up some autonomy and control
• Funding to support collaborative activity	
• Identification of at least one benefit for each partner	
• Realism: start small while thinking big	• Culture of co-operation in collaborating organizations
• Staff support and interest in partner organizations	• Effective communication is essential – between individuals, organizations, and all stakeholders
• Strategic planning to facilitate sustainability	
• Time: the collaborative process is time consuming; it may take time to develop,	• Equality: all collaborators should be able to identify benefits for themselves

Continued on next page

Table 11.1 *Continued*

Factors relating to collaborative activities	Factors relating to collaborators
implement and see results; and the pace of change may be different for each partner	• Local champions • Maintenance of organizational integrity • Organizational and senior management commitment • Positive process of human interaction • Shared vision and clarity of purpose to ensure that focus and enthusiasm are maintained • Skills in collaborative working • Strong leadership – preferably with status and authority • Trust between stakeholders • Understanding of context of partnership working and potential barriers

A number of writers have attempted to provide a structure for partnership working, including Hawkins and Malley (1999) and Nankivell, Foster and Ellkin (1999). Childs and Banwell (2001) propose a generic model of partnership, the Developmental Process of Successful Partnership Working. This was revised slightly in the light of the experience of the establishment of the Durham and Teesside Health Libraries Alliance (Childs and Dobbins, 2003). The resulting model consists of the following elements:

A *Starting the process* – identifying a champion, a vision and starting to work together in a joint venture

B *Achieving agreement* – a process that requires an 'implementer' and involves communication, establishing ownership and trust; funding is acquired and a partnership pattern is agreed which is clear to all involved

C *Creating a self-sustaining partnership independent of the presence of specific individuals and robust in a climate of change* – this stage focuses on embedding the partnership and establishing an infrastructure for future activities

D *Implementation* – identifying an implementer, producing a strategy, continuing to promote the partnership and seeking to extend the partnership further

E *Time, time, time.*

The complexity of working in partnership is recognized and, although the model is presented in a linear list of separate steps, in reality these 'turn back on themselves in a spiral. The overall partnership can be seen as a complex braid of these individual spirals.'

Skills in collaborative working

'Skills' is a key area, yet one that is often overlooked. Using skill sets identified by TFPL for the information services workforce (Skelton and Abell, 2001), it is possible to identify and categorize a number of skills necessary for effective collaborative working. These are outlined in Table 11.2.

Table 11.2 Key skills for collaborative working

Skills set	Skills
Personal attributes	• Creative/innovative • Breadth of vision • Confident • Collaborative • Flexible
Interpersonal skills	• Communication • Influencing • Team working • Facilitation • Networking • Advocacy and lobbying
Organization-specific skills	• Understanding the sector/industry • Understanding the organization (including partnerships)
Business skills	• Planning • Leadership • Financial management • Bidding • Project management • Marketing and promotion • Media and public relations • Presentation • Management and strategic planning • Team development

This skill profile represents a shift from traditional library and information skills to those more focused on strategic management and leadership. Skelton and Abell (2001) provide not only a useful breakdown of many of these skills, but also practical guidance on key organizations to contact and development methods for individuals, teams and groups.

Conclusion

Collaborative working is essential to enable health information professionals to respond to the growing demands of users and employers. Significant benefits have been realized through collaborative activity that has taken place, and is currently taking place, particularly in terms of improving the effective use of resources and the quality of services and widening access to information resources. However, this approach presents many challenges, and an under-standing of the potential barriers will help those considering a collaborative approach. An examination of the success factors presented in this chapter will provide a useful starting point, particularly if considered systematically in the form of a framework such as that proposed by Childs and Banwell (2001). By underpinning these steps with the development of specific skills and compe-tencies needed for successful collaborative working, the considerable effort required to work collaboratively will be rewarded.

Key points

- Collaborative working is not a 'nice-to-do' activity; it is essential to ensure the delivery of high-quality health-information services.
- Collaborative working is not easy, and major barriers can hinder progress. An understanding of these challenges can lead to more effective joint work-ing.
- Successful collaborative working is built on strong foundations – success factors that should be taken into account when embarking on any venture.
- Collaborative working requires a range of skills that can be developed.

References

Banks, P. (2002) *Partnerships under Pressure: a commentary on progress in partnership-working between the NHS and local government*, Kings Fund, www.kingsfund.org.uk/pdf/PartnershipsUnderPressure.pdf.

Blackburn, N. (2001) Building Bridges: towards integrated library and information services for mental health and social care, *Health Information and Libraries Journal*, **18** (4), 203–12.

The British Library, www.bl.uk.

Brophy, P. (2001) *The Library in the Twenty-first Century: new services for the information age*, London, Library Association Publishing.

Childs S. and Banwell L. (2001) *Partnerships in Health: effective access models to higher education and National Health Service libraries for health professionals and students*, A British Library Project funded under the Co-operation and Partnership Programme, Final Report, Information Management Research Institute, School of Information Studies, University of Northumbria.

Childs, S. and Dobbins S. (2003) *The Research–Practice Spiral: description of a partnership between the Information Management Research Institute, Northumbria University, and the Durham and Teesside Health Libraries Alliance*, unpublished.

Collins (2002) *Collins English Dictionary: 21st century edition*, 5th edn, Glasgow, HarperCollins.

Comptroller and Auditor General (2001) *Joining Up to Improve Public Services*, HC 383 Session 2001–2, 7 December 2001, London, The Stationery Office.

Crisp, N. and Newby, H. (2002) *Statement of Strategic Alliance for Health and Social Care*, Department of Health and the Higher Education Funding Council for England, www.doh.gov.uk/research/documents/strategicallianceapril2002.doc.

Gibbens, S. (2003) *National Core Content – Announcement of Award: press release from the National Core Content Group*, National Core Content Group, www.nelh.nhs.uk/news_ncc.asp.

Great Britain. Department of Health (1998) *Partnership in Action (New Opportunities for Joint Working between Health and Social Services): a discussion document*, London, Department of Health, www.doh.gov.uk/pub/docs/doh/partners.pdf.

Great Britain. Department of Health (2002) *Learning for Everyone: a development plan for NHSU*, London, Department of Health, www.nhsu.nhs.uk/pdf/document_005.htm.

Hawkins, M. and Malley, I. (1999) *Joint Service Delivery Arrangements as the Basis of Cooperation between Library Authorities*, London, Library and Information Commission.

Health Libraries Network (HLN), http://stlis.thenhs.com/hln/index1.htm.

HELICON, www.helicon-info.com.

Information and Library Service Development. NHS South West Workforce Development Confederations (2002) *Annual Report 2001–2002*, www.adgw-wdc.nhs.uk/pdf/library_svces_sw_ar_2001-2.pdf.

London Health Libraries Strategy and Development Group and London Workforce Development Confederations (2003) *Business Plan Agreement 2003–2004*, www.londonlinks.ac.uk/lsdg/business_plan_april2003.pdf.

Lord, J. (2002) Developing the RCN Information Strategy: a process of partnership and collaboration, *Inform*, **13** (2), 6–7.

Melling M. and Little, J. (2002) Developing a Service Culture through Partnerships.

In Melling M. and Little, J. (eds), *Building a Successful Customer-service Culture: a guide for library and information managers*, London, Facet Publishing.

Middleton, A. and Rowell, J. (2002) *Health and Education Northumbria Students Access to Learning Resources (HENSAL) Project*, http://online.northumbria.ac.uk/faculties/art/information_studies/imri/rarea/hi/cpcl/HENSALpp1.ppt.

Moore, N. and Carpenter, J. (2002) Mapping the Co-operative Landscape. In Pilling, S. and Kanna, S. (eds), *Co-operation in Action: collaborative initiatives in the world of information*, London, Facet Publishing.

Müller, A. et al. (2002) Transfer of Knowledge: a Nordic/Baltic cooperation programme for medical libraries, *Health Information and Libraries Journal*, **19** (3), 166–8.

Nankivell, C., Foster, W. and Ellkin, J. (1999) *People Flows*, British Library Research and Innovation Centre Report 167, London, The British Library.

NHSU, www.nhsu.nhs.uk/index.htm.

NISO Committee AX (2003) *The OpenURL Framework for Context-sensitive Services Standard (version 1.0)*, Bethesda MA, National Information Standards Organization, http://library.caltech.edu/openurl/PubComDocs/Announce/20030416-Announce-Trial.htm.

Normington, D. and Crisp, N. (2003) *Health and Education Strategic Partnerships*, Department of Education and Skills and Department of Health, www.doh.gov.uk/hrinthenhs/learning/section4a/hesps.htm.

North East Museums, Libraries and Archives Council (NEMLAC), www.nemlac.co.uk.

Nursing Union List of Journals (NULJ), http://nulj.50megs.com/.

Pampling, D., Gordon, P. and Pratt, J. (2000) Practical Partnerships for Health and Local Authorities, *British Medical Journal*, **320**, 1723–5.

Pearson, D. and Rossall, H. (2001) Developing a General Practice Library Resulting from Collaboration between a GP and Librarian, *Health Information and Libraries Journal*, **18** (4), 192–202.

SEEK, www.shef.ac.uk/seek/.

Shaw, J. G. (2001) Health Library Partnership Programmes between Resource-poor Countries and Western Europe, *Health Information and Libraries Journal*, **18** (4), 220–7.

Shemilt, C. and Lockett, G. (2002) Building a New Relationship on Common Ground: the development of a multi-professional education and training development (ETD) forum, *Inform*, **13** (2), 1–3.

Skelton, V. and Abell, A. (2001) *Developing Skills for the Information Services Workforce in the Knowledge Economy: a report on the outcomes of eight scenario planning workshops*, Commissioned by the information services National

Training Organisation (isNTO), London, TFPL.

Stutz, A. (2002) Mapping Medicine: collaborative collection management for biomedical resources: review of the literature, *Health Information and Libraries Journal*, **19** (4), 226–9.

Thornhill, J. (2003) *Users First: removing barriers to knowledge access across NE and the NHS*, NHS/HE Forum, www.ucl.ac.uk/Library/nhsforum.htm.

Three Confederations Electronic Library for Health and Social Care, www.telh.nhs.uk.

Twidale, M. et al. (1997) *Collaboration in Physical and Digital Libraries, British Library Research and Development Report No. 64*, London, British Library Research and Innovation Centre.

Wildridge, V. (2002) What's in a Name?: partnership working terminology, *Inform*, **13** (2), 8–9.

12

Developing innovative services and managing change

Graham Walton

Introduction

Healthcare library and information services (LIS) face continual change. Nationally, geographical boundaries are altered and layers of management are introduced or jettisoned to impact ultimately on individual LIS. Locally, mergers between hospitals occur with previously unrelated library services being amalgamated. Within individual organizations, the reporting lines for the library can be completely changed resulting in new line management with different ideas and approaches. The librarians can find themselves part of a new umbrella structure with new colleagues and processes. Existing co-operative schemes can end with LIS being forced to locate new collaborators and partners. Software companies can develop new interfaces to databases necessitating wholesale changes to user education and documentation. As health professionals embrace evidence-based practice, a new portfolio of services is required to support this trend. A larger organization can decide that the library needs to physically move to new accommodation. The range of external environmental factors that can impact on libraries is documented in a complete issue of *Health Libraries Review* (Day and Walton, 1995). Most of the changes that are identified were unavoidable and required a response from the health LIS.

This chapter explores change within the health LIS context and demonstrates the centrality of innovative practice. The drive to innovate has existed for many years. Indeed Machiavelli was aware of the pressure in the Middle Ages: 'There is nothing more difficult to carry out, nor more doubtful of success, nor more dangerous to handle, than to initiate a new order of things.'

Machiavelli's vision was limited by his failure to acknowledge that innovation can be managed as part of the change process. Innovation and change management are complex and intertwined concepts. Many books, articles and research projects have explored innovation and change. This chapter aims to provide a broad introduction to key trends and concerns. The nature of change in the twenty-first century is described together with the imperative this places on innovative service development. There then follows an exploration of creativity within the context of innovation. Approaches to the facilitation and management of innovative services are outlined. The chapter concludes by discussing resistance to change, and ways in which such resistance can be overcome.

Nature of change

Charles Handy (1991), the management guru, tells us:

> Thirty years ago most people thought that change would mean more of the same, only better. That was incremental change and to be welcomed. Today we know that in many areas of life we cannot guarantee more of the same … [we] cannot even predict with confidence what will be happening in our own lives.

Uncertainty engendered by rapid and unpredictable change is evident for anyone working in healthcare. Lloyd and King (2002) review changes faced by health services across the world. Unparalleled change has occurred to structures, procedures and personnel. Woodsworth, Maylone and Sywak (1992) argue that LIS are the point where the impacts of change (be they political, educational or organizational) are most acutely concentrated, and where information technology is the most potent change agent of all. This impact is further emphasized by Drake (2000) who proposes that technology is the prime driver in the ways that people work, seek information and communicate. This accelerated technological change is even more heightened when it occurs at the same time as growing expectations of high-quality services and shrinking budgets (Paul, 2000). Health LIS wrestle with challenges resulting from moving to electronic delivery while at the same time working with the same (at best) resource level and having to demonstrate service quality

Management writers such as Drucker and Handy argue that people have to develop an increased understanding of change. In the past ten years change has become discontinuous and not part of a pattern. Technological, economic and political factors contribute to this discontinuity. Standing still at times of discontinuous change is simply not an option. People need to consciously manage this current unpredictability and future instability (Johannessen, Olsen and Olaisen, 1999). The health librarian cannot escape from the double pressures of the intense turbulence of the health sector and the LIS sector itself.

Innovation and service development

If a healthcare LIS does not alter its services and show innovation its manager faces the real danger of the services becoming obsolete. Drucker sees innovation as involving the application of knowledge to produce new knowledge. The European Commission (1996) has concluded that innovation is to do with:

- renewal and enlargement of the range of products and services and the associated markets
- establishment of new methods of production, supply and distribution
- introduction of changes in management, work organization and the working conditions and skills of the workforce.

All of the above are practical issues that impact on health LIS that are faced with users looking for an ever-increasing range of services to support them in their clinical work. LIS staff have to establish how such services can be developed and expanded to meet these needs. The internet has transformed the way that services are supplied and delivered because they are increasingly being developed electronically and distributed via the world wide web. This requires changes in the ways in which LIS are managed and structured together with the need for LIS staff to acquire new skills.

Within this context, innovation is concerned with the successful implementation of creative ideas that generate value and address unmet needs or gaps. Innovation starts with creativity whereby novel ideas are produced. These creative ideas are then sieved to identify those that will lead to new services in the library, or new ways to organize the library or new ways to manage the services. Berwick (2003) has investigated innovation in healthcare and he argues that various key factors will influence acceptance of change. Individuals have to feel that the innovation will help. It also must be compatible with a person's values/beliefs/past history and current needs. The more simple an innovation is, the more likely it is to be accepted quickly. It should be piloted initially at a small-scale level to establish its likely level of achievement.

Role of creativity in innovation

Creativity is the process of human thought that can lead to new ideas (Burke, 1994). When creativity is not present in an organization, the potential for new ideas is lost (Amabile, 1998). Ensuring that health LIS staff are creative in their work increases a library's ability to respond to new and diverse situations. As information technology takes over many clerical tasks the levels of creativity displayed in the service and staff become increasingly important. Creativity can bring new ways of seeing things together with new ideas. There are three stages in the creative management process: the identification of the idea, the development of the idea into something tangible and then the introduction of the development into the service. The truly creative ideas have lasting impact and are perceived as being worthy by others. Being different is not enough; the outcomes of creativity have to be appropriate and practical. Kletke et al. (2001) have identified those conditions where creativity is shown in problem solving:

- The product must have novelty and value.
- The thinking is unconventional.
- The thinking requires motivation, persistence and high intensity over a period of time.
- The initial problem is vague or ill defined so problem solving is part of the solution.

For creativity to flourish requires a climate conducive to creative thinking. Processes must be put in place whereby these ideas can be communicated; procedures are required to ensure the innovations that result from the creativity can be managed. In these days of uncertainty there needs to be a structured way to solving problems and using creative approaches to provide these solutions. The first stage is to redefine and analyse the problem. Once this has been achieved then different ideas must be identified to take this forward. Kesselman (1994) has considered various techniques for generating ideas from within the library context. A process is then needed to evaluate and select the ideas. After the chosen idea and solution have emerged they need to be implemented. VanGundy (1988) has produced a useful book that lists various creative approaches around this problem-solving structure.

A librarian has to become sensitive to, and aware of, external events as well as recognizing patterns and trends in their working environment. This allows intuition to become very effective in creatively developing services.

Managing the innovative process

Machiavelli's perceptions on the importance of innovation have been alluded to, along with his lack of insight into the ability to manage the process. This section explores how innovation and creativity can be managed in library and information services. Innovation is not achieved by flicking a switch; it is hard work. Neither is it to be seen as a response to a crisis or a way to fight fires. It is more appropriate if it is built into libraries as a modus operandi and is consciously managed. Four separate features contribute towards embedding innovation within a library service: the role of leadership, the mixture of skills/team members, the structure and the understanding of the environment. Institutional creativity and innovation are seen as the desired target. When they occur, the organization has harnessed the power of individuals to make a creative benefit across the board that is greater than the sum of individual efforts.

Role of leader in innovative practice

Tensions exist in the difference between leadership and management. Management is concerned with the maintenance of the existing organization (Kotter and Schlesinger, 1979). Leadership, on the other hand, is more concerned with change. A leader is expected, first and foremost, to develop the vision as to where the library is heading. Akeroyd (2000) proposes that the key factor in changing to electronic provision is the leader's clear, articulated vision. Paul (2000) identifies the attributes of the library manager necessary to allow innovation to flourish. They need to be candid, highly communicative and open to participation by others in decision-making processes. An ability and willingness to co-operate extensively on an equal basis with other staff members is also important. They should lead by example by showing initiative and innovation themselves. Managers have to be prepared for resistance and be prepared to begin change with their staff. As Hayes (2002) points out, they need to keep the systems operating effectively (manage) as well as simultaneously vitalizing the system to ensure that it will remain effective over the longer term (lead).

Team skills mix and innovation

Innovation cannot be expected to develop and be diffused unless an appropriate mixture of skills and team members is present. Successful, innovative teams are made up of people from different backgrounds, who have different angles to issues and who are not clones. Having a team completely made up of creative individuals would not be productive. Assembling the mixture of different characteristics required by a performing team will permit multiple approaches and will increase the cross-fertilization of ideas. Personality characteristics will also influence the adoption and spread of change. They can be divided into five main categories (Berwick, 2003):

- *Innovators* (2.5% of population) – they are the fastest adopting group. They are not opinion leaders and can be seen as mavericks. They are small in number.
- *Early adopters* (13.5%) – They are opinion leaders and have resources and risk tolerance of new things.

- *Early majority* (34%) – They learn from people they know and watch the early adopters. They are more prepared to hear about innovations relevant to their current, local situation rather than more general innovations.
- *Late majority* (34%) – The late majority look to the early majority first. When an innovation appears to have become part of the status quo, it will be adopted as long as there is local proof. Scepticism may abound.
- *Traditionalists* (16%) – For this group the point of reference is the past.

Being aware of these different attitudes towards innovation will help team members to both appreciate and work around any variances that will emerge. Innovation will occur where there is diversity of perspective, expertise and experience.

Organizational structure and innovation

For many years, libraries have relied on hierarchical, bureaucratic organizational structures (Walton and Edwards, 2001). Bureaucracies are typically created for stability and not for creativity and innovation. Innovation makes it increasingly important that mechanisms exist to allow interaction within the organization. Collaboration between different units and wide employee participation are central. In a large organization there is greater depersonalization and a decrease in lateral/vertical communication. The challenge is to address those barriers that bureaucracies and large organizations can present to innovation. This can be done by setting up project teams involving members from different disciplines or by introducing a matrix structure. The small size of many health libraries provides an inherent advantage for innovation.

Awareness of outside world and innovation

A fourth strand to managing innovation is awareness and understanding of the outside world. Libraries tend to focus on short-term pressures and immediate objectives and actions (Hudner, 2002). Such a focus can limit the development of a deep understanding of how the world is changing. A health librarian requires a detailed knowledge of the following: customer, services/products, market, competition, technology, competencies and trends in society as a whole. Haldane (2003) illustrates how intelligence about health LIS user behaviour can inform and develop improved services. Information, ideas and intelligence must be brought back into the library from outside. The climate within the library then has to be managed to allow this awareness to feed into the innovation and creativity. If people are controlled and threatened then innovation will not flourish. Attending meetings and conferences, along with involvement in professional activities, can help in gathering this intelligence. Awareness of issues being faced by different health professions is also invaluable.

Resistance to innovation and overcoming the resistance

Reasons for resistance

It is not easy to integrate innovation into strategic and management processes in LIS (Hudner, 2002). There will be resistance at various levels to the applications of innovative ideas and approaches. Some see innovation and change as a threat because they represent the unknown. They may challenge the status quo and are not welcomed by those with powerful vested interests in maintaining the current position. Introducing innovation can also mean an extra workload. One study on innovation in the NHS convincingly shows that resistance is a reaction against the burden of additional work (King and Andersen, 1995). Resistance exists at the individual, group and organizational levels. At the individual level, people resist change because of a mixture of personality factors and prior experiences. Those people who have had previous negative experiences of change may very well set up barriers. They may lack trust in colleagues; they may misunderstand the purposes of the changes; and they may have different perspectives on the change. Others may suffer from 'change fatigue' and struggle to find the energy and enthusiasm to become engaged in innovative practice. Others may find that their own personal self-interests are threatened by the proposed innovations. If people feel that they will lose something of value they will resist the change (Hayes, 2002). Innovation can be seen to be a threat to power and influence.

Resistance can also occur as part of the group process and dynamics. The 'groupthink' phenomenon, identified by Janis (1982), can occur when a group does not have power. Any change from outside this group is seen as a threat to the status quo. Other factors that can influence group resistance are the level of involvement in the innovation process and the level of self-determination. At the organizational level, factors contributing to resistance are the structure, the culture and the strategic direction chosen for the institution.

Overcoming resistance

The seminal investigation on overcoming resistance to change and innovation was produced by Kotter and Schlesinger (1979). They identify six methods for dealing with resistance to change:

1 *Education and persuasion* – People need to be educated about the need for innovation and change. Ideally an unbiased presentation of the facts should allow a rational justification of action. Another approach is to encourage people to develop an awareness of the fallibility of current practices so they can see more clearly the need for change.

2 *Participation and involvement* – If people are involved in the innovation process, they can develop a shared perception of the need for change. Decision making can also benefit from wider input. Participation in the process can lead to people accepting innovations because they 'own' them as a group.

3 *Facilitation and support* – Resistance can manifest itself as fear and anxiety in the individual. If people are provided with training in new skills, given time off after demanding periods or listened to and provided with emotional support, they may become less resistant.

4 *Negotiation and agreement* – Rewards can be given for those behaviours that facilitate change. If it is clear that an individual will lose out after the change, then a reward strategy can overcome their resistance.

5 *Manipulation and co-option* – A person can be given a key role in the design of the innovation with the purpose of securing their endorsement (rather than gaining from their expertise). Manipulation is the attempt to influence others to change and it can involve the deliberate biasing of messages. The manipulation and co-option approach can lead people to feeling tricked.

6 *Direction and reliance on explicit and implicit coercion* – Managers of innovation and change can use their power to withhold valued outcomes from people in order to motivate them to change. This approach may result in a willingness to comply and go along with the changes, but long-term commitment may be low.

The final two are not recommended because they can be counter-productive and result in negative outcomes.

Conclusion

This chapter has examined change management specifically from the perspective of innovation (and creativity). Health libraries are being challenged in all areas of work where uncertainties abound. Librarians cannot assume that they will navigate these changes by chance or by inaction. Others could take over roles that have traditionally been the remit of health librarians. Having started with a quotation from history this chapter will end with an even earlier one. In AD 288 a worried Roman called Servaeus Africanus wrote:

It is apparent from the accounts alone that a number of people, wishing to batten on the estates of the Treasury have invented titles for themselves whereby they procure no advantage to the Treasury but swallow up the profits

The imperative is to always ask 'What is the next step?' Innovation is not reformation, it is about introducing useful change. Consciously managing this change, when introducing innovation and creativity, increases the likelihood that the health library will continue to meet its users' needs.

Key points

* Change is unpredictable and varied and forces health LIS to be innovative.
* Innovation and creativity are about generating value and addressing unmet needs or gaps.
* Innovations can be managed by developing the leadership role, having a diverse team, making structures less bureaucratic and by having an in-depth knowledge of the outside world.
* Resistance will occur to innovation and change at personal, group and organizational levels.
* There are various approaches that can be taken to overcome resistance to change.

References

Akcroyd, J. (2000) The Management of Change in Electronic Libraries, *66th IFLA Council and General Conference*, 13–18 August 2000, www.ifla.org/IV/ifla66/papers/037-110e.htm.

Amabile, T. (1998) How to Kill Creativity, *Harvard Business Review*, (Sept–Oct), 78–87.

Berwick, D. M. (2003) Disseminating Innovations in Health Care, *JAMA*, **289** (15), 1969–78.

Burke, M. E. (1994) Creativity Circles in Information Management, *Librarian Career Development*, **2** (2), 8–12.

Day, J. and Walton, G. (1995) Current Issues in Library and Information Services: responses to health service changes, *Health Libraries Review*, **12** (4), 233–4.

Drake, M. A. (2000) Technological Innovation and Organizational Change Revisited, *Journal of Academic Librarianship*, **26** (1), 53–9.

European Commission (1996) Green Paper on Innovation, *Bulletin of the European Union*, Supplement **5**/95.

Haldane, G. (2003) LISTENing to Healthcare Students: the impact of new library facilities on the quality of services, *Health Information and Libraries Journal*, **20** (Suppl. 1), 59–68.

Handy, C. (1991) The Age of Unreason. In Henry, J. (ed.), *Creative Management*, London, Sage Publications.

Hayes, J. (2002) *The Theory and Practice of Change Management*, Basingstoke, Palgrave.

Hudner, E. (2002) Seeking Innovation: librarians help push organizations ahead, *Information Outlook*, **6** (1), 10–13.

Janis, I. L. (1982) *Groupthink*, 2nd edn, Boston MA, Houghton Mifflin.

Johannessen, J.-A., Olsen, B. and Olaisen, J. (1999) Aspects of Innovation Theory based on Knowledge-management, *International Journal of Information Management*, **19**, 121–39.

Kesselman, M. (1994) Ideas Come from Everywhere Generating Creativity for Your Library, *Wilson Library Bulletin*, **68** (9), 42–4.

King, N. and Andersen, N. (1995) *Innovation and Change in Organizations*, London, Routledge.

Kletke, M. G. et al. (2001) Creativity in the Organization: the role of individual creative problem solving and computer support, *International Journal of Human Computer Studies*, **55** (3), 217–38.

Kotter, J. P and Schlesinger, L. A. (1979) Choosing Strategies for Change, *Harvard Business Review*, (March–April), 106–14.

Lloyd, C. and King, R. (2002) Organisational Change and Occupational Therapy, *British Journal of Occupational Therapy*, **65** (12), 536–43.

Paul, G. (2000) Mobilising the Potential for Initiative and Innovation by Means of Socially Competent Management, *Library Management*, **21** (2), 81–5.

VanGundy, A. B. (1988) *Techniques of Structured Problem Solving*, 2nd edn, New York, Van Nostrand Reinhold.

Walton, G. and Edwards, C. (2001) Flexibility in Higher Education Libraries: exploring the implications and producing a model of practice, *Journal of Librarianship and Information Science*, **33** (4), 199–208.

Woodsworth, A., Maylone, T. and Sywak, M. (1992) The Information Job Family: results of an exploratory study, *Library Trends*, **41** (2), 250–68.

13

Continuing professional development

David Stewart

Introduction

In a working environment where change is a constant, it is vital that all library information staff take their continuing professional development seriously. Not just because organizational change is almost an annual event in the NHS but also because customer expectations, information technology and the role of the librarian are also subject to rapid change. The Chartered Institute of Library and Information Professionals' (CILIP) code of professional ethics reinforces this by stating that 'information professionals should . . . undertake continuing professional development to ensure that they keep abreast of developments in their areas of expertise' (CILIP, 2003). Jordan and Lloyd (2002) say that training and development 'enable staff to cope with acquiring the new skills which they need today and . . . to be comfortable with the fact that this skill set will change and evolve continuously throughout their working lives'.

This chapter considers personal, organizational and managerial responsibility for continuing professional development (CPD). It explores the development of a co-ordinated approach to CPD. The range of CPD activities is reviewed as are the different levels of provision.

Personal responsibility for continuing professional development

The Medical Library Association of the United States (1991) has succinctly summarized an individual's responsibility: 'in the continuum of learning, the single most important variable is the individual professional'. This is explored further by Corral and Brewerton (1999) who propose 'developing your personal capacity to perform effectively at work and in other areas of your life is vital if you wish to survive and thrive in a rapidly changing and highly competitive market'. Another commentator (Watts, 1996) has argued that being employed is really about renting out your skills, rather like a contract; you provide your skills to the organization and in return the organization provides you with opportunities to extend and develop those skills.

Corrall and Brewerton (1999) also help us to understand that responsibilities for an individual's CPD are shared: by the employing organization, the manager and, perhaps most importantly, the individual themselves. They say: 'the individual as an employee has personal responsibility for being an active (rather than passive) participant in this process and for approaching his or her development in a collaborative spirit'.

Walton (2000) has noted the key issue for library managers here: 'the health LIS manager has to develop a work environment where staff have the time and space to undertake staff development activities'. For the solo librarian, there are different challenges which have been identified and examined by Bryant (1995).

Organizational and managerial responsibilities

At a theoretical level, Pluse (1998) indicates that 'assuming an employer sets clear and focused skill requirements at recruitment and selects successfully against these, then subsequent training and development will revolve around what skills and knowledge need adding and/or updating from time to time'. In practice, he also acknowledges that it is often a case of serendipity, of 'what comes up' and 'Who can we send on this?' rather than a thought-through process of training needs analysis.

Management also has a role in maintaining regular routine dialogue between managers and their staff to ensure the success of any training strategy. This could be part of 'regular review/appraisal but also at specific times such as induction, job change, below par performance or to support the delivery of new services/equipment' (Pluse, 1998). Many health librarians face a range of challenges that make a co-ordinated and long-term approach to CPD difficult. These are the frequent organization changes that affect the NHS and also low staffing levels in many health libraries which make it difficult to allocate time for CPD. There is often a lack of specific training budgets in most health libraries which must therefore rely on an organization-wide fund for training that is often thinly stretched.

Developing a co-ordinated approach to continuing professional development

Training needs analysis (TNA)

A variety of debates attempt to distinguish between needs and wants. Library managers are encouraged to try to identify the CPD needs of their staff, in other words those courses or programmes that will help an individual member of the team do their job better. CPD 'wants' are often seen as the icing on the cake, 'nice to have but is it really relevant?' Reid and Barrington (1999) provide a thorough explanation of the varying techniques of analysis. They identify six steps in analysing a job for training purposes:

* Gain the co-operation of all concerned as this 'ensures a better chance of obtaining commitment to any training programme which might result'.
* Carry out a pre-analysis investigation to ensure that the problem is really a lack of training rather than other issues such as excessive workload or poor organization.
* Decide the appropriate analytical approach.
* Analyse the job including the identification of responsibilities and tasks. There is a wide range of techniques available, including observation by the manager, self-observation, questionnaire, interview and even doing the job yourself to see what is involved.
* Write or check the job description to ensure that it matches the manager's and employee's perceptions of what is required and how the job is done.
* Write a training specification which details the skills and knowledge required for the job and what training is required for the individual.

For library managers wanting a recent and more library-focused summary of this subject then Williamson's (1993) *Training Needs Analysis* is an excellent place to start.

Appraisal and personal development plans (PDP)

The Department of Health's paper *Working Together, Learning Together: a framework for lifelong learning for the NHS* (Great Britain. Department of Health, 2001) highlights another key tool in finding out what CPD is needed, that of appraisal. All NHS organizations are required to 'ensure that a major outcome of the appraisal process for all staff is the agreement of personal development plans [PDPs] which should link individual learning need to the skills and competencies to meet organisational priorities as well as valuing and recognising learning which is not always work related'.

While it is clear that not all health-library staff are appraised and also that the introduction of PDPs in the NHS is somewhat patchy, the formal appraisal process provides a mechanism for library managers to meet with all their staff to discuss work objectives and training needs and agree an action plan for the coming year.

Range of continuing professional development activities

Internal courses

Most health organizations provide a range of internal courses that library staff can attend including induction programmes and short courses. Induction programmes can last for half a day, a whole day or can be extended over several weeks. Components could include health and safety, manual handling, pay, annual leave, sickness process as well as introductions to various departments such as human resources.

e-Learning

There is significant potential for e-learning to address some of the barriers to CPD. Learning material can be easily delivered and access becomes less of an issue. E-learning has been defined as 'the provision of learning content delivered or enabled by electronic technology. E-learning offers flexibility in enabling learning which can be immediate and delivered by an "online" instructor, or self-paced where the learner is able to access pre-packaged learning material at any time, and for a time duration which is most convenient for them' (Cheshire and Merseyside WDC, 2003). There is considerable growth in the number and availability of e-learning courses, packages and resources and these are likely to offer library information staff access to new ways of learning. Various universities offer graduate and postgraduate programmes in health informatics primarily delivered in the e-learning environment. A number of formal courses have been developed by the School of Health and Related Research (ScHARR) at the University of Sheffield. These include courses on applying diagnosis, aetiology, prognosis and therapy, on methodological filters to retrieving the evidence and also one around evaluation and project management.

Electronic discussion groups

The number of e-discussion groups has grown enormously over the last few years and does rather lend support to the view that wherever two librarians gather together there will be a working party and a subgroup. However, discussion groups are an increasingly important way of sharing ideas and experience and for asking for help and advice. Key for health librarians at national level are:

- lis-medical@jiscmail.ac.uk
- evidence-based-libraries@jiscmail.ac.uk
- lis-nursing@jiscmail.ac.uk
- hlg-members@jiscmail.ac.uk.

Most regions also have discussion groups to bring their networks closer together (e.g. lihnn@jiscmail.ac.uk for the North West of England's health librarians).

Mentoring and coaching

While these terms are not interchangeable they both represent the renewed interest in the value of experienced staff helping others to think through a wide range of work and career issues. Mentoring involves 'advising, counselling and sometimes acting as a role model' (Reid and Barrington, 1999). Coaching is much more work and job-based and has been summarized as 'the purposeful and skilful effort by one individual to help another achieve specific performance goals' (Metz, 2001). A coach will normally be in the same department as the individual being coached and will provide almost day-to-day support in the early days of employment. However, coaching is more than 'sitting next to Nellie and watching what she does'; it should be structured around specific activities and functions and allow the coach and coachee to have time together for discussion.

Shadowing

Opportunities to shadow other staff in the health sector are relatively few and where patient confidentiality is involved then it is likely that permission will be required from local ethics committees. Shadowing provides a means of staying with another member of staff – another librarian or a member of a clinical or managerial team – for a period of time in order to see how they manage their job and the challenges they are faced with and how they deal with them. Library staff in Liverpool have shadowed a number of community-based clinical staff primarily to determine information needs and flows; however, they have found the experience useful in the wider CPD setting. In addition, Lancashire Teaching Hospital's new clinical librarian has shadowed clinical librarians in Leicester as part of her induction programme.

Groups and committees

Getting involved in local, regional or national groups is an ideal way of meeting colleagues and beginning to develop a range of skills such as contributing to meetings, chairing, minute taking and so on. As a by-product you will begin to build up your personal network of people who can help you in the future.

Visits, personal networks and reading

Newly qualified professionals will find visits to other health libraries an essential part of developing not only their skills but also the services for which they are responsible. Visits can range from the purely informal to being part of a full-fledged benchmarking exercise. Building your personal network of contacts will be invaluable throughout your career. Such a network will often provide you with a range of people to turn to for advice, information and sometimes mentoring. A well-ordered approach to collecting business cards, e-mail addresses and telephone numbers is essential for this to be a lifelong resource. Staying in touch with the professional literature is a central part of managing continuing professional development. Health information now has a number of professional journals (such as *Health Information and Libraries Journal*) with an increasing emphasis on trying to improve the research base of the profession.

Continuing professional development: regional, national and international provision

Regional

Until recently most English NHS regions had a regional library unit which included responsibilities for NHS librarians' CPD. Workforce Development Confederations (WDC) were established; they had similar responsibilities but WDCs are being merged with Strategic Health Authorities at the time of writing. Courses have been run and continue to be run for librarians in a geographical region around such areas as strategic planning, marketing the library service, skills training and managing transition. Such courses are normally free for delegates who have only to find travel costs.

Professional bodies such as CILIP and Aslib have regional branches that provide CPD opportunities. ASSIST (www.assist.org.uk) is a national organization established in 1993 to provide a network for those involved in health informatics. In theory ASSIST has a UK-wide branch structure though in practice some areas of the UK have no active branch. Some branches, however, run a busy CPD programme which health librarians should find useful in terms of the wider IT agenda and also as a way of meeting IT colleagues.

National

Chartered Institute of Library Information Professionals (CILIP)

CILIP accredits undergraduate courses in librarianship and, while they lie outside the remit of this chapter on CPD, readers can find details of these courses on the CILIP website (www.cilip.org.uk/qualifications/where.html). CILIP's CPD programme is varied and extensive, covering such areas as managing a distributed team, assertiveness and supervisory skills. A resource factor that has to be considered is the time and money needed to travel to what are primarily London-based activities.

CILIP has a busy conference programme that includes the biannual Umbrella conference bringing librarians from all sectors together. In addition, CILIP groups offer considerable CPD targeted on their particular membership. The Health Libraries Group (HLG) (www.cilip.org.uk/groups/hlg/) holds a series of seminars each year as well as a biannual conference. HLG has two subgroups: Libraries for Nursing (LfN) (www.cilip.org.uk/groups/hlg/lfn/) and Information for the Management of Healthcare (IFMH) (www.cilip.org.uk/groups/hlg/ifmh/), both of which have seminar programmes.

CILIP's other important role for library information staff is as the regulatory body for the profession. A core part of this is the awarding of chartered membership to members once they have their initial qualification. In order to qualify for chartered membership candidates must hold an academic qualification in librarianship and information management that is approved by CILIP, be a member of CILIP for a minimum of one year and have a period of practical professional experience on which to base an application.

Fellowship is the highest professional qualification available to CILIP members. It is open to any chartered member who has been on the register and in professional practice for at least five years. Fellowship candidates have to demonstrate that they have built on the potential identified by the award of chartered member through developing the ability to carry out demanding tasks and handle complex professional issues and by making a contribution to all or part of the profession. Evidence may be presented to CILIP in any format and, if awarded, chartered fellows may use the postnominals FCLIP.

Opportunities for library assistants, para-professionals and other library support staff

All of the issues around taking personal responsibility for CPD apply equally to both library assistants and to professionally qualified librarians. Many of the techniques outlined above and many of the courses and conferences mentioned in this chapter are likely to be of value to health-library assistants. In the small teams typical of many health libraries, the line between senior library assistant and assistant librarian is, in truth, too fine to draw.

There is, however, a range of opportunities in terms of formal qualifications that are particularly relevant to library assistants. These are City and Guilds courses and National Vocational Qualifications (NVQs). Within the English NHS individual learning accounts (www.doh.gov.uk/nhslearningaccount/) have made up to £150 per person available annually for CPD. A number of colleges of further and higher education offer the City and Guilds Library Information Work Certificate (scheme number 7370). Details of institutions offering these courses can be found at www.city-and-guilds.co.uk/. Scottish and National Vocational Qualifications (S/NVQs) are competency, work-based qualifications awarded either by the City and Guilds Institute or the Scottish Qualifications Authority (SQA). The City and Guilds Institute offers levels 2 and 3, while the SQA offers levels 2 to 4. A useful guide to S/NVQs is Arundale's (1999) *Getting your S/NVQ: a guide for candidates in the information and library sector.*

NHS Libraries Adviser (NHSLA)

In England the post of NHS Libraries Adviser was established in 1994 and has been important in developing a more strategic approach to libraries and librarians' professional development. One of the post's key roles is skills development for NHS staff with funding provided for such CPD opportunities as the Folio courses and National electronic Library for Health (NeLH) master classes. Details can be found at www.nelh.nhs.uk/dlnet/ and www.doh.gov.uk/ipu/nhsla/.

Sector Skills Councils (SSCs)

A new network of Sector Skills Councils is being established at the time of writing. These replace the former National Training Organisations (NTOs). SSCs are employer-led bodies with a strategic responsibility to identify and tackle skills, productivity and employability issues for the private, public and voluntary sectors they represent. Their boards will include representatives from employers, trade unions and professional bodies. The former Information Skills National Training Organization (isNTO) is currently negotiating with other NTOs to form a new Sector Skills Council that will then include the interests of library information staff.

Aslib: the association for information management

Aslib is a corporate membership organization that promotes best practice in the management of information. Among its range of activities is a very busy CPD programme including short courses and conferences. In June 2003 alone Aslib offered at least 17 courses including time management, knowledge mapping and health and medical information on the internet. Details can be found at www.aslib.com.

A university for the NHS (NHSU)

The creation of a university for the NHS was announced in the Department of Health's (2001) *Working Together, Learning Together: a framework for lifelong learning for the NHS*. It is currently being established and was formally launched in the autumn of 2003. It is intended that the NHSU (www.nhsuniversity.nhs.uk) will have various responsibilities relevant to CPD activities for health librarians. It will cover all settings in which NHS provided or funded care is delivered. Extensive use will be made of e-learning. There is widespread acknowledgement that the NHSU is an extremely ambitious enterprise and the exact way it will function is still being determined. Nevertheless, it is likely to become a central part of the CPD infrastructure of the NHS in England and health librarians will need to be aware of the opportunities it provides.

International

Many countries and even some continents have professional bodies that bring together library information professionals. A number of these are health specific. They include the Medical Library Association (MLA) (www.mlanet.org/index.htm) in the United States, the Canadian Health Libraries Association (CHLA) (www.chla-absc.ca/) and the European Association for Health Information and Libraries (EAHIL) (www.eahil.org/). All three offer major annual or biannual conferences that are valuable ways of meeting overseas colleagues and getting an insight into delivering health information in other countries. In addition the internet makes the learning resources of these organizations easily available in the UK.

Every five years a country hosts the International Medical Libraries Conference (ICML). ICML8 was in London in 2000 and ICML9 will be in Sao Paulo, Argentina, in October 2005, hosted by the Latin American and Caribbean Centre on Health and Social Sciences (www.bireme.br/icml9). ICML8 brought together nearly 1500 librarians from around the world and offered a busy programme of lectures, seminars and social events.

Conclusion

The purpose of this chapter has been to establish the importance of continuing professional development for the health librarian and to consider how it can be effectively delivered. An effective CPD programme helps to ensure that the library and its staff provide the services that users value and appreciate. Special mention should be made of a resource that brings together CPD opportunities available to health librarians in the UK. Fiona Maclean produces a website that is updated monthly that lists current opportunities (www.cilip.org.uk/groups/hlg/nonhlg.html).

Key points

- Continuing professional development is important because it enables library information staff to keep abreast of changes in practice, technologies and the wider environment.
- Continuing professional development is a shared responsibility between the individual and their manager and employer.
- Training needs analysis is an important tool for managers and employers to determine what training staff need and in what format it should be delivered.
- While formal courses, internal and external, are valuable, there are many other ways to address CPD needs such as visits, committee work, coaching and mentoring, and shadowing.
- The opportunities provided via the internet, e-learning and electronic discussion groups seem to be growing all the time and may be especially useful for solo-librarians or those staff a long way from population centres.
- CILIP as the professional body is central to CPD in terms of its role as the regulatory body and is a major provider of CPD opportunities.
- Formal opportunities for para-professional staff are still rather limited and the infrastructure around S/NVQs and City and Guilds is not very robust.

Acknowledgements

The author is grateful for the advice and support of the following in writing this chapter: Linda Ferguson, Deputy Director of Health Libraries: CPD, NW Health Care Libraries Unit; Veronica Fraser, NHS Libraries Adviser, Department of Health; and health library staff in the North West Region.

References

Arundale, J. (1999) *Getting your S/NVQ: a guide for candidates in the information and library sector*, 2nd edn, London, Library Association Publishing.

Bryant, S. L. (1995) *Personal Professional Development and the Solo Librarian*, London, Library Association Publishing.

Cheshire and Merseyside Workforce Development Confederation (WDC), Cumbria and Lancashire WDC (2003) *Delivering e-Learning in the NHS: getting the blend right: a strategic approach for the north west*, Preston, Cumbria and Lancashire Workforce Development Confederation.

CILIP (2003) *Code of Professional Ethics: draft for consultation*, London, Chartered Institute of Library and Information Professionals.

Corrall, S. and Brewerton, A. (1999) *The New Professional's Handbook: your guide to information services management*, London, Library Association Publishing.

Great Britain. Department of Health (2001) *Working Together, Learning Together: a framework for lifelong learning for the NHS*, London, Department of Health.

Jordan, P. and Lloyd, C. (2002) *Staff Management in Library and Information Work*, 4th edn, Aldershot, Ashgate.

Medical Library Association (1991) *Platform for Change: the educational policy statement of the MLA*, Chicago, Medical Library Association.

Metz, R. (2001) *Coaching in the Library: a management strategy for achieving excellence*, Chicago IL, American Library Association.

Pluse, J. (1998) Human Resource Management. In Prytherch, R. (ed.), *Handbook of Library and Information Management*, Aldershot, Gower.

Reid, M. and Barrington, H. (1999) *Training Interventions: promoting learning opportunities*, 6th edn, London, Chartered Institute of Personnel and Development.

Walton, G. (2000) Providing Direction and Management for Health Library and Information Services. In Booth, A. and Walton, G. (eds), *Managing Knowledge in Health Services*, London, Library Association Publishing.

Watts, T. (1996) *Careerquake*, London, Demos.

Williamson, M. (1993) *Training Needs Analysis*, London, Library Association Publishing.

14

Providing hybrid information services

Steve Rose and Angela Gunn

Introduction

After defining the hybrid information service and tracing its development, this chapter explores a number of issues which the information professional must address in developing hybrid services. These include the paper–electronic mix, technical requirements and trade-offs between access and control. Different models for costing hybrid services are examined as well as implications for the information professional and the end users. Findings from evaluations of the hybrid library environment are detailed and ways forward considered.

Definition

Knight (1997) gives the following definition of the hybrid library service:

> The hybrid library is a library which can provide a one-stop-shop for both hardcopy and electronic resources. Its information systems should provide the end user with a seamless interface that will allow them to locate paper books and journals held locally and at neighbouring sites at the same time as being available to find relevant online resources, electronic publications and digitised material. To do this, the user needs to be provided with a front end that can access information in a variety of databases which are widely distributed and can contain a variety of information in different formats.

For many libraries, the hybrid information environment has begun at the local level, the catalyst being the creation of a web-enabled catalogue. This has enabled the provision of an interface which gives the user access to the physical information resources of the library, digital copies of physical information resources where available, databases and information resources freely available on the internet. The concept can be extended to develop regional or national initiatives. Within the context of health libraries, these can range from shared union catalogues through to national projects such as the National electronic Library for Health (NeLH).

Development of the hybrid library concept

The development of hybrid libraries in the UK can be traced to the early 1990s, an unlikely catalyst being the abolition of the 'binary divide' between the older universities and the polytechnics (Rusbridge and Royan, 2000). Concerns over the historical underfunding of the former polytechnic libraries questioning their capacity to support the research that university status brought resulted in the Follett Report (Joint Funding Councils' Library Review Group, 1993). This report focused on the need for substantial IT investment, and responsibility for the implementation of recommendations was delegated to the HE Funding Councils' Joint Information Systems Committee (JISC) who in turn handed implementation over to a subcommittee, the Follett Implementation Group for IT (FIGIT).

Electronic Libraries Programme (eLib)

The Electronic Libraries Programme (eLib) came out of FIGIT's response to implementing the IT agenda in the Follett Report. The first two phases yielded nearly 60 projects. Although not hybrid projects themselves, they laid the foundation for eLib phase 3. Phase 3 was concerned with converting successful eLib projects into self-sustaining services and, in doing so, exploring the feasibility of the hybrid library. Five eLib hybrid library projects began in January 1998 as part of phase 3. Various papers describe the background to these (Pinfield et al., 1998; Rusbridge and Royan, 2000).

Apart from the catalyst of educational reforms, other change agents add impetus for the development of the hybrid model. The increased provision of higher education using distance-learning models means that users need access to library-related resources away from centralized buildings. The growth of the internet has reflected the need to change the way information is delivered in many sectors. In health specifically, the NHS reforms of the late 1990s have shifted the balance of power for the commissioning and provision of healthcare to the primary sector. This has increased the need for access to the evidence of a multidisciplinary group of health professionals, previously underserved by the library sector, who often work in remote areas far away from repositories of library collections. All of these drivers mean that the momentum towards electronic delivery of information, at the point of need and in the place where it is required, has gathered pace.

As well as the eLib projects, the Consortium of University Research Libraries (CURL) has a number of other national initiatives driving the advancement of hybrid information services (www.curl.ac.uk/projects/).

Provision of a paper–electronic mix

There are a number of issues that the information professional must grapple with when managing a paper–electronic mix and when making decisions regarding the balance in developing traditional resources against investment in digital alternatives. Despite the national drivers highlighted above, evidence suggests that these are not paving the way for totally digital library and information services. Wake and Lisgarten (2002) explore hybrid library developments within the School of Pharmacy, University of London, and pinpoint a number of reasons why the library must remain hybrid rather than opt to become exclusively digital. Included are uncertainties which need to be addressed with publishers of electronic resources; archiving arrangements; the timeliness of electronic editions compared to paper copy alternatives; continuing access to volumes paid for if a title is cancelled; and restrictive licence conditions.

Issues around licensing issues are especially pertinent for libraries serving multi-sector user groups. For example, access to digitized journals for NHS users through the National Core Collection does not automatically transfer to users within higher education. Therefore, the information professional is not always able to decide between electronic versus hard copy, but may need to retain access to both so that no user group is disadvantaged. It is also evident that many publishers are unwilling to give permission for digitization. It has been found that 35–40% of requests are refused (SCONUL, 2000). Despite the vast growth of the internet, Herring (2001) concludes that only about 8% of all journals are online and only a fraction of books are available. Therefore, with regard to access to scientific literature, it has been argued (Weston, 2002) that the web can complement traditional libraries, but will not replace them.

Nevertheless, there is evidence that library and information professionals are tackling some of the issues proactively, and looking to overcome some of the barriers. A targeted approach to e-texts has been identified (Roberts and Appleton, 2003), and a number of papers of the 2002 University of Oklahoma conference, focus on the theme of electronic resources and collection development in academic libraries (Thomas, 2002; Lee, 2002).

Access, control and technological issues

As has been noted, providing access to networked resources has tended to be through the library web pages. The emergence of web OPACs has led to the cataloguing of all non-print resources, making the library catalogue the main interface for discovering and accessing electronic resources. This has implications for network security because anyone with walk-in access could use the catalogue to gain access to resources which require only Internet Protocol (IP) authentication. The same issue arises where networked computers are on open access. Remote users also need access to resources which may be provided to on-site users via IP authentication. This could be addressed by providing a username and password but would not be practical for a large number of resources. Some IP-checked resources are, in addition, Athens compliant and a third option would be to authenticate users by remote log-in to the campus network. The latter has resource implications if a large number of users need access via this route.

We have come a long way since the start of free-at-the-point-of-use end-user searching in the 1980s when each year of a database or journal volume had to be searched separately. Now several sources such as bibliographic databases and journals can be searched simultaneously with the removal of duplicates possible in some cases. While these are important in the development of a search interface by information providers, the next logical step in the eyes of the user would be to have a single search interface providing access to a wide variety of resources. This would avoid the need to repeat searches on systems hosted on other networks and adapting the searches to suit.

In the NHS the portability issue has been addressed, partially, by the development of the National electronic Library for Health (NeLH) and the National Core Collection. Although the same interface is available from different locations, searching collections of electronic journals, databases, the internet and local library catalogues all require separate interfaces. The academic/NHS divide is also a barrier here as resources and interfaces used by students often differ from those they will use in their working lives even when using the same library/information centre.

A key issue for the long term is interoperability in the interrogation of diverse resources. The user wants to search for, discover, evaluate, locate and view all the relevant information seamlessly. This requires the adherence to standards such as Z39.50 and metadata formats such as Dublin Core. Darmoni et al. (2001) describe the use of Dublin Core in a structured health resource guide on the internet. The integration problems of various metadata systems are discussed by Yu, Lu and Chen (2003) who propose a model using an XML system framework to overcome the constraints of different metadata information. The application of XML to digital library systems is described by Kim and Choi (2000) who also compare the main features of XML with those of HTML. Whittaker (2003) describes the use of portals to link disparate databases for searching in museums archives and libraries. Bekaert et al. (2002) review the use of metadata to access multimedia and archive collections. These papers all highlight that there is still much work to be done.

Costs

Costs too become a key factor in deciding on the balance between hard copy and electronic formats. The option of a free electronic version of a title with the print subscription is becoming rare. It has been estimated (Pinfield, 2001) that electronic journals can cost 7–8% on top of printed versions. Other related costs include that of ensuring that adequate IT facilities are available, including provision for replacements and upgrades, within the library environment. When considering IT requirements, it is also necessary to consider whether the current technology will become transient or obsolete. An evaluation of practical experiences of digitization notes how costs can accrue very quickly because of the intensive use of staff resources involved in developing digitization products (Hampson, 2001). Printing costs too can become prohibitively expensive if they are offered free or are subsidized. As users prefer to print off copies of full-text articles, this problem is likely to be exacerbated as more digitized resources become available.

User needs

When deciding on the balance between paper and electronic resources, it is important not to lose sight of who is really important here – the end user. There are a number of potential disadvantages to the hybrid library. For example, users can be confused about different access routes to resources, about differing licensing arrangements, whether titles can be accessed remotely or within the library and with the plethora of passwords needed for various resources. Tenopir and King (2001) estimate that identifying and locating electronic resources takes up more time than identifying and locating print resources. As information professionals, we need to be wary of what Day describes as the 'satisfied inept' (Law, 1997), the user who believes they have searched the internet and found all they need, when their knowledge of sources and search skills is lacking.

The importance in investing in user education and training programmes cannot be overestimated. One of the ten steps to success to emerge from the evaluation of one hybrid-library project (HyLiFe project) is to plan training and support for users and ensure that they have the confidence to use information technology (Wynne, Edwards and Jackson, 2001). The revision of user education programmes to support hybrid-library developments is described by Wake and Lisgarten (2002); the challenges suggest that user education in the hybrid library may be regarded as 'double trouble'. Therefore user education programmes need to be much more sophisticated. They need to recognize that users are not a heterogeneous group, a conclusion drawn from an evaluation of the MALIBU project (Cave et al., 2001), when discussing user testing. Many authors (Loven, 1998; Powell, 1999; Gibson and Silverberg, 2000; Kaplowitz and Yamomoto, 2001) provide practical examples of how they have developed user education programmes tailored to the hybrid-library environment. A workshop developed to teach end users about electronic resources has also been developed at the University of Buffalo Health Sciences Library (Brower, 2002).

Evaluations from the hybrid library environment.

A toolkit was produced from the evaluation of the HyLiFe project in the form of ten steps to success (Wynne, Edwards and Jackson, 2001). These include securing the support of senior institutional managers, and working collaboratively with a range of people, for example technical staff and academics. With regard to the latter, it is possible to tie hybrid-library developments into wider developments – for example the creation of virtual learning environments (VLEs) (Emly and Ryan, 2001; Ekmekcioglu and Brown, 2001). Effective collaborative working is also seen as a key to success in the MALIBU project with reference to the importance of overall project management (Cave, et al., 2001).

It is also important to consider those more traditional facets of a library service, when involved in hybrid-library developments. Two of HyLiFe's ten steps to success are worth noting here: the need to concentrate on resolving authentication and copyright issues and the need to devise policies on the provision of services such as loans, photocopying and document delivery. For example, if the hybrid library is to adequately support distance learners, then flexibility is required by introducing postal book loans, adding electronic request forms to the web and offering an article-photocopying service. Remote access resources do not stand alone without this form of backup from the library.

Flexibility is a key word when considering the role of the information professional. This was seen to be central in an evaluation of the eLib projects, with particular reference to HyLiFe (Walton and Edwards, 2001). Information professionals need not only to be flexible in embracing change, forging new working relationships with those associated with hybrid-library developments; they need to keep users' interests central and serve a population which demands increased flexibility.

Even though the growth of the hybrid information service requires information professionals to adopt new ways of working, the role of the information professional should not be seen as under threat. The Agora evaluation (Pinfield et al., 1998) highlights a central role for the information professional in facilitating the creation of navigable information landscapes. Research looking into the information professional's role in supporting health service managers shows that going totally virtual is not a reality (Rose, 2002).

Conclusion: hybrid developments in the future

Although, in the short term, we are not moving to a totally digital environment, increased digitization, within the hybrid model, is likely. This will be brought about not only by the adaptation of lessons from the eLib projects and others, but by key changes in other areas. For example, the academic publishing industry is undergoing evolutionary change. Initiatives such as BioMed Central, a commercial publisher of online biological and medical titles, paves the way here. Through various income-generating activities, which include charging authors or their institutions for publishing, BioMed Central offers free open access to peer-reviewed biomedical research electronically. Further evidence of how librarians can engage in new methods of publishing has been highlighted with reference to the development of a library–faculty partnership at Virginia University (Watson, Login and Burns, 2003).

Key points

- Evidence from the literature suggests that the future will remain hybrid rather than digital.
- Findings from the eLib projects offer important ways forward for information professionals in developing hybrid library and information services.
- There are a number of issues related to access, control and technology which the library and information professional must address.
- Library and information professionals must adopt a flexible approach in developing services to meet users' needs, when working within the hybrid model. However, there are clear roles for the profession which will not be overshadowed by developments in digitization.
- A proactive approach to working with users is vital. Within this context, information-skills training is very important.
- There is a need to engage with innovative approaches to electronic publishing. This could help overcome some of the barriers presented by costs.

References

Bekaert, J. et al. (2002) Metadata-based Access to Multimedia Architectural and Historical Archive Collections: a review, *Aslib Proceedings*, **54** (6), 362–71.

Brower, S. (2002) Teaching e-Journals: building a workshop for an academic health sciences library, *Serials Review*, **28** (2), 88–92.

Cave, M. et al. (2001) Travelling at the Speed of Discovery: the MALIBU project's most valuable lessons, *Ariadne*, (January), www.ariadne.ac.uk/issue26/malibu.

Darmoni, S. J. et al. (2001) The Use of Dublin Core Metadata in a Structured Health Resource Guide on the Internet, *Bulletin of the Medical Library Association*, **89** (3) 297–301.

Ekmekcioglu, F. C. and Brown, S. (2001) Linking Online Learning Environments with Digital Libraries: institutional issues in the UK, *Libri*, **51** (4), 195–208.

Emly, M. and Ryan, C. (2001) Adding Value to Student Learning: integrating the hybrid library into the virtual learning environment, *New Review of Information Networking*, **7**, 225–35.

Gibson, K. E. and Silverberg, M. (2000) A Two-year Experience Teaching Computer Literacy to First Year Medical Students Using Skill-based Cohorts, *Bulletin of the Medical Library Association*, **88** (2), 157–64.

Hampson, A. (2001) Practical Experiences of Digitisation in the BUILDER Hybrid Library Project: case study, *Program*, **35** (3), 263–75.

Herring, M. (2001) 10 Reasons Why the Internet is No Substitute for a Library, *American Libraries*, **32**, 76–8.

Joint Funding Councils' Libraries Review Group (1993) *Report*, Bristol, HEFCE.

Kaplowitz, J. R. and Yamomoto, D. O (2001) Web-based Library Instruction for a Changing Medical School Curriculum, *Library Trends*, **50** (1), 47–57.

Kim, H. H. and Choi, C. S. (2000) XML: how it will be applied to digital library systems, *The Electronic Library*, **18** (3), 183–9.

Knight, J. (1997) The Hybrid Library: books and bytes, *Ariadne*, (September), www.ariadne.ac.uk/issue11/knight/intro.html.

Law, D. (1997) Parlour Games: the real nature of the internet, *Serials*, **10**, 195–201.

Lee, S. H. (2002) Electronic Resources and Collection Development, *Journal of Library Administration*, **36** (3), 1–120.

Loven, B. (1998) Information Skills for Distance Learning, *Medical Reference Services Quarterly*, **17** (3), 71–5.

Pinfield, S. et al. (1998) Realizing the Hybrid Library, *D-Lib Magazine*, (October).

Pinfield, S. (2001) Managing Electronic Library Services: current issues in UK higher education institutions, *Ariadne*, (September), www.ariadne.ac.uk/issue29/pinfield/intro.html.

Powell, C. A. (1999) Educational Needs Assessment: revitalizing a user education programme, *Medical Reference Services Quarterly*, **18** (4), 71–8.

Roberts, S. and Appleton, L. (2003) e-Texts: a targeted approach, *Serials*, **16** (1), 83–7.

Rose, S. (2002) *Going Virtual, Is It a Reality?: experiences and ways forward in providing library services to support the health services management function in the UK*, Proceedings of the eighth European Conference of Medical and Health Libraries, 16–21 September 2002, Cologne, Germany, www.zbmed.de/eahil2002/proceedings/rose-proc.pdf.

Rusbridge, C. and Royan B. (2000) *Towards the Hybrid Library: developments in UK higher education*, 66th IFLA Council and General Conference, Jerusalem, www.ifla.org/IV/ifla66/papers/001-142e.htm.

SCONUL (2000) The e-University: a briefing note, www.sconul.ac.uk/bfgnote.doc.

Tenopir, C. and King, D. W. (2001) The Use and Value of Scientific Journals: past, present and future, *Serials*, **14**, 113–20.

Thomas, S. E. (2002) Think Globally, Act Locally: electronic resources and collection development, *Journal of Library Administration*, **36** (3), 93–107.

Wake, M. and Lisgarten, L. (2002) *User Education in the Hybrid Library: double trouble?*, Proceedings of the 8th European Conference of Medical and Health Libraries, 16–21 September 2002, Cologne, Germany, www.zbmed.de/eahil2002/proceedings/wake-proc.pdf.

Walton, G. and Edwards, C. (2001) Flexibility in Higher Education Hybrid Libraries: exploring the implications and producing a model of practice, *Journal of Librarianship and Information Science*, **33** (4), 199–208.

Watson, L. A., Login, I. S. and Burns, J. M. (2003) Exploring New Ways of Publishing: a library–faculty partnership, *Journal of the Medical Library Association*, **91** (2), 245–7.

Weston, W. (2002) Access to Scientific Literature: the web can complement libraries, but not replace them, *Nature*, (November), 19.

Whittaker, D. (2003) Interoperability in the MAL sector, *Update*, **2** (4), 44–5.

Wynne, P., Edwards, C. and Jackson, M. (2001) HyLiFe: ten steps to success, *Ariadne*, (March), www.ariadne.ac.uk/issue27/hylife/.

Yu, S.-C., Lu, K.-Y., and Chen, R.-S. (2003) Metadata Management System: design and implementation, *The Electronic Library*, **21** (2), 154–64.

15

Creating portals and gateways

Susan Roe

Introduction

If one assumes that the information on the internet is comprehensive and holds fast-growing deposits of the world's knowledge, it is apparent that such information should be harvested to the benefit of society. This chapter discusses attempts to raise the quality of information by filtering out low-value data, and making it more accessible and recognizable. After defining portals and subject-based information gateways (SBIGs) differences are explored and an example is given of current selection criteria for an SBIG. There follows an analysis of current literature, allowing evaluation of the usefulness of SBIGs. Recommendations for improvement are then given and an attempt is made to counter misconceptions that emerge from the literature analysis. The future for personalized browser-based information systems is briefly discussed before considering the challenges posed for NHS knowledge-management teams.

As surfers wake up to the vast store of information, readily accessible from their desktops, many realize that 'the sheer enormity of the information . . . can prove a barrier' (Rowley, 2000). Surfers recognize that much-needed data is out there, but their expectations are often frustrated. The internet has grown through accretion, not design. The structure of information on the internet is haphazard, mainly because it represents the whole spectrum of creators of websites, ranging from commercial interests and advertising to education and academics. By the same token, the quality of data varies.

Early on it was realized that the exponentially growing internet was a valuable information channel. Its content soon expanded to resemble a gigantic self-updating encyclopaedia, but it was formless and therefore unwieldy. An initial attempt at making information accessible involved setting up collections of subject-specific links called portals, targeting specific groups of users. Portals allow surfers to limit their exploration to subject-specific areas, to experience a higher rate of relevant hits and thus feel more adept at finding information. However, most portals serve commercial interests, where the main concern is not to sift and evaluate information for quality. The diluting effect of low-value information led to delays and failure in retrieving relevant high-quality data. Koniger and Janowitz (1995) maintain:

> Information is only valuable to the extent that it is structured. Because of the lack of structure in the creation, distribution and reception of information, the information often does not arrive where it is needed and is therefore useless.

Rowley (2000) adds that 'the ever-present need to structure information has become more pressing'. Within the NHS, comparatively little training in searching is available, and when staff search and do not retrieve appropriate resources they become sceptical about the quality of available information.

Portals and subject-based information gateways

In response to the need for more sophisticated filters, the NHS Information Strategy (NHSIS) raised portal technology to another dimension with the National electronic Library for Health (NeLH): a collection of quality-assessed health-related electronic resources (see Chapter 5). The NeLH strategy paper stresses the importance of providing only highest-quality resources:

> The underlying principle on which the NeLH will be based is that every source of knowledge or Website to which the NeLH directs its readers must have an explicit method of quality assurance.
>
> (NHS Information Authority, n.d.)

Academic institutions pursue similar objectives in owning and maintaining subject-based information gateways, subject-specific catalogues of internet resources, quality-assessed by specialists within the subject area. They constitute a system for filtering and signposting internet data. Detailed descriptions of each resource are entered into a searchable database with resources considered for inclusion being assessed according to rigorous criteria. Figure 15.1 shows a sample selection and indicates the effort required to ensure that only high-quality resources are included.

1   Scope policy: Considering your users
    • information coverage
    • access
    • cataloguing policy
    • geographical issues

2   Content criteria: Evaluating the information
    • validity
    • authority and reputation of source
    • substantiveness
    • accuracy
    • comprehensiveness
    • uniqueness
    • composition and organization
    • currency, and adequacy of maintenance

3   Form criteria: Evaluating the medium
    • ease of navigation
    • provision of user support
    • use of recognized standards
    • appropriate use of technology
    • aesthetics

4   Process criteria: Evaluating the system
    • information integrity (work of the information provider)
    • site integrity (work of the web-master/site manager)
    • system integrity (work of the systems administrator)

5   Collection management policy: Considering your service
    • collection coverage and balance
    • availability of internet resources
    • availability of library resources

Figure 15.1 Quality selection criteria: a reference tool for internet
            subject gateways

A more detailed reference tool can be found at www.ukoln.ac.uk/metadata/
desire/quality/report-1.html.

SBIGs provide a browsable virtual library in a format that resembles a traditional library. Users can choose a subject tree and work down its branches.
Academic communities draw on a strong network of links, permitting a collaborative approach to SBIGs. They can then apply common quality assurance
and database construction across gateways, enabling users to cross-search over
several subject gateways, combinations referred to as networks. The Resource

Discovery Network (RDN) combines nine SBIGs (see Table 15.1) and provides cross-searching facilities (Martin, 2003).

Table 15.1 Resource Discovery Network subject-based information gateways

Name	Subject area	Web address
ADAM	art, design, architecture and media	http://adam.ac.uk/
BUBL	library and information science	http://bubl.ac.uk/
EELS	engineering	http://eels.lub.lu.se/
EEVL	engineering, mathematics and computing	www.eevl.ac.uk/
HUMBUL	humanities	www.humbul.ac.uk/
OMNI	medicine	http://omni.ac.uk
PSIgate	physical sciences	www.psigate.ac.uk/
RUDI	urban design	www.rudi.net/news.cfm
SOSIG	social sciences	www.sosig.ac.uk/

Other academic institutions have developed SBIGs, tailored to the needs and interests of their information communities, including those mentioned in Table 15.2.

Table 15.2 Other subject-based information gateways

Name	Subject area	Web address
Academic Info	academic resources	www.academicinfo.net/index.html
AERADE	aerospace and defence studies	http://aerade.cranfield.ac.uk/
AGRIGATE	agriculture, forestry, environment, food science, horticulture	www.agrigate.edu.au/
AHDS	arts and humanities	http://ahds.ac.uk/
ALTIS	hospitality, leisure, sport, tourism	www.altis.ac.uk/
Biogate	biological sciences	http://biogate.lub.lu.se/
BIOME	health and life sciences	http://biome.ac.uk/
Biz/ed	business and economics	www.bized.ac.uk/
Chemdex	chemistry	www.chemdex.org/
DutchESS	various subject areas	www.konbib.nl/dutchess/
EdWeb	educational reform and information technology	www.edwebproject.org/
Gateway to Educational Materials (GEM)	educational resources	http://thegateway.org/
Geo-Information Gateway	geography, geology, the environment	www.geog.le.ac.uk/cti/info.html

Continued on next page

Table 15.2 *Continued*

Name	Subject area	Web address
History	historical studies	www.ihrinfo.ac.uk/
iLoveLanguages	language-learning and linguistics	www.ilovelanguages.com/
infolaw	law	www.infolaw.co.uk/
IDB	botany	www.botany.net/IDB/botany.html
INFOMINE	various subject areas	http://infomine.ucr.edu/
LAWLINKS	law	http://library.ukc.ac.uk/library/lawlinks
Links for Chemists	chemistry	www.liv.ac.uk/Chemistry/Links/link.html
The Math Forum	mathematics	http://mathforum.org/library/
MCS	media and communication studies	www.aber.ac.uk/media/Functions/mcs.html
MedHist	history of medicine, and allied sciences	http://medhist.ac.uk/
Meta Matters	various subject areas	http://dcanzorg.ozstaging.com/mb.a
NetEc	economics	http://netec.mcc.ac.uk/NetEc.html
NOVAGate	forestry, food, veterinary, and agricultural sciences	http://novagate.nova-university.org/
PADI	preserving access to digital information	www.nla.gov.au/padi/
PATW	philosophy studies	http://users.ox.ac.uk/%7Eworc0337/phil_index.html
Philosophy in Cyberspace	philosophy	www-personal.monash.edu.au/~dey/phil/
PhysicsWeb Resources	physics	http://physicsweb.org/resources/
psci-com	communication of science, science in society	www.psci-com.org.uk/
Psych Web	psychology	www.psychwww.com/
RDN	various subject areas	www.rdn.ac.uk/
Renardus	various subject areas	www.renardus.org/
Sapling	architecture, planning and landscape	www.sapling.org.uk/
SciCentral	science	www.scicentral.com/index.html
World Wide Arts Resources	the arts	http://wwar.com/
WWW Virtual Library	various subject areas	www.vlib.org.uk/

SBIG networks and the NeLH share common attributes. They value quality, as opposed to quantity, of information and concern themselves not only with knowledge but also the skills to apply it. But NeLH has two further dimensions: it is equally open to patients, clinicians, the public and managers; it sets out to create and sustain communities of users (NHS Information Authority, n.d.). This makes it proactive and dynamic, and involves users in development of the gateway.

The NeLH 'is continually evolving to meet changing needs, as laid out in government policies and initiatives for the health sector' (Urquhart et al., 2001) and provides 'a solid foundation for the development of online communities, where health professionals can exchange valuable information and ideas and create new resources for others to use' (NHS Information Authority, n.d.). These extra attributes constitute a knowledge-management portal.

Analysing the literature

A 'comprehensive scan of the literature' reveals 'very little in the way of user evaluation of on-line subject gateways' (Monopoli and Nicholas, 2000). The literature on SBIGs is vast; titles and abstracts of 886 relevant references were assessed and 35 papers were examined. The author selected studies for review if they contained user evaluation of SBIGs, recruited people representative of the target audience and included views of satisfied participants (Table 15.3).

Table 15.3 Evaluations of subject-based information gateways

Authors	Coleman and Amber (2002)
Title	*The Resource Discovery Network (RDN): evaluation report*
Description	The RDN provides access to high-quality internet resources for learning, teaching and research.
Evaluation	Positive. The RDN was praised for its usability. Many users liked the combination of a range of resources under one umbrella. There was strong praise for the high quality of the content of RDN, which was the main reason for preferring this site to commercial search engines. There was further praise for the accessibility, clear description and good identification of relevant material. Most participants acknowledged they had found useful resources.
	Mixed. Both high praise and disappointment about the range of the data. A few at interview complained of 'limited resources' and 'lack of depth', but this was not reflected in the online questionnaire.
	Negative. Some reservations about the additional navigation and the difficulty of blending distinct interfaces.

Continued on next page

Table 15.3 *Continued*

Authors	King and Moffat (1996)
Title	*Evaluation of the EEVL Pilot Service*
Description	The Edinburgh Engineering Virtual Library (EEVL) aims to improve access to quality internet engineering resources.
Evaluation	Positive. Users were impressed by the focus on engineering; the leanness of hits; and the scanning-for-quality of resources. Applauded were the ease of locating information in areas of interest; the time saved by descriptions which pointed to relevant sites; and the excellent overview of subjects gained by browsing. The focus group praised subject bases as a springboard for research; and liked the consistent relevance of links. Negative. A few users complained of lack of content in their area.
Authors	Monopoli and Nicholas (2000)
Title	*A User-centred Approach to the Evaluation of Subject Based Information Gateways: case study SOSIG*
Description	Social Science Information Gateway (SOSIG) is an online catalogue of internet resources on subjects related to the social sciences such as education, philosophy and politics.
Evaluation	Users felt SOSIG saved time, provided more accurate and direct information, and encouraged exploration. Material was authoritative and relevant.
	Unfortunately, uptake of newly developed information systems such as SOSIG is generally poor. People tend to stick with systems they feel most comfortable with. Many users are unable to evaluate the system in terms of their own needs. This was evidenced in a growing increase in requests for clarification; and in low percentage use – 46% of users accessed the service occasionally, 33% weekly and only 3% daily. Need for promotion, training and awareness-raising exercises, followed by further evaluation.
Authors	Mackie and Burton (1999)
Title	*The Use and Effectiveness of the eLib Subject Gateways: a preliminary investigation*
Description	The eLib programme seeks to maximize benefits of the internet to academics. Three gateways were investigated to find out how often they are used and whether they are seen to be effective in locating quality information.

Continued on next page

Table 15.3 *Continued*

Evaluation	Out of 64 respondents, less than 30% had used any of the gateways, indicating that a further study is desirable. Most respondents found gateways 'very easy' or 'fairly easy'; only one found them fairly difficult. Difficulty was not a reason for poor uptake. 70% of respondents found the gateways were effective search tools some of the time. 66% found the subject-based approach compared favourably to general search engines. Others were uncertain, again pointing out the need for further study.
Authors	Monopoli and Nicholas (2001)
Title	*A User Evaluation of Subject Based Information Gateways: case study ADAM*
Description	The Art, Design, Architecture and Media Gateway (ADAM) aims to help search the internet for art and design topics.
Evaluation	There was a favourable response: 63% of users preferred the service to a traditional library. Positive. Gateways gave quicker access and more comprehensive and up-to-date information. Negative. Usage was irregular and light. 21.5% accessed the service 'hardly ever' or 'occasionally'. 38.15% said it was their first time using the gateway. As with the SOSIG gateway, re-evaluation of ADAM is required following promotion, training and awareness raising.

Points for SBIGs

The following attributes were identified from the literature as features that helped to manage information overload:

• relevant
• appropriate to interests/needs
• free of duplication
• up to date
• accessible 24 hours
• of trustworthy quality
• quality-checked by experts
• useful as a one-stop shop
• a spur to research

- convenient for locating information in the area of interest
- excellent for getting an overview of the topic
- more effective than other search tools for browsing subject areas
- produced leaner hits
- and the thesaurus permitted sophisticated searches.

Suggested improvements illustrate perceived limitations of the gateways:

> The most significant disadvantage (and the area most often covered by work-shop participants) is the lack of resources compared to search engines.
> (Mackie and Burton, 1999)

Mackie and Burton assert that 'this opinion . . . could be counteracted by adequate promotion of the services so that ... the users will see that the aim of SBIGs is to be a selective rather than a comprehensive collection, pointing only to high quality Internet information resources'.

Points against SBIGs

Negative points include the following:

- limited range of data (contradicted in the 'points for' section)
- limited resources (presumably a limitation in the number of topics)
- lack of depth (firmly contradicted in the 'points for' section)
- difficulties in blending interfaces (a technical problem which might be solved by technicians)
- need for extra navigation time (more than balanced by the large number of claims that gateways save browsing time).

Apparently the main 'disadvantage' is based on the misconception that commercial search engines use language for identical reasons and at the same level of sophistication as SBIGs. In reality, search engines and SBIGs are different entities. Once this misconception is cleared away, it is easier to characterize the two principal components of the new gateways: structural transformation of the knowledge content and reorganization of human resources. With regard to structural transformation, these gateways represent more than just special-interest catalogues. More convenient access to information stems not merely from concentrating on a subject area, although this does help to limit searches. More important is the way the information is organized. In this respect, the title 'SBIG' is unintentionally misleading, because it advertises subject bases and ignores structure. The significant difference between commercial search engines and the new gateways is akin to the difference between a pocket dictionary and a chapter in a medical textbook. Both have limitations. The medical dictionary is limited in scope compared with the *New Oxford English Dictionary*, which reaches out more broadly. For the textbook chapter to be useful for browsing it needs to be indexed in great detail, with extensive cross-referencing. Differences in ways of acquiring knowledge are best understood as a continuum of levels, ranging from the simple (one word) to the complex (connected discourse). The new gateways are moving along the continuum; yet the simple structures are still valid. In accepting this continuum searchers must recognize that different ways of accessing knowledge are complementary. Both the pocket dictionary and the textbook chapter are useful and necessary, not mutually exclusive. Information hunters already combine different systems and must add new systems to this repertoire.

The future

Human-resource issues have important implications for information management. Looking to the future, Collins (2003) recommends the addition of 'a third dimension' – co-operation among searchers:

> The essence of knowledge management is in the sharing of information within an information community, [but unfortunately] the most valuable information assets are scattered among people, processes and content. The ultimate goal is to create an enterprise-wide environment that seamlessly connects these [assets] together.

What if dictionary, textbook chapter, whole textbook, thesaurus, encyclopaedia and networks, etc. were brought together within a dedicated sharing community? The latest portal technology seeks to do just that. It is called an Enterprise Portal (EP). It seeks to be a knowledge portal comprised of 'multiple types of portals blended into a composite solution'. The EP is a personalized browser-based system that lets surfers access information, collaborate with each other, make decisions in all aspects of their jobs and take action on all business-related information, regardless of the users' virtual location, the location of the information, or the format in which the information is stored. This dynamic way of accessing information helps overcome barriers people encounter when retrieving data, embracing 'roles, work processes, work flow, collaboration, content management, data warehouses, learning, enterprise applications and business intelligence' (Collins, 2003).

Unfortunately, in the NHS, this remains a dream. NHS workers are familiar with new technology which goes nowhere, seeds of innovation which bear no fruit. Those who espouse information sharing contend against those who hoard it in their own silo. The NHS includes disparate organizations, with conflicting goals and aspirations, making it difficult to locate its most valuable information assets. Identification of these is prerequisite to developing an EP.

The enterprise portal is a platform on which to implement knowledge management initiatives. Success within the NHS thus requires a knowledge management strategy, embedded within the NHS information culture. Until that time, realization of such benefits remains out of reach (Collins, 2003).

Conclusion

Recent improvements in gateways and portals reveal much cause for hope and enormous potential. Nevertheless, misconceptions remain together with obstacles to surmount. The inertia of deep-rooted habits is yet to be overcome, requiring consciousness raising, tuition and teamwork. However, the urgent and escalating demand for efficient knowledge management is a strong imperative that may ultimately prove relentless.

Key points

- Information portals create collections of subject-specific links targeted at specific user groups.
- Subject-based information gateways are subject-specific catalogues of internet resources, quality-assessed by specialists within the subject area.
- Academic communities are able to employ a collaborative approach to SBIGs; applying common quality assurance and database construction across multiple gateways, enabling cross-searching.
- The National electronic Library for Health (NeLH) raises portal technology to another dimension, providing quality-assessed health-related electronic resources.
- Subject-based information gateways are an efficient response to information overload, but more is needed to raise awareness of resources and the sophisticated way by which resources are captured.
- The enterprise portal is a personalized browser-based system that lets surfers collaborate with each other, regardless of users' location, the location of the information, or the format in which the information is stored.
- For the NHS to take full advantage of enterprise portals, it must absorb knowledge management principles into its information culture.

References

Coleman, P. and Amber, L. (2002) *The Resource Discovery Network: evaluation report*, University of Bristol Information Services, www.rdn.ac.uk/publications/evaluation/evalreport02.pdf.

Collins, H. (2003) *Enterprise Knowledge Portals: next-generation portal solutions for dynamic information access, better decision making, and maximum results*, New York, AMACOM.

King, I. and Moffat, M. (1996) *Evaluation of the EEVL Pilot Service*, Heriot-Watt University, www.eevl.ac.uk/evaluation.htm.

Koniger, P. and Janowitz, K. (1995) Drowning in Information, but Thirsty for Knowledge, *International Journal of Information Management*, **15** (1), 5–16.

Mackie, M. and Burton, P. F. (1999) The Use and Effectiveness of the eLib Subject Gateways: a preliminary investigation, *Program*, **33** (4), 327–37.

Martin, R. (2003) *Turning Gateways into Portals, Library & Information Update*, (June), www.cilip.org.uk/update/issues/jun03/article3june.html.

Monopoli, M. and Nicholas, D. (2000) A User-centred Approach to the Evaluation of Subject Based Information Gateways: case study SOSIG, *Aslib Proceedings*, **52** (6), 218–31.

Monopoli, M. and Nicholas, D. (2001) A User Evaluation of Subject Based Information Gateways: case study ADAM, *Aslib Proceedings*, **53** (1), 39–52.

NHS Information Authority (n.d.) *NeLH Strategy Paper*, www.nhsia.nhs.uk/nelh/pages/strategy1.asp.

Rowley, J. (2000) Knowledge Organisation for a New Millennium: principles and processes, *Journal of Knowledge Management*, **4** (3), 217–23.

Urquhart, C. et al. (2001) *NeLH Pilot Evaluation Project: final report*, DILS, University of Wales, Aberystwyth, and ScHARR, University of Sheffield.

16

Managing intellectual property

Susannah Hanlon

Introduction

For users of information, the digital age has revolutionized opportunities for authorized and unauthorized reproduction of 'novel or previously undescribed tangible output of any intellectual activity' (NHS, 1998). Intellectual property (IP) 'has an owner, it can be bought, sold or licensed and must be adequately protected' (NHS, 1998). For public-sector managers, with intense budget pressures, the protection and exploitation of intellectual property is taking on renewed economic significance. The pressure for the information professional is that incorrect advice could result in a prosecution. The most they, or any information user, can be expected to do is to demonstrate that every effort has been made to avoid breaching IP legislation.

This chapter identifies key developments in approaches to IP in the health sector, and in the IP legislative framework, principally in patents and copyright, and identifies resources of particular use to the health-information professional. Resources for obtaining timely information are included at the end of the chapter in addition to links to the relevant legislative or regulatory mechanisms.

Developments in the NHS

In 1998, the NHS developed an introductory handbook on the management of intellectual properties. This is primarily for R&D managers and advisers in NHS trusts and independent providers of NHS services (NHS, 1998). The handbook deals with a range of intellectual properties, but its primary focus is on patents. Section 5 (Income Generation) of the Health and Social Care Act 2001 was implemented in order to foster income generation from innovation. It allows 'the Secretary of State and NHS trusts and Primary Care Trusts to form or invest in companies in order to facilitate income generation'. This prompted the drive for the NHS to be seen as an 'Innovative Organisation' (Great Britain, Department of Health, 2002). Figure 16.1 lists the key UK legislation around intellectual property; Table 16.1 details the relevant European legislation; and Figure 16.2 the key international conventions and treaties.

Patent Act 1977

Copyright, Designs and Patents Act 1988 and related amendments in the form of statutory instruments to implement EU Directives (see Table 16.2)

The Patent Rules 1990 (statutory instrument)

Trade Marks Act 1994

Health and Social Care Act 2001

Copyright (Visually Impaired Persons) Act 2002

Figure 16.1 UK legislation around intellectual property

Spin-off companies have been proposed to facilitate the exploitation of IP; NHS trusts are not allowed to hold equity in companies. 'A licensing agreement between a spin-off company and its "parent" provider, which specifies licence fees and royalty rates, is an appropriate substitute' (NHS, 1998). In 2002, the Department of Health developed its *Framework and Guidance on the Management of Intellectual Property in the NHS*. The 1998 document still applies, but the 2002 document emphasizes the commitment of the Department of Health to actively exploiting IP. Innovation can occur through 'the

Table 16.1 European legislation around intellectual property

Directive	Subject
89/104/EEC	trademarks
98/71/EC	legal protection of designs
91/250/EEC	legal protection of computer programs
92/100/EEC	rental right and lending right and certain rights related to copyright in the field of intellectual property
93/83/EEC	co-ordination of certain rules concerning copyright and rights related to copyright applicable to satellite broadcasting and cable retransmission
93/98/EEC	harmonizing the term of protection of copyright and certain related rights
96/9/EC	legal protection of databases
2001/29/EC	harmonization of certain aspects of copyright and related rights in the information society

Berne Convention for the Protection of Literary and Artistic Works (originally
  1886; most recent revision 1979)
Universal Copyright Convention (1952)
Patent Law Treaty (PLT) (2000)
World Trade Organization (WTO) Trade Related Aspects of Intellectual
  Property Rights (TRIPS) (1994)
World Intellectual Property Organization (WIPO) Copyright Treaty (WCT)
  (1996)
World Intellectual Property Organization (WIPO) Performance and
  Phonograms Treaty (WPPT) (1996)

Figure 16.2 Key international conventions and treaties on intellectual
property

delivery or management of patient care, in the education or training of employees or through an R&D programme' (Great Britain. Department of Health,
2002).

There are two particularly useful sections in the *Framework and Guidance*
document, which may be of use to IP enquirers. The first of these is Part 3, the
Employment Guidance, which gives guidance on handling IP rights in a range
of employment and contractual situations, whereby IP has been generated. IP
generated by full-time employees of any organization in the natural course of
their employment does not belong to them, but to their organization. However,
in order to stimulate creativity in employees, both universities and the NHS in
some circumstances waive these rights, or at least award a portion of the proceeds of exploitation to their employees. For all other contracts the situation is
more complex, but this Employment Guidance provides useful guidelines
(Great Britain. Department of Health, 2002).

The NHS handbook also contains a chapter on sharing income from
exploitation (NHS, 1998). Following on from the Employment Guidance is
Part 4, Statement of Partnerships. This is also useful, in that it sets out 'the prin-
ciples under which NHS Trusts, Primary Care Trusts and Independent
Providers of NHS Services, their funding partners and universities should treat
IP that is generated by joint work' (Great Britain. Department of Health, 2002).
The Department of Health is in the process of establishing a network – intel-
lectual property hubs or 'IP hubs' (Clouston, 2001). The North Central
London IP Hub is set up (NCLIH, 2003) but this is not the case elsewhere.

An NHS Innovations website has also been established. This has an excellent FAQ section, with information about how the IP hubs are supposed to
work, and how the NHS views the exploitation of IP. The FAQs on employee
issues complement and simplify some of the issues raised in the Department of
Health *Framework and Guidance* document (Great Britain. Department of

Health, 2002). Table 16.2 identifies the types of intellectual property in the NHS.

Table 16.2   Categories of intellectual property relevant to the NHS

IP type	Duration, years
Patents	20 (+5)
Copyright	70
• typographical works	25
• database rights	15
Know-how (e.g. trade secrets)	indefinite
Unregistered design rights (e.g. drawings of prototype medical instruments)	15
Trademarks	10 years (+10)

Patents

The issue of patents is very thoroughly dealt with in the NHS handbook (NHS, 1998). However, to ensure an up-to-date response to an enquirer, it is advisable to consult the website of the UK Patent Office for UK developments, the European Union online website on intellectual property (Europa) or the World Intellectual Property Organization (WIPO) for international developments. The UK Patent Office website also deals with copyright, design and trademark issues and legislation. The NHS refers to the following legislation relating to patents:

• Copyright, Designs and Patents Act 1988 and Patent Act 1977 as amended by the former
• The Patent Rules 1990 (statutory instrument).

To qualify for consideration to patent, items must be 'inventions, each embodying a new idea capable of being applied or used by industry and involving a non-obvious step'. Suggested examples of patentable material are medical diagnostics, dental materials, orthopaedics and anti-cancer drugs. There are also some excluded classes, such as surgical procedures and scientific theories.

The decision about seeking patent protection is made 'jointly by you, the inventor, and your IP Adviser on behalf of your employer' (NHS, 1998). If the invention is created during the normal course of the employee's work, the IP rights belong to the employer. However, health employers, wishing to encourage creativity and wealth generation through IP rights, often share the economic benefit of the patent. It is advisable for the employee concerned to check their contract of employment. An NHS intellectual property adviser, appointed by the NHS Executive, co-ordinates and supports the implementation of the policy. The final word about exploiting the IP lies with the adviser and patent agent, after the patents database has been checked. The UK Patent Office website provides a database search facility.

In the majority of countries, a patent application cannot be made after publication of the invention – 'first to file'. However, if the invention has already been published, it is possible to file a patent with the US Patent Office – 'first to invent'. BTG plc, a company specializing in technology commercialization, has published a number of pamphlets advising on various aspects of patenting. Its pamphlet on keeping a laboratory notebook details how the 'first to invent' principle works and how to submit a patent to the US Patent Office (BTG, 2002). Once a patent has been published, the IP owner, with advice, determines the licensing conditions for the patent. The NHS handbook provides a chapter on various licensing options. The NHS is conscious that an enquiry regarding IP should include the will to follow up the process of exploitation. However, it is also aware that many patentable inventions cannot be guaranteed commercial success, and advises caution in determining whether or not to file the invention (NHS, 1998).

Copyright

Copyright legislation has changed its colour many times through the centuries. Gillian Davies gives a lively and succinct historical discussion of the philosophical, ethical and practical debates leading to our current regulatory framework (Davies, 2002). Authors have moral rights, of paternity, integrity, false attribution and disclosure, which are independent of the economic rights of copyright. These rights are outlined in the Copyright, Designs and Patents Act 1988, but it is worth examining the right of paternity in further detail. This right is the right of the author to be identified as such, unless the work is generated in the course of employment (S.77–7). It is important for an organization to be clear about its approach to both economic and moral rights. Employees could potentially become disenfranchised, resulting in a reduced level of creativity.

Article 9(2) of the Berne Convention focuses on the awareness of user access needs. This supports the principles of fair dealing and library privilege as expressed in the Copyright, Designs and Patents Act 1988. The Copyright (Visually Impaired Persons) Act 2002 means visually impaired people will now have better, faster access to information and literature. Alternative formats of copyright material such as large print, Braille and audio, can now be provided without the need to ask the permission of the copyright holder.

The Copyright, Designs and Patents Act 1988 is currently undergoing amendments in response to the EU Directive on the Harmonization of Certain Aspects of Copyright and Related Rights in the Information Society 2001. Fair dealing will only exist for non-commercial research or private study. If the user is aware, at the time of copying, that they are copying material required for commercial research, then they will be in breach of copyright. The challenges for librarians in monitoring this have been highlighted by Norman (2003). Table 16.3 lists various websites which can be used to ascertain current developments regarding copyright and other intellectual property issues.

Table 16.3   Useful websites relevant to intellectual property

ASLIB
   www.aslib.com

BioMed Central Open Access Publishers
   www.biomedcentral.com

Chartered Institute of Library and Information Professionals (CILIP)
   www.cilip.org.uk

CILIP Libraries and Archives Copyright Alliance
   www.cilip.org.uk/laca

Copyright Licensing Agency (CLA)
   www.cla.co.uk

European Bureau of Library, Information and Documentation Associations (EBLIDA)
   www.eblida.org

Eur-Lex *Portal to European Union law*
   www.europa.eu.int/eur-lex/en/index.html

Europa European Union On-line *Intellectual Property* pages
   http://europa.eu.int/comm/internal_market/en/intprop/index.htm

Her Majesty's Stationery Office (HMSO) HMS Online
   www.hmso.gov.uk

Intellectual Property (Government-backed home of UK Intellectual Property on the internet)
   www.intellectual-property.gov.uk

Joint Information Systems Committee Legal Information Service (JISCLIS)
   www.jisc.ac.uk/legal

Joint Information Systems Committee Plagiarism Advisory Service (JISCPAS)
   www.northumbria.ac.uk/jiscpas

Continued on next page

Table 16.3 *Continued*

NHS Innovations
www.innovations.nhs.uk
Patent Office
www.patent.gov.uk
United States Patent and Trademark Office
www.uspto.gov/
WIPO
www.wipo.int

Copyright in the digital environment

In the digital environment, copying has become infinitely easier, leading to the growing temptation to breach copyright. Websites still have automatic copyright, unless this is waived in a copyright statement, accessed through the website. One web page could contain several separate copyright items – text, graphics, movies and music. Some websites provide clear guidance to users about copyright. If in doubt, users need to contact the webmaster for permission to copy or to link to that website. It is preferable for links to be to the home page or index page, and the linked website should open in a new window, so that the URL of the linked site is clearly visible. To link to a page other than the home page, or to use framing, permission needs to be obtained from the webmaster.

Materials from books, journals and periodicals should not be posted or scanned without written consent from the copyright holder. Pedley (2000) points out that, even with e-mails, it is necessary to be careful about sending published material as an attachment without obtaining copyright permission.

The EU Directive on the Harmonization of Certain Aspects of Copyright and Related Rights in the Information Society 2001, mentioned earlier, developed from two new WIPO treaties, aimed at bringing 'international copyright law into the digital age' (WIPO, 2001). The Directive makes provision for the use of digital rights management systems (DRMS); circumvention is only authorized to facilitate exceptions. There is a fear that DRMS will be misused, and authorized users may find themselves unable to access material. This concern has been fuelled all the more by the EU's most recent proposal.

The European Bureau of Library, Information and Documentation Associations (EBLIDA) is involved in exploring access issues around DRMS (EBLIDA, 2003). DRMS technologies include subscription access, use of watermarks or use of 'dongles', which limit the amount of downloadable or printable information from each issue or disk. Some websites have disabled the 'cut and paste' function. Other rights holders apply digital object identifiers (DOIs). These take the searcher straight to copyright owner for authentication.

Open-access publishing

An interesting development is in the area of open-access publishing. Several publishing houses, including Elsevier, are requesting a re-examination of the way research is funded, in order to allow them to charge for publishing. With the publishing costs economically covered, publishers can then facilitate open-access publishing, rather than a subscription approach (Hyams, 2003). BioMed Central already operates as an online open-access publisher of peer-reviewed biomedical research. Authors retain their moral rights to protection of the integrity of their work. The future for publication of research will probably be a mixture of open-access publishing, subscription journals and a hybrid. The theory behind open-access publishing is that instead of having too much information, which is only minimally accessed, there would be fewer publications, because of the rigorous peer review process, but their quality would be assured, and access would increase (Hyams, 2003).

Copyright and databases

There are rights to copyright in the case of databases. Where the selection and arrangement of content of a database is the author's own intellectual creation, this is covered by copyright. There is also a 'database right', when the above is not the case and where someone has made the investment in obtaining, verifying and presenting the contents of the database, thereby protecting the investment of money, time or effort that goes into compiling databases (Pedley, 2000). This right provides protection from unfair extraction and reutilization of the contents of the database for 15 years (Norman, 2003).

The Copyright Licensing Agency and the NHS

The Copyright Licensing Agency's (CLA) website is of particular relevance to health-information professionals. Implementation of copyright both in the NHS and in higher education (HE) is carried out primarily through copyright licenses, agreed with the CLA. Its website details the NHS and Higher Education Institution (HEI) copyright licences, it also lists excluded works. The NHS licence details what can be copied, how much can be copied (for example, for journal clubs or internal committees), what to do in the cases of library privilege and interlibrary loans. If the copying required is above the CLA limits, then the person requesting the copy is referred to the CLA's Rapid

Clearing Service (CLARCS). CLARCS then investigates the fee set by the copyright holder, and charges the user accordingly. Licensing agencies are still working on their strategies for digitization, such as scanning or e-mail.

The CLA provides user guidelines for the HE digitization scheme. The context for licensed digitization is to provide digitized copies for staff and students over a network. Before anything can be scanned, it needs to be authorized through CLARCS, which determines how fees are charged, whether they are per student or as a flat fee. Under this HE scheme, there are strict conditions for permission to digitize, including who is allowed to digitize, how access is decided, how to present the material and what software is to be used to digitize the material. The Higher Education Resources ON-demand project (HERON) invites HEI members to subscribe and request material from HERON's digital resources, for clearance and digitization. HERON works closely with the CLA. So far, the licence applies only to literary material. There are, as yet, no guidelines for other organizations, such as the NHS, but the CLA has a general leaflet and welcomes responses.

Commentators on copyright

Copyright commentators who regularly provide useful information for information professionals are Graham Cornish (2001), Paul Pedley (2000), Sandy Norman (1999, 2002, 2003) and Charles Oppenheim (2002). Norman and Oppenheim contribute to the discussion on copyright in the particular context of health libraries. Norman is currently in the process of updating guidelines for health librarians. Pedley provides brief examples of case law and a list of FAQs. He also has a website (Pedley, 2000). The Chartered Institute of Library and Information Professionals has its Libraries and Archives Copyright Alliance (LACA) website with up-to-date information, particularly about changes to UK copyright legislation, resulting from the relevant EU Directives.

Plagiarism

Plagiarism, or the passing off of work as one's own, is not always deliberate, and for some individuals, not necessarily perceived as the academic misconduct it is deemed to be. In 2002, in a drive to raise awareness of the issues surrounding plagiarism, the Joint Information Systems Committee (JISC) funded a Plagiarism Advisory Service, based in the Information Management Research Institute at Northumbria University. The Service aims to provide advice on the prevention and detection of plagiarism. A website (JISCPAS) has been established to provide guidance on areas such as academic and teaching practice, policies and procedures, and study skills.

Conclusion

The NHS and its partner organizations have taken a serious look at how to best manage the IP generated by its stakeholders. Stakeholders' awareness of what is available to them tends to vary according to time constraints, priorities at the time, and awareness and culture of their own and surrounding work teams. The health-information professional has a useful role in facilitating this awareness. The impact of electronic developments is reigniting issues about copying and introducing new issues. This could be regarded as an exciting, albeit confusing, time for all information professionals.

Key points

- Health information professionals need to have a strategy that enables them to remain responsive to new developments in approaches to intellectual property, and supportive to their users.
- Librarians need to ensure they are up to date with regulations.
- It is imperative that librarians ensure their advice is not taken as legal advice.
- Librarians working within the NHS should be aware of its resources and advice points for IP issues and policies.

Acknowledgements

The author thanks Diana Jones PhD BA MCSP, Principal Lecturer, Faculty of Health, Social Work and Education, Northumbria University, and Sue Raine, MCSP, Senior I Physiotherapist, Hunters Moor Regional Neurological Rehabilitation Centre, Northgate and Prudhoe NHS Trust, for sharing their experiences at the NHS, and some of their findings and resources.

References

BTG (2002) *Keeping a Laboratory Notebook*, www.btgplc.com.

Clouston, G. (2001) Intellectual Property Affects You, *NHS Executive Refocus Northern and Yorkshire*, **16**, (August).

Copyright, Designs and Patents Act 1988, www.hmso.gov.uk/acts/acts1988/Ukpga_19880048_en_1.htm.

Cornish, G. P. (2001) *Copyright: interpreting the law for libraries, archives and information services*, revised 3rd edn, London, Library Association Publishing.

Davies, G. (2002) *Copyright and the Public Interest*, 2nd edn, London, Sweet & Maxwell.

EBLIDA, European Bureau of Library, Information and Documentation Associations (2003) *Position on Digital Rights Management Systems*, (February), EBLIDA topics and position papers, www.eblida.org/topics/topics.htm.

Great Britain. Department of Health (2002) *The NHS as an Innovative Organisation: a framework and guidance on the management of intellectual property in the NHS*, NHS, www.innovations.nhs.uk/nhs_ip_guidance.htm.

Health and Social Care Act 2001, Chapter 15, www.legislation.hmso.gov.uk/acts/acts2001/20010015.htm.

Hyams, E. (2003) Scholarly Publishing on the Road to Damascus, *Library and Information Update*, **2** (7), 20.

NCLIH (2003) *North Central London Innovation Hub*, www.nclih.co.uk.

NHS (1998) *The Management of Intellectual Property and Related Matters: an introductory handbook for R&D managers and advisers in NHS trusts and independent providers of NHS services*, www.innovations.nhs.uk/nhs_ip_guidance.htm.

Norman, S. (1999) *Copyright in Health Libraries*, 3rd edn, London, Library Association Publishing.

Norman, S (2002) *Copyright: impending changes and how are we going to deal with them?: presentation to Copyright Consultation Meeting on 2 October 2002*, www.managinginformation.com/copyright_directive.htm.

Norman, S. (February 2003) Copyright Changes and Challenges, *He@lth Information on the Internet*, **31**, 3–4, www.hioti.org.

Oppenheim, C. (2002) *Practical Difficulties posed by the Directive for Information Professionals*, www.managinginformation.com/copyright_directive.htm.

Pedley, P. (2000) *Copyright for Library and Information Service Professionals*, 2nd edn, London, Aslib.

WIPO (2001) Directive 2001/29/EC of the European Parliament and of the Council of 22 May 2001 on the harmonisation of certain aspects of copyright and related rights in the information society, *Official Journal*, L.167, 22/06/2001, P. 0010–0019.

Part 3
Using the knowledge base effectively: information sources and skills

17

Accessing the knowledge base

Maria J. Grant

Introduction

Since the early 1990s healthcare practitioners have become aware of the need to use evidence in informing their decision making. While questions are often driven by an effectiveness agenda, that is, seeking to identify which are the best treatments for particular conditions (Glanville, Haines and Auston, 1998), this represents only one aspect of evidence-based practice. A growing interest in service delivery and organization of care has led practitioners to develop and embrace methods for accessing a broader range of evidence such as qualitative research, and outcome and process studies in seeking to address why treatments are effective.

In 1997, the Department of Health emphasized the importance of access to the health knowledge base in 'the delivery of high quality healthcare' (Great Britain. Department of Health, 1997), a point reiterated in *Information for Health* (Great Britain. Department of Health, 1998). These themes were restated in 2002 when the Department of Health stressed the role of information in ensuring clinicians are able to deliver the best possible care (Great Britain. Department of Health, 2002).

Librarians are central in smoothing the progress of clinical effectiveness by facilitating access to information, and this chapter proposes a structured approach to accessing this information, or knowledge base, in whatever forms that knowledge may take. At first glance, the process recommended appears linear. However, a flexible and iterative approach to searching is encouraged. This chapter outlines the approach and methodologies of key organizations involved in increasing access to the evidence base, and considers how the reader may utilize this work in their own practice. Whole articles (Counsell, 1997; Glanville,

Haines and Auston, 1998), chapters (Falzon, 2000) or indeed entire books (Gash, 2000; Brettle and Grant, 2003) have been devoted to each of the elements outlined below.

How to structure a search for evidence

When searching for research evidence there are several issues to consider. These include clarifying who the information is for and why they are seeking evidence, defining a meaningful search question, determining the type of evidence sought, structuring a search strategy, and identifying which sources to search (Gash, 2000; Brettle and Grant, 2003). How each issue is approached determines the type of information required from the knowledge base, what form the search will take, and ultimately how successful the search process will be.

Who wants to know?

Before initiating a search it is vital to consider the perspective of the person requesting the information. The intended audience will often determine the format in which information is presented. The audience might be a traditional grouping such as policy makers, practitioners or researchers, where information may adopt a technical or academic approach. It might also include the patient, necessitating a more accessible tone.

The patient perspective has received greater consideration in recent years, with organizations such as the Patients Forum (2003) established specifically with this in mind. Policy documents encourage patient involvement, not only in relation to their own treatment, but also in commissioning and in informing research agendas (NHS Executive, 1999; Great Britain. Department of Health, 2000, 2001). Organizations such as the Evidence for Policy and Practice Information and Co-ordinating Centre (EPPI-Centre, 2003) include patient involvement as an explicit organizational goal, and seek to involve patients in prioritizing review questions, appraising research evidence, and in disseminating research findings. The EPPI-Centre has produced guidelines for involving patients in the review process to assist others in following a similar model.

Reasons for searching

Reasons for searching will determine how systematic (and indeed how comprehensive) an approach should be in accessing the knowledge base. For example, locating a few references to support an argument requires a different approach to that for a thorough or systematic literature review. The former can probably be answered by a 'quick and dirty' search of perhaps a single resource, while a more structured approach is necessary when seeking to inform decision making, implement evidence-based practice or conduct any review. Where missing parts of the knowledge base might have serious implications for the conclusions drawn, an iterative approach to searching is particularly appropriate.

The NHS Centre for Reviews and Dissemination (Khan et al., 2001), and the Cochrane Collaboration (Clarke and Oxman, 2003) have both produced guidelines on how to undertake a literature search for a systematic review. However, as with any comprehensive search for information, it should be acknowledged that, while time may constrain what is realistically possible, the aim should be to search as exhaustively as possible within the original scope of the project (Fulop et al., 2001).

An iterative approach to searching

Achieving a deep and comprehensive understanding of the health management and organizational literature is challenging. The evidence base will likely come from a range of disciplines such as business, medicine, sociology, each with differing perspectives on the same subject and terminology. This can prove challenging in defining the scope, both of the topic and of any subsequent search of the knowledge base. An iterative approach to searching makes it possible to develop a deeper understanding of the available knowledge base (Grant and Brettle, 2000). Initially this manifests itself when identifying key concepts underpinning the subject area, ascertaining the main sources to search, and the types of evidence likely to be available (Fulop et al., 2001). This enhanced insight is then fed back into the search process, on an ongoing basis, to enable increased clarity and understanding of the subject area and its associated knowledge base. This will inform subsequent revisions of the search strategy. Depending on how comprehensive a search is required, such enhanced clarity can also assist in improving the precision (the proportion of relevant information retrieved in relation to all information retrieved) and recall (the proportion of relevant information retrieved in relation to all relevant information potentially available) of database searches.

For comprehensive searches, the search strategy should be extended to include hand searching of key resources, citation tracking from key papers, consultation with experts in the subject area, and searches of grey or unpublished knowledge sources. Regardless of whichever knowledge source is being interrogated, an iterative approach can result in a more targeted and ultimately more 'successful' search being achieved (Grant and Brettle, 2000).

Defining a meaningful search question

Before accessing the knowledge base, it is important to clarify the search topic and define a clearly focused search question (Counsell, 1997; Booth, 2000). While a thorough reference interview will usually be sufficient in discovering the information needs of a user, Ross, Nilsen and Dewdney (2002) suggest that the 'phenomenon of the ill-formed query . . . [can lead] to erroneous inferences'. Not only may the question being asked not truly convey or represent the context or underlying reason for the request, but each party may bring their own unspoken, and possibly different, understanding and perception to a topic area. Although the principles remain the same regardless of the search being undertaken, the ubiquitous presence of electronic media and the apparent ease of database searching have exacerbated the need to ensure that a 'true' and meaningful search question is uncovered when accessing the knowledge base.

Two systems have emerged to assist in formulating a search question. Encapsulated in a mnemonic each system provides a structured approach to clarifying the search topic and subsequent search plan. The two acronyms are PICO and ECLIPSE.

PICO

Developed by clinicians (Richardson et al., 1995), PICO provides a set of structured categories to consider in seeking evidence in response to clinical questions such as:

> Is St John's wort an effective anti-depressant?

or

> Are hospital at-home schemes effective in the rehabilitation of patients after stroke?

PICO comprises the following components:

- P – defining the patient or problem under consideration
- I – defining the intervention or treatment under consideration
- C – defining the comparison intervention or treatment under consideration
- O – defining the clinical outcome/s or outcome of interest.

Table 17.1 takes the clinical question 'Is St John's wort an effective anti-depressant?' as an example, and illustrates how PICO might be used to structure this question into search concepts.

Table 17.1 A PICO search: Is St John's wort an effective anti-depressant?

Acronym	Letter represents	Search concepts
P	Patient and/or problem	Depressed adults
I	Intervention	St John's wort
C	Comparison	Traditional anti-depressant drugs
O	Outcomes	Levels of depression

The clinical nature of scenarios structured via the PICO acronym lends itself to research evidence that is primarily quantitative in nature. However, for broader types of questions its categories may be unnecessarily restrictive. For example, when seeking to identify why a particular intervention is effective a closer investigation of that intervention may be considered, and therefore no comparison is required. The PICO system can be used without the need for a comparison (P – Patient; I – Intervention; and O – Outcome). Alternatively, the ECLIPSE acronym may prove helpful.

ECLIPSE

Developed by librarians (Wildridge and Bell, 2002), ECLIPSE provides a set of structured questions or categories to elucidate the elements of non-intervention search questions that are, by nature, broader in construct than clinical questions. For example:

> What are users' perceptions of gastro-intestinal clinic waiting times?

As with PICO, ECLIPSE is an acronym. It represents the following words or categories:

- E – What type of information is expected from the search? e.g. models of good practice; how to improve service; how to organize a service
- C – Which client group is the service aimed at?
- L – What is the location of the service?
- I – What impact is the change in the service, if any, which is being looked for? What would constitute success? How is this being measured?
- P – Which professional groups are involved in providing/improving the service?
- SE – For which service is the information being sought?

Table 17.2 takes the non-intervention search question 'What are users' perceptions of gastro-intestinal clinic waiting times?' as an example, and illustrates how ECLIPSE might be used to structure this question into search concepts.

Table 17.2   An ECLIPSE search: What are users' perceptions of gastro-intestinal clinic waiting times?

Acronym	Letter represents	Search concept
E	Expectation	Models of good practice
C	Client	Patients with colitis
L	Location	Out-patients department
I	Impact	Organization of appointments
P	Professionals	Administrators
SE	SErvice	Gastro-intestinal clinic

The ECLIPSE acronym provides a framework when searching for management and policy related questions, in both the health and social care fields. This type of research evidence is likely to be more qualitative in nature than that sought using PICO.

Determining the type of evidence sought

As illustrated by the PICO and ECLIPSE acronyms, some questions naturally lend themselves to a particular type of knowledge source or research evidence. However, for complex or multidimensional search questions, perhaps encompassing a range of perspectives, an appreciation of the potential contribution of a range of research evidence types is required. Organizations such as the Cochrane Collaboration (Khan et al., 2001) have focused on quantitative research to identify the effectiveness of particular interventions. However, as the nature of the questions being asked and the subjects being investigated has broadened (to include social interventions, education and policy), qualitative research evidence is increasingly being sought. Qualitative and quantitative research evidence can represent different perspectives of the same issue, and can complement each other in producing richer, more rounded, and ultimately more reliable results. Growing recognition that the research question should determine the research method adopted is increasingly evident in systematic reviews (Silverman, 1997; Sackett and Wennberg, 1997).

Methods for synthesizing evidence from qualitative research alongside quantitative research are emerging (EPPI-Centre, 2003), and organizations such as the EPPI-Centre, University of London (EPPI-Centre, 2003), the Centre for Evidence Based Social Services, University of Exeter (Centre for Evidence Based Social Services, 2003) and the Health Care Practice Research and Development Unit, University of Salford (Health Care Practice Research and Development Unit, 2003) have adopted such approaches in their own practice.

Identifying which sources to search

Clarifying the responses to the previous four issues (who wants to know?, reasons for searching, defining a meaningful search question, and defining the type of evidence sought) will inform sources to be searched.

The reason for undertaking a search should inform the choice of the most appropriate information source for answering a query or question, be it a book, journal article, professional organization or bibliographic database. NeLH, the National electronic Library for Health (National electronic Library for Health, 2003), provides access to an increasingly wide knowledge base, via the NHS Workforce Development Confederation's funded National Core Content project, and the Specialist Libraries. An increasing number of dedicated resources cover particular elements of the health management and policy field including the C2-SPECTR (Campbell Collaboration's Social, Psychological, Educational and Criminological Trials Register – Campbell Collaboration, 2003), CareData (Social Care Institute of Excellence, 2003), HMIC (Health Management Information Consortium) and REEL (Research Evidence in Education Library – EPPI-Centre, 2003) databases.

From an access perspective, the more commonly known databases, e.g. CINAHL and MEDLINE, are often the first, and perhaps only, source interrogated. Each database has a specific coverage area, and optimal search strategies can enhance the effectiveness of a search. However, even when searching in a relatively clearly defined subject area such as psychiatry, the majority of relevant journal literature may not be covered by the most commonly available databases (McDonald, Taylor and Adams, 1999). The dispersed nature of the published knowledge base indicates that searches of multiple sources may be required to facilitate the desired level of coverage (Grant, 2004).

Depending on the reasons for and required comprehensiveness of a search, the iterative search process will require that database searches be supplemented by recourse to additional knowledge sources such as experts in the field, professional organizations and sources of grey literature.

Optimal search strategies

Since they were first proposed in 1994 (Haynes et al., 1994), a range of optimal search strategies (OSS) has been compiled to facilitate thorough database searches, often in shortening the time-frame for such searches. These pre-prepared search strategies, previously referred to as 'search filters', 'quality filters', 'hedges' or 'optimal search strategies' (Paisley, 2000), have been developed (and usually tested) for use with particular databases and/or search interfaces to retrieve specific types of evidence, study design or clinical information more effectively.

Until recently, OSSs were available only for the more commonly used databases, e.g. CINAHL and MEDLINE. The range and availability of OSSs is continually expanding and can now facilitate enhanced searches on EMBASE and PsycInfo (McKibbon, Eady and Marks, 1999). The organizations listed in Table 17.3 have produced predesigned search strategies to optimize searches for specific types of knowledge or study design.

Table 17.3 Optimal search strategies

Organization	Type of information/ study design	Database/ search interface
Centre for Evidence Based Medicine, Oxford, UK (www.cebm.net/searching.asp)	• Aetiology • Diagnosis • Prognosis • Therapy	• Ovid • WinSPIRS
Health Care Practice Research and Development Unit, Salford, UK (www.fhsc.salford.ac.uk/hcprdu/ projects/qebp_2001.ppt)	• Qualitative research	• MEDLINE (Ovid)
NHS Centre for Reviews and Dissemination, York, UK (www.york.ac.uk/inst/crd/search.htm)	• Meta-analysis • Reviews	• CINAHL (Ovid/SilverPlatter) • MEDLINE (Dialog/Ovid/ SilverPlatter)
Public Health Resource Unit, Milton Keynes, UK (www.phru.org.uk/~casp/filters.htm)	• Aetiology • Diagnosis • Prognosis • Therapy	• CINAHL (Ovid) • EMBASE (Ovid) • MEDLINE (Ovid/ SilverPlatter) • PsychINFO (Ovid)
UK Clearing House on Health Outcomes, Leeds, UK (www.leeds.ac.uk/nuffield/ infoservices/UKCH/sheets.html)	•Outcome measurement • Outcome measures	• CINAHL (Ovid) • MEDLINE (Ovid)
University of Rochester, Canada (www.urmc.rochester.edu/)	• Aetiology • Diagnosis • Meta-analysis • Prognosis • Qualitative research (CINAHL only) • Therapy	• CINAHL (Ovid) • MEDLINE (Ovid)

Conclusion

This chapter has focused on accessing the knowledge base and, although the steps outlined seem relatively straightforward and self-contained, searching for information is seldom as clear cut as it might first appear. There is always room for improving a search, whether through redefining a search question or searching alternative or additional sources of information. Searches can and should be continually refined in light of information obtained – time and resources permitting.

Although a search topic may be deconstituted into quantifiable components, searching is ultimately an iterative process. Initial investigations of the knowledge base may provide an overview of the available evidence, but are likely to necessitate the refinement of the search structure, and perhaps even the search question. Having followed the steps proposed, a modicum of artistry, professional judgement, and knowledge of the context in which the search is being undertaken should all inform how a search proceeds.

Key points

- Access to the knowledge base is important in the delivery of high-quality healthcare.
- The context of the search topic will inform any decisions made during the search process.
- Define a focused and meaningful search question before commencing the search. PICO and ECLIPSE can assist in the process.
- Predesigned search strategies exist to optimize searches of the knowledge base by type of information or study design.
- An iterative approach to searching is recommended, informed by the results of initial and subsequent enquiries.
- A range of complementary information sources should be used, particularly in answering complex or multidimensional search questions.
- The dispersed nature of the knowledge base may necessitate searches of multiple sources to facilitate the desired level of coverage.

References

Booth, A. (2000) Formulating the Question. In Booth, A. and Walton, G. (eds), *Managing Knowledge in Health Services*, London, Library Association Publishing, 197–206.

Brettle, A. and Grant, M. J. (2003) *Finding the Evidence for Practice: a workbook for health professionals*, London, Churchill Livingstone.

Campbell Collaboration (2003) *Welcome*, www.campbellcollaboration.org/.

Centre for Evidence Based Social Services (2003) *Centre for Evidence Based Social Services*, www.ex.ac.uk/cebss/.

Clarke, M. and Oxman, A. D. (eds) Cochrane Reviewers Handbook 4.2.0 (updated March 2003), www.cochrane.dk/cochrane/handbook/hbook.htm.

Counsell, C. (1997) Formulating Questions and Locating Primary Studies for Inclusion in Systematic Reviews, *Annals of Internal Medicine*, **127**, 380–7.

EPPI-Centre (2003) *EPPI-Centre: introduction*, http://eppi.ioe.ac.uk/.

Falzon, L. (2000) Searching the Databases. In Booth, A. and Walton, G. (eds), *Managing Knowledge in Health Services*, London, Library Association Publishing.

Fulop, N. et al. (2001) *Studying the Organisation and the Delivery of Health Services: research methods*, London, Routledge.

Gash, S. (2000) *Effective Literature Searching for Research*, 2nd edn, Aldershot, Gower.

Glanville, J., Haines, M. and Auston, I. (1998) Finding Information on Clinical Effectiveness, *British Medical Journal*, **317**, 200–3.

Grant, M. J. (2004) Which Database, Which Interface? In Booth, A. and Brice, A. (eds), *Evidence Based Practice: a handbook for information professionals*, London, Facet Publishing.

Grant, M. J. and Brettle, A. (2000) *Developing a Review Question: a spiral approach to literature searching*, 3rd Symposium on Systematic Reviews: Beyond the Basics, Oxford, 3–5 July 2000.

Great Britain. Department of Health (1997) *Library and Information Services*, Health Service Guideline, HSG (97) 47.

Great Britain. Department of Health (1998) *Information for Health: an information strategy for the modern NHS 1998–2005. A national strategy for local implementation*, London, Department of Health.

Great Britain. Department of Health (2000) *The NHS Plan: a plan for investment, a plan for reform*, London, Stationery Office.

Great Britain. Department of Health (2001) *Health and Social Care Act 2001*, London, Stationery Office.

Great Britain. Department of Health (2002) *Learning from Bristol: the DH response to the report of the public inquiry into children's heart surgery at the Bristol Royal Infirmary 1984–1995*, London, Department of Health.

Haynes, R. B. et al. (1994) Developing Optimal Search Strategies for Detecting Clinically Sound Studies in MEDLINE, *Journal of the American Medical Informatics Association*, **1** (6), 447–58.

Health Care Practice Research and Development Unit (2003) *HCPRDU: Health Care Practice Research and Development Unit*, www.fhsc.salford.ac.uk/hcprdu/.

Khan, K. S. et al. (2001) *Undertaking Systematic Reviews of Research on Effectiveness: CRD's guidance for those carrying out or commissioning reviews*, CRD Report 4, York, University of York.

McDonald, S., Taylor, L. and Adams, C. (1999) Searching the Right Database: a comparison of four databases for psychiatry journals, *Health Libraries Review*, **16**, 151–6.

McKibbon, A., Eady, A. and Marks, S. (1999) *PDQ: evidence-based principles and practice*, Hamilton, Ontario, B.C., Decker.

National electronic Library for Health (2003) *National electronic Library for Health*, www.nelh.nhs.uk.

NHS Executive (1999) *Patient and Public Involvement in the New NHS*, London, Department of Health, HSC 1999/210.

Paisley, S. (2000) Filtering the Literature. In Booth, A. and Walton, G. (eds), *Managing Knowledge in Health Services*, London, Library Association Publishing.

The Patients Forum (2003) *The Patients Forum*, www.thepatientsforum.org.uk/.

Richardson, W. S. et al. (1995) The Well Built Clinical Question: a key to evidence based decisions, *ACP Journal Club*, **123** (2), A12–13.

Ross, C. S., Nilsen, K. and Dewdney, P. (2002) *Conducting a Reference Interview: a how-to-do-it manual for librarians*, London, Facet Publishing.

Sackett, D. L. and Wennberg, J. E. (1997) Choosing the Best Research Design for Each Question, *British Medical Journal*, **315**, 1636.

Silverman, D. (1997) The Logics of Qualitative Research. In Miller, G. and Dingwall, R. (eds), *Context and Methods in Qualitative Research*, London, Sage.

Social Care Institute of Excellence (2003) *eLSC Library of Social Care*, www.elsc.org.uk/.

Wildridge, V. and Bell, L. (2002) How CLIP Became ECLIPSE: a mnemonic to assist in searching for health policy/management information, *Heath Information and Libraries Journal*, **19** (2), 113–15.

18

Appraising the literature

John Blenkinsopp

Introduction

Evidence-based medicine, and consequently evidence-based healthcare (EBHC), involves 'turning clinical problems into questions and then systematically locating, appraising, and using contemporaneous research findings as the basis for clinical decisions. . . . Critical appraisal can be used to determine the validity and applicability of the evidence, which is then used to inform clinical decisions'(Rosenberg and Donald, 1995). EBHC means 'Integrating the best available research evidence with information about patient preferences, clinician skill level, and available resources to make decisions about patient care' (Ciliska et al., 2001). It thus ensures that patient care is based upon critically appraised best evidence rather than personal opinion.

This chapter examines how librarians can involve themselves in the critical-appraisal process. It discusses how the librarian's role can be extended by identifying resources already available, by using existing skills to enhance the appraisal process, by producing guides and digests and by involvement in training. It introduces terms used in critical appraisal, the practicalities of librarian involvement, the appraisal process and issues around training.

The importance of critical appraisal

According to Sackett et al. (2000), there are five steps to evidence-based practice (see Figure 18.1).

Step 1	Convert the need for information into answerable questions.
Step 2	Track down the best evidence with which to answer that question.
Step 3	Critically appraise that evidence for its validity (closeness to the truth).
Step 4	Integrate the critical appraisal with our clinical expertise.
Step 5	Evaluate our effectiveness and efficiency in executing steps 1–4 and seek ways to improve them for next time.

Figure 18.1 The evidence-based practice process

Critical appraisal (step 3) underpins the whole process. Failing to appraise the evidence may actually cause harm to patients – in fact, if a patient's treatment is based on evidence that has not been appraised, it is probably worse than treatment based on no evidence at all. Critical-appraisal skills are needed 'to assess the quality of evidence in support of a treatment and to maintain clinical skills' (Anderson, 2000).

Greenhalgh (2001) refers to critical appraisal as 'reading the right papers at the right time'. In practice, critical appraisal combines common sense, high-quality research and clinical expertise to identify a treatment that is patient orientated, clinically effective and efficient. This involves bringing research into practice by finding the right papers, reading them, judging whether the results are believable and trustworthy and then deciding whether that evidence base can be used to change local practice.

Clinicians would have to read 19 papers 365 days a year to keep up to date in internal medicine (Strauss and Sackett, 1998). The concept of 'quality not quantity' means that librarians no longer measure the success of a literature search by the amount of paper generated – instead they supply small numbers of high-quality papers that can be used to improve practice in the local area. This is why knowledge of critical appraisal is vital. Critical appraisal is also required for the 'scientific' component of many membership examinations for clinical staff. Clinical staff need critical appraisal to keep up with changes in their specialist area: 'As clinicians we feel that, provided the topic is important to us and common, critically appraising the evidence . . . is an efficient method of keeping ourselves up to date' (Lancaster and Weingarten, 2001).

The role of the librarian

Librarians have an important role to play in supporting critical-appraisal activities within their organization (Bexon and Falzon, 2003). This may be as part of continuing education, clinical governance or clinical librarianship. They are also responsible for gathering and sifting the information required for EBHC as well as appraising such materials. This can raise both the profile and credibility of health librarians within the organization, extending 'the librarian's role beyond identification of the literature to involvement in practicing and teaching quality filtering and critical appraisal of the literature' (Scherrer and Dorsch, 1999).

EBHC can extend the librarian's role beyond simply identifying the literature to involvement in evaluating its quality and impact on the local setting. These 'value added' activities require librarians to acquire new knowledge of the processes or resources available and to develop new skills as trainers. Within health librarianship, librarians should not see critical appraisal as an 'add on' instead of being core to services provided. As use of, and access to, information sources change, it is vital that health librarians move beyond the bounds of what is perceived as traditional practice. Involvement in critical appraisal may place librarians more centrally within their organization and reduce the risk of their becoming marginalized.

Often librarians find it difficult to become involved in critical appraisal because others in the organization see it as their own responsibility. Appraisal has the unfair reputation of being a daunting subject which is too academic and mathematics based. When appraising a paper terms such as 'odds', 'numbers needed to treat' or 'confidence intervals' are often encountered. With practice, such terms can be understood allowing appraisers to concentrate on the 'bottom line' of a paper – what it really says and whether the intervention it discusses will help to change practice for the better.

Librarians can contribute specialist experience to critical-appraisal processes. Their involvement may range from teaching health professionals how to effectively search 'unscreened' resources (e.g. MEDLINE and Cinahl) and screened resources (Cochrane Library, Best Evidence)' (Wong et al., 2000), to producing digests and providing group facilitation.

Locating Studies for appraisal

Before appraising any article, it is useful to identify the question to be answered. The PICO formula can be used to identify the patient (P), the intervention being given (I), a comparison with a placebo or another treatment (if necessary) (C) and the patient outcome (O) (see Chapter 17). This can assist a librarian when planning the search strategy because it helps to formulate the question into a manageable search.

Once the literature search has been conducted it is necessary to identify the right papers to appraise. Unfortunately, not every area of research has clear evidence to support it. In reality, much research is of variable quality – only a very small amount of published material is clinically relevant. Evidence should be the best available. In a patient-centred NHS, any treatment must be acceptable to the patient, effective for the health professional and cost efficient for the

NHS manager. Two ways to identify the quality of a study involve the use of checklists and application of hierarchies of evidence.

Hierarchies of evidence

Hierarchies of evidence are useful for quickly classifying the quality of studies. Each paper can be categorized and a literature search can thus be sorted according to the quality of papers found. As a general rule, the higher the paper is on the hierarchy (see Figure 18.2), the stronger the evidence.

Meta-analysis and systematic review
Randomized controlled trials
Cohort studies
Case-controlled studies
Case reports
Letters/opinion

Figure 18.1 The evidence-based practice process

Applying this approach we would assume a systematic review to be a starting point for evidence-based practice locally. Systematic review and meta-analysis – 'a statistical analysis which combines or integrates the results of several independent clinical trials considered by the analyst to be combinable'(Huque, 1988) – are secondary research techniques which synthesize a comprehensive evaluation of available research in an area. Systematic reviews are being 'used increasingly to guide practice, strengthening the link between research results and improved health outcomes' (Cook, Levy and Heyland, 1998).

The best known systematic review collection, the Cochrane Library, is a relatively small database and systematic review is still developing as a methodology. Reviews can 'take between 6 months and a year to produce and cost between £20,000 and £50,000 to conduct' (North and Booth, 1999). Consequently, most clinical questions rely on primary research for their answers. Where a meta-analysis or systematic review is unavailable, we move down the hierarchy of evidence to primary studies such as randomized controlled trials (RCT), cohort studies and so on.

Checklists

While using a hierarchy is a quick way of identifying studies for appraisal, measuring the validity, applicability and quality of a primary study requires use of a checklist. Checklists are invaluable in structuring the appraisal process – they help to identify the agenda for discussion. For example, RCTs are considered the 'gold standard' of research, but the quality of these varies considerably, making it important to identify any shortcomings. From the variety of good checklists available it is important to find the one that best suits you and your users. A good starting point is the CASP (Critical Appraisal Skills Programme) set of appraisal checklists. These are produced by the Public Health Resource Unit based in Oxford and are freely available at www.prhu.org.uk/~casp/casp.htm. Seven CASP checklists are currently available and these can be used to ascertain the reliability and clarity of results and to isolate personal opinions.

Irrespective of study design, each checklist asks important questions to help the reviewer decide whether a paper is of sufficient quality to be applied locally. For example, the checklist for randomized controlled trials asks whether the research question is clearly formulated, whether there is random allocation of patients to intervention and comparison groups, whether patients and health professionals are blinded to the group to which the patients have been allocated and that there are no obvious biases.

CASP uses multidisciplinary scenarios to help non-medical personnel to use the 'users' guides to medical literature' to interpret research findings, by stripping criteria down to essential issues. Users' guides exist for most types of study design ranging from systematic review and RCT to guidelines and cohort studies. They grew out of a series of 25 articles published in the *Journal of the American Medical Association* over a ten-year period. The authors, Guyatt and Rennie (2002), recognize that 'every few years the literature doubles in size . . . every day the task of taming the literature becomes more hopeless'. The checklists offer a practical guide to help make sense of clinical papers and can be used as the basis for training in critical appraisal.

Useful resources for clinical appraisal

Many good starting points for critical appraisal are freely available on the internet. Bandolier (available at www.jr2.ox.ac.uk/bandolier/whatnew.html) produces bullet points of evidence-based information; it also produces simple guides to aspects of critical appraisal such as how to calculate numbers needed to treat. BestBets (available at www.bestbets.org) provides best evidence topics (BETS) in a database of appraised topics. The Centre for Evidence Based Medicine (available at www.cebm.net/) gives advice on teaching critical appraisal and includes an EBM toolbox which explains the main concepts of appraisal. Articles by Trisha Greenhalgh on how to read a paper (available at http://bmj.com) are also useful. ScHARR's Netting the Evidence (available at www.nettingtheevidence.org.uk) offers a searchable database of evidence-based information available on the internet.

Producing information to support EBHC

One main role of the librarian in EBHC is to produce information to support critical appraisal. This may take the form of digests, critically appraised topics (CATS), subject guides or even specific lists of resources available. Many libraries produce digests summarizing clinically relevant articles and others provide access to published digests. Examples include the *BMJ*'s evidence-based journals (*Evidence Based Medicine*, *Evidence Based Mental Health* and *Evidence Based Nursing*) which alert clinicians to important advances by sum-marizing and appraising them. Such journals apply detailed criteria to appraisal of included papers.

The *BMJ* also publishes a weekly POEM (Patient Oriented Evidence that Matters) which summarizes a valid piece of research that is important to doc-tors and patients. Over 100 journals are searched and articles are evaluated for validity. The full database of POEMS is available commercially (at www.infopoems.com/index.cfm).

To help libraries produce clinically relevant digests, many versions of MEDLINE limit searches to specific levels of evidence such as meta-analysis or RCTs. Many also allow you to update such searches by setting an alert for your search strategy. For instance, in updating a stroke-care pathway you could save your search strategy as an e-mail alert. Whenever MEDLINE is subsequently updated, the system sends an e-mail listing additional papers at the level of evi-dence you require. Results can be incorporated into a digest and circulated to relevant users.

Exemplar CAT sites include Evidence Based On Call (available at www.eboncall.co.uk) and the Centre for Evidence Based Medicine Catbank (available at www.cebm.net/cats.asp). The catbank also allows you to download 'catnipper' software which enables you to create your own CATs. CATs are short and summarize the main issues – you can build up a collection of CATs on common questions and circulate them to relevant staff to give them a good overview of appraised research in their subject areas. Librarians are often the first to see clinically relevant journal articles and are well positioned to publi-cize these papers as they arrive. It can be helpful to monitor newspaper and television coverage of major clinical papers and publicize access via a newsletter digest or an intranet page.

Training in critical appraisal

Librarians have a valuable role to play in critical-appraisal teaching and train-ing. Involvement can range from attending or facilitating specialist journals clubs or 'taster sessions' to participating in week-long evidence-based practice workshops. According to Richard Smith (2003) 'most doctors don't read or understand medical research – but they can be trained to do so without too much effort'.

Specialist journals clubs

Journals clubs proliferate throughout the NHS – often as a means for getting busy health professionals to meet on a regular basis and share experience. Although it is sometimes difficult for librarians to gain acceptance in such groups, they can bring invaluable expertise in finding and appraising the evidence. The librarian image can be a major barrier – especially where critical appraisal is traditionally seen as the responsibility of the consultant or departmental head. Benefits of librarian involvement include providing a platform to publicize the library services to a wider audience, to offer training on bibliographic databases and to increase credibility.

Multidisciplinary journals clubs

Multidisciplinary journals clubs and evidence-based networks are often initiated by librarians and enable staff from all areas of the organization to meet on a regular basis to develop and refresh their appraisal skills. Multidisciplinary clinical practice – such as stroke – can be usefully discussed within such groups so that all participants feel able to contribute. These sessions often allow experimentation meaning that members are able to tackle papers in difficult or new areas such as diagnostic testing or decision analysis. It can be useful to take these groups out of the acute or primary care settings and involve members from all aspects of the health service. Examples are the Sheffield Evidence Based Networking Group (ShEBaNG) and the Teesside Evidence Based Group (TEBaG). Results from these appraisal sessions can be made available to a wider audience within a digest, as with ShEAFS (the Sheffield Evidence Appraisals From ShEBaNG) (available at www.shef.ac.uk/~scharr/ir/sheafs/).

'Taster' sessions

Taster sessions are usually full training days aimed at staff who understand basic concepts of critical appraisal but want to develop more understanding. They can be aimed at specific groups such as pharmacists or librarians and can be introductory or more advanced. For example, the BMA's Basic and Advanced Critical Appraisal Skills Workshops (details at www.bma.rg/ap.nsg/Content/LIBCASWorkshops) act as an introduction to staff wanting to attend the more advanced week-long courses offered throughout the country.

Librarians can be involved in identifying the resources available to support critical appraisal and in facilitating small-group work. Such workshops offer an ideal environment for staff to practise their skills away from the workplace

Residential workshops

More advanced sessions often take the form of week-long residential workshops. In these workshops, attendees have an opportunity to lead a group in appraising a paper and to learn about small-group work. Librarians are often involved throughout these workshops, particularly during literature-search sessions that train participants in the use of databases such as MEDLINE and the Cochrane Library and search filters to improve the quality of search results (Crumley, Bayley and Bhatnagar, 2002). Towards the end of such week-long sessions, the focus often shifts from formulating the question and appraising the evidence towards implementing results into clinical practice.

Facilitation of a group

Teaching critical-appraisal skills often works well within small groups – especially where there are varied levels of understanding. According to Sackett and Parkes (1998), larger groups have not worked well: 'Forced to confine themselves to pre-clinical curricula, and often trapped in vast lecture halls, they seldom brought joy to either side of the lectern and often found themselves talking in their students' sleep.'

Groupwork should be conducted in a 'safe' environment to ensure that participants may develop skills and make mistakes without anyone outside the group becoming aware. A good way to encourage nervous participants is to establish clear ground rules at the start of each session to ensure that all members of the group are supportive and that no discussion or gossip about the session leaves the room. Facilitation of groups is a real skill which enables members to interact and participate thereby maximizing benefits from the appraisal process.

To facilitate a relevant and open discussion, it is helpful to develop a scenario. Scenario writing can be a skill in itself – it needs to be realistic, involving a situation to which all group members can relate. It often helps if you can inject humour to help make it a more enjoyable process. It can be challenging to keep all in a group interested and involved and to handle those who do not contribute to the discussion or those who want to dominate it. EBHC is still controversial; many continue to view it as 'cookbook medicine' whereby healthcare professionals follow a 'recipe' to treat their patients rather than use their clinical skills. Instead it should be viewed as a supplement to, rather than substitute for, clinical practice. Woolf (2000) argues that excessive critical appraisal can 'harm patients because knowledge is rejected that can save (or improve lives)'. This may explain why 'Many healthcare professionals continue to base practice around traditions of rituals, despite research evidence demonstrating the contrary' (McSherry and Haddock, 1999).

Conclusion

Rather than providing a guide to critically appraising a paper this chapter focuses on the many ways in which health librarians can involve themselves in resourcing and applying critical appraisal to the benefit of the whole process. At this relatively early stage of librarian involvement, librarians need to recognize the importance of appraisal in the clinical setting, understand its key concepts, provide resources to support it and be involved in developing appraisal within their organization: 'The destination has not been reached, but the journey is going in the right direction' (Paisley, 2000).

Key points

- Critical appraisal is a major part of evidence-based healthcare.
- Librarians have an important part to play in the critical-appraisal process.
- Critical appraisal can give librarians a more centralized role in the organization.
- Identifying high-quality papers is easier if we use hierachies of evidence and checklists.
- Librarians have a key role in identifying resources and providing training to support critical appraisal.

References

Anderson, J. D. (2000) Need for Evidence-based Practice in Prosthodontics, *Journal of Prosthetic Dentistry*, **83** (1), 58–65.

Bexon, N. and Falzon, L. (2003) Personal Reflections on the Role of Librarians in the Teaching of Evidence-based Healthcare, *Health Information and Libraries Journal*, **20** (2), 112–15.

Ciliska, D. K. et al. (2001) Resources to Enhance Evidence-based Nursing Practice, *AACN Clinical Issues*, **12** (4), 520–8.

Cook, D., Levy, M. and Heyland, D. (1998) How to Use a Review Article: prophylactic endoscopic sclerotherapy for esophageal varices, *Critical Care Medicine*, **26** (4), 692–700.

Crumley, E., Bayley, L. and Bhatnagar, N. (2002) Librarian Integration into McMaster's 2001 Evidence-based Clinical Practice Workshop, *Bibliotheca Medica Canadiana (BMC)*, **23**, 87–9.

Greenhalgh, T. (2001) *How to Read a Paper: the basics of evidence-based medicine*, 2nd edn, London, BMJ Publishing.

Guyatt, G. and Rennie, D. (2002) *Users' Guides to the Medical Literature*, Chicago IL, American Medical Association Press.

Huque, M. F. (1988) Experiences with Meta-analysis in NDA Submissions, *Proceedings of the Biopharmaceutical Section of the American Statistical Association*, **2**, 28–33.

Lancaster, T. and Weingarten, M. (2001) Critical Appraisal. In Silagy, C. and Haines, A. (eds), *Evidence-based Practice in Primary Care*, 2nd edn, London, BMJ Publishing.

McSherry, R. and Haddock, J. (1999) Evidence-based Health Care: its place within clinical governance, *British Journal of Nursing*, **8** (2), 113–17.

North, G. and Booth, A. (1999) Why Appraise the Evidence?: a case study of vitamin C and the healing of pressure sores, *Journal of Human Nutrition and Dietetics*, **12** (3), 237–44.

Paisley, S. (2000) Filtering and Evaluating the Knowledge Base. In Booth, A. and Walton, G. (eds), *Managing Knowledge in Health Sciences*, London, Library Association Publishing.

Rosenberg, W. and Donald, A. (1995) Evidence Based Medicine: an approach to clinical problem-solving, *British Medical Journal*, **310** (6987), 1122–6.

Sackett, D. and Parkes, J. (1998) Teaching Critical Appraisal: no quick fixes, *Canadian Medical Association Journal*, **158** (2), 203–4.

Sackett, D. L. et al. (2000) *Evidence-based Medicine: how to practise and teach EBM*, 2nd edn, London, Churchill Livingstone.

Scherrer, C. S. and Dorsch, J. L. (1999) The Evolving Role of the Librarian in Evidence-based Medicine, *Bulletin of the Medical Library Association*, **87** (3), 322–8.

Smith, R. (2003) Do Patients Need to Read Research?, *British Medical Journal*, **326**, 1307.

Strauss, S. and Sackett, D. (1998) Using Research Findings in Clinical Practice, *British Medical Journal*, **317**, 339–42.

Wong, R. A. et al. (2000) Evidence-based Practice: a resource for physical therapists, *Issues on Aging*, **23** (3), 19–26.

Woolf, S. H. (2000) Taking Critical Appraisal to Extremes: the need for balance in the evaluation of evidence, *Journal of Family Practice*, **49** (12), 1081–5.

19

Creating effective web pages

Steve Ashwell

Introduction

Websites can be broadly characterized as web publishing (sites that are magazine-like and present a typical corporate brochure) and web-based services (sites that do a specific job, for example keep a record of somebody's interests and send out automatic e-mails after updates) (Greenspun, 1999). This chapter focuses on the web-publishing type of site. Increasingly, however, such web-based services as content management systems and e-communities are finding applications in the health sector. These do not require authors to know anything about hypertext markup language (HTML). An information worker without programming skills can usually handle web administration and will typically perform this specific job very well. Many established health sites fall within the web-publishing category and the speed and ease with which these sites can be set up probably guarantees them a niche for years to come.

This chapter begins by examining the value of websites for health organizations. After describing the value of hypertext it reviews recent research on the characteristics of health information on the internet. Moving to a consideration of website development it identifies methods of needs assessment and usability testing. Key factors in marketing a website are also identified.

Value of the web for health organizations

The world wide web is an effective distribution mechanism for health information. Table 19.1 outlines resources that health organizations might wish to share on the web.

Table 19.1 Objectives and examples of web publishing for health organizations

Objective	Examples
Provide a channel for corporate communication	• Recruitment notices • Annual reports • Location map • Plan of campus/building • Address, phone, fax details • Car parking • Specialist services (i.e. specialties) • Public accountability information (minutes of trust board meetings)
Provide information to patients	• Disease fact sheets • Outpatient information (clinic times, telephone numbers) • Wheelchair access information • Hospital campus development plans • Public consultations • News on issues affecting the organization • Quality improvement online surveys • Health improvement advice and surveys (e.g. links with leisure facilities, online data-collection forms)
Provide web resources for internal organization (intranet)	• Detailed staff contact directory • Policies and procedures documents (e.g. human resources policies) • News • Internal reports (e.g. audits, studies) • Repository for internal documents (e.g. local guidelines, local handbooks) • Online noticeboards
Provide easier access to clinical services	• Meeting requirements set out in *Information for Health* • Online booking of appointments • Reducing laboratory-result waiting times • Register to receive appointment reminders automatically via e-mail • Combining appointment information/test results with links to evidence
Provide access to resources for education	• Links to resources available via NeLH • Links to NHS core content (e.g. online journals, health databases) • Links to e-learning content

Hypertext and creating web pages

The world wide web implements a vision that has been around since the time the NHS was founded (Naughton, 1999). Key thinkers had advanced a vision of distributed teams, sharing knowledge and documents from a pool of resources that are always available. Unlike searches performed using a relational database, the WWW uses hypertext to make associations or links within or between pages. Hypertext links are inserted into text created by the author of a page. The author decides which words are the triggers and which pages, locally or remotely stored, are the destination of links.

Web pages are expressed in hyper text markup language and, once text is marked up using HTML, it can be displayed in a web browser such as Microsoft Internet Explorer™. Creation of a web page is made easier by using software editors that allow an author to create hypertext in a similar way to creating a document using a word processor. Online tutorials in HTML include a high-quality course on the basics of creating web pages on the NCSA website. There are also numerous books on the subject. *HTML and XHTML: the definitive guide*, is a handy reference volume (Musciano and Kennedy, 2002).

The advantages of HTML over other file formats are that it is a cross-platform language, it can be created easily, it is not difficult to learn and it allows pages to be linked easily.

Unfortunately, the ease and speed with which web pages can be created and published (Griever, 2001) can mean that standard editorial practices are abandoned. Within health, where there is a professional onus for accuracy and peer review, this can be dangerous and even deadly.

Health web pages

Several surveys (Boseley, 1999; Health On the Net Foundation, 2001; BBC News, 2002) suggest that health web pages are among the most frequently accessed documents on the web. Well over half of all people with internet access use the web to search for medical information. Breast cancer is one of the most common search topics (Meric et al., 2002).

Many studies attempt to evaluate the quality of health information on the web (Silberg, Lundberg and Musacchio, 1997; Eysenbach and Köhler, 2002; Meric et al., 2002; Eysenbach et al., 2002). Many highlight problems with most sites surveyed, revealing gaps or failures in very basic areas. A literature review (Williams et al., 2002a) identifies common criteria used to assess the information quality of health websites and notes that accuracy and authority of content are particularly important in health. Silberg and colleagues (1997) set out standards that health websites should follow, now known as the 'JAMA benchmarks'. These include authorship, attribution, disclosure and currency. The Health On the Net Foundation (HONF) has a code of conduct for website authors, which contains eight principles. These include transparency of sponsorship, honesty in advertising and attribution, so it is clear where the information comes from. Health websites that follow these principles are entitled to display the HONF logo but other studies have shown that such self-regulation does not work. The DISCERN project (www.discern.org.uk/) has produced a tool to help consumers determine information quality (Charnock et al., 1999; Shepperd, Charnock and Cook, 2002; Rees, Ford and Sheard, 2002).

A systematic review of studies attempting to evaluate health-information quality on websites (Eysenbach et al., 2002) highlights gaps between health information on the web and evidence-based health knowledge. Meric et al. (2002) investigated the popularity of certain breast cancer websites. Popularity was based on results in the Google (www.google.com) and AltaVista (www.altavista.co.uk/) search engines. Google rank and the number of external websites linking to the site (found by using the link:URL search method) were used to determine the popularity of websites; JAMA benchmarks were used to assess the quality of the most popular websites. The study found no correlation between popularity of health websites and quality of content. More popular breast cancer sites were more likely to include information about ongoing trials, results of randomised controlled trials, results of other breast cancer research, information on legislation and advocacy, and information on opportunities for psychosocial adjustment. They also allowed interaction via a message board service.

Website development

The person responsible for managing a website-development project must be able to gauge how much that website will cost and how long it will take to build. PRINCE (PRojects IN a Controlled Environment) project management methodology can be applied to website-development projects (see Chapter 10). Establishing a project board, with the power to make executive decisions, lends greater weight to governance of a website project. The board should be user-heavy rather than supplier-heavy to increase the probability that the project delivers a product that meets user needs. The project manager ensures that the board's decisions are implemented and oversees the work of the project team.

Fleming (1998) identifies six stages in website development: information gathering, strategy, prototyping, implementation, launch, and maintenance and growth. AMS Technology Group (n.d.) suggests questions to inform the initial information-gathering stage:

- What is the purpose of the website?
- Who is your target audience?
- Is everyone in the organization going to have input into the website and use it to improve business processes?
- How will the website integrate with your traditional communication vehicle and marketing plans?
- What is your budget and expected return on investment?
- How will you capture information about visitors to your site? What will you do with that information?
- Who will refresh material on your website, and how? How often will this be done?
- Does your company have the operational processes in place to support the website demands and requests for information generated by the website?

Grunwald (2002) points out that the strategic phase of web development provides an opportunity to rethink the organization's whole strategic plan. When developing plans it is worth building in extra time to allow for 'iterative design'. For example, having built a prototype, you may need to rethink some aspect of your original idea. Making the Net Work has devised ten guidelines for nonprofit organizations creating a website including 'Know what you want BEFORE designing the site', 'Develop a wish list of web features' and 'Design your website from the perspective of your audience; not your organization'.

Solo professional librarians may be tasked with developing a website. Still (2003) offers much sensible advice and focuses on delivering a website that communicates the right message, meets users' needs and is presented in a simple and clear way. Larger-scale projects may require more formal project-management processes (Friedlein, 2000; Strauss and Hogan, 2001; Shelford and Remillard, 2002).

Identifying needs, testing and usability

Work by Eysenbach and Köhler (2002) examined how consumers search the web for health information. The study used unobtrusive observational techniques to study how consumers searched to find answers to common internet health questions and in-depth interviews to investigate decision-making processes and criteria for selection of a particular site. Credibility criteria emerged:

- sites from 'official' authorities
- professional layout
- understandable and professional writing
- citation of scientific references.

Specific criteria emerged that are helpful to web developers:

- accessibility
- site map
- search capabilities
- user-friendly, uncluttered, speedy interface
- ability to send e-mail to site owner
- outbound links to further recommended websites.

Williams and colleagues (2002b) used participant observation, protocol analysis and interviews to gather data about one website, Surgery Door. In contrast to the study by Eysenbach and Köhler which used 21 lay people, Williams's sample comprised 20 MSc information science students who did not regularly search the web and who had not studied medicine. The small sample size of both studies might suggest low power, however web usability guru Nielsen (2000a) argues that over 75% of a website's usability problems can be identified with only five users testing it. Such user-centred studies can be useful when assessing an existing website or those of possible competitors. The main messages from Williams and colleagues are:

- Pages should not be too crowded with text.
- Commercial features on health sites are not well received.
- A large number of contents lists, site maps and indexes do not always aid navigation.
- Avoid changes in menu structure between areas of the site.
- Avoid use of frames because the individual page cannot be bookmarked.

Usability studies can assist in the site redesign process. Fuller and Hinegardner (2001) describe a usability study to aid the redesign of the Health Sciences and Human Services Library of the University of Maryland. A first prototype was developed following suggestions and comments from a usability test. A second usability test was conducted to refine the prototype. Nielsen (1998) advises that user tests by inexperienced testers can take as long as 39 hours including planning the test, defining the tests, recruiting test users, conducting tests with five users, analysing the results and writing the report. Fuller and Hinegardner describe using a web survey but state that the response rate was statistically insignificant. Such surveys should not be used merely because they are cheap.

Williams and colleagues (2002b) offer generic advice on home-page design, based on comments on the Surgery Door home page, echoing observations by Nielsen (2000a) and Krug (2000). The home page is an important feature of any site. The name of the company or site should be very prominent and should normally appear in the upper left of the screen where it is easy to spot, although it need not be the largest design element on the page. Krug outlines why home-page design is sometimes a compromise:

- The home page is like the most expensive real-estate property and everyone with something to promote wants their piece of it.
- Everybody has an opinion about it, even the chief executive.
- Unlike lower-level pages, the home page has to appeal to all visitors.

According to Krug (2000), compromises over home-page decisions mean that the big picture is often not communicated. A home page should answer five basic questions:

- What is this?
- What can I do here?
- What do they have here?
- Why should I be here – and not somewhere else?
- Where do I start?

Website promotion and marketing

The launch of a new website is clearly the most important milestone in a development project. Following PRINCE project methodology, a communications plan will help the project manager to factor marketing costs into the financial plan. However, regardless of budget there are simple steps by which web developers can ensure that their website is found by searchers. Eysenbach and Köhler (2002) found that, when asked to find answers to specific health questions, people used general search engines instead of medical portals, medical society or library websites. They also used sub-optimal search strategies and only 35% of searches used more than one word. Participants in the study usually clicked on a resource on the first page of results, very few looked at the second page. The majority (97%) clicked on a link within the first ten results and 71% clicked on a link within the first five results. What can a web manager learn from these results?

- Ensure that a website is indexed by search engines.
- Voluntarily register your website with search engines.
- Title the pages correctly.
- Use hidden meta fields on your pages, used by search engines to index sites.

The Central Medical Library (CMK) website at the University of Ljubljana in Slovenia analysed automatically created log files to understand users' behaviour and to redesign its website (Rozic-Hristovski, Hristovski and Todorovski, 2002). Log files usually include:

• number of pages viewed
• frequency of visits to particular sites
• length of session/page view time.

Web-hosting companies often bundle statistics packages within their hosting fees but many free programs are equally as good.

Greenspun (1999) describes how log files can identify 'hidden sites', pages which do not receive maintenance that might contain out-of-date content. Log files can identify external sites that refer visitors and words used for searching in search engines. Checking such search engines can tell you how highly your website is ranked. Database-driven web applications may have statistics built in as standard reports. These could include:

• numbers of registered users in different user classes
• numbers of users signed up to e-newsletters or other content sent out (pushed) automatically to registered users
• keywords typed in the search facility.

Host-name lookup functions convert Internet Protocol (IP) addresses of machines loading a website into domain-name information, e.g. turning 18.30.0.217 into lilac.lcs.mit.edu. This can be useful in 'cleaning' log file data: removing bias in the data by stripping out details of internal users. It can also help a web manager to stratify the market by providing a human-readable indication of where visitors are coming from. Log files can be used to triangulate results from other methodologies (Williams et al., 2002a) but should be used with caution because some form of 'data cleaning' will always be required. When used in conjunction with qualitative data such statistics can help in marketing and redesigning websites.

Every web page should include metadata in the header section of the HTML source code. Hock (1999) states that title and URL are the highest value 'fields' in search-engine indexes so it is worth coming up with good descriptive titles. Other meta fields include 'description' and 'keywords'. Some search engines provide annotations or abstracts with titles in their results pages, taken from the description field. Nielsen's advice (2000b) is to keep descriptions short and, when completing the keywords field, think of as many synonyms for the topic of your page as you can.

Conclusion

A well planned and well designed website is a considerable asset for any organization. This is particularly true for healthcare organizations, given their service function and public interest in health information. Regardless of the scale of a website project, benefits can be realized from careful attention to project management, usability testing and marketing. Developing effective web pages can now be considered an essential feature in exploiting knowledge for health services.

Key points

* Health information is among the most popular content on the world wide web.
* Studies assessing the quality of health information for consumers vary greatly in methodology and rigour.
* Project-management methodologies provide a helpful framework for website development.
* Websites should be prototyped with a minimum of five testers.
* Lay searchers prefer to use general internet search engines rather than established medical databases and indexes.
* Metadata information within the web document header improves search-engine ranking.

References

AMS Technology Group (n.d.) *Building a Website Foundation*, www.amsgrp.com/webdesign.html.

BBC News (2002) Health Websites Gaining Popularity, 14 September 2002, *BBC News website*, http://news.bbc.co.uk/1/hi/health/2249606.stm.

Boseley, S. (1999) Web Life: health, *Guardian Unlimited*, (16 December), www.guardian.co.uk/Archive/Article/0,4273,3942029,00.html.

Charnock, D. et al. (1999) DISCERN: an instrument for judging the quality of written consumer health information on treatment choices, *Journal of Epidemiology and Community Health*, **53** (2), 105–11.

Eysenbach, G. and Köhler, C. (2002) How Do Consumers Search for and Appraise Health Information on the World Wide Web?: qualitative study using focus groups, usability tests, and in-depth interviews, *British Medical Journal*, **324**, 573–7.

Eysenbach, G. et al. (2002) Empirical Studies Assessing the Quality of Health Information for Consumers on the World Wide Web: a systematic review, *JAMA*, **287** (20), 2691–700.

Fleming, J. (1998) *Web Navigation: designing the user experience*, Sebastapol, CA, O'Reilly & Associates.

Friedlein, A. (2000) *Web Project Mmanagement: delivering successful commercial web sites*, San Francisco, CA, Morgan Kaufmann.

Fuller, D. M. and Hinegardner, P. G. (2001) Ensuring Quality Website Redesign: the University of Maryland's experience, *Bulletin of the Medical Library Association*, **89** (4), 339–45.

Google search engine, www.google.com/.

Greenspun, P. (1999) *Philip and Alex's Guide to Web Publishing*, San Francisco, CA, Morgan Kaufmann.

Griever, M. (2001) Build a Simple Web Site for Your Practice in Less than an Hour, *CMAJ*, **164** (6), 860.

Grunwald, T. (2002) *Planning a Web Site: navigating the maze of opportunities*, www.makingthenetwork.org/toolbox/tools/webguide.htm.

Health On the Net Foundation (2001) *Survey on the Evolution of Internet Use for Health Purposes: raw data for the survey February–March 2001*, www.hon.ch/Survey/FebMar2001/.

HONF (Health On the Net Foundation) HON Code of Conduct for Medical and Health Web Sites, www.hon.ch/HONcode/Conduct.html.

Hock, R. (1999) *The Extreme Searcher's Guide to Web Search Engines: a handbook for the serious searcher*, Medford NJ, CyberAge Books.

Making the Net Work (n d.) *10 Guidelines for Web Design: planning a site; navigating the maze of opportunities*, www.makingthenetwork.org/tools/webguide.htm.

Meric, F. et al. (2002) Breast Cancer on the World Wide Web: cross sectional survey of quality of information and popularity of websites, *British Medical Journal*, **324**, 577–81.

Musciano, C. and Kennedy, B. (2002) *HTML and XHTML: the definitive guide*, Sebastopol, CA, O'Reilly.

Naughton, J. (1999) *A Brief History of the Future: the origins of the internet*, London, Weidenfeld & Nicolson.

NCSA website, *A Beginner's Guide to HTML*, http://archive.ncsa.uiuc.edu/General/Internet/WWW/HTMLPrimerAll.html.

Nielsen, J. (1998) Cost of User Testing a Web Site, *Jakob Nielsen's Alertbox*, (3 May), www.useit.com/alertbox/980503.html.

Nielsen, J. (2000a) Why You Only Need to Test with 5 Users, *Jakob Nielsen's Alertbox*, (19 March), www.useit.com/alertbox/20000319.html.

Nielsen, J. (2000b) *Designing Web Usability: the practice of simplicity*, Indianapolis, Ind., New Riders.

Office of Government Commerce (2002) *Managing Successful Projects with PRINCE 2 CD ROM*, revised edn, London, The Stationery Office.

Rees, C. E., Ford, J. E. and Sheard, C. E. (2002) Evaluating the Reliability of DIS-CERN: a tool for assessing the quality of written patient information on treatment choices, *Patient Education and Counselling*, **47** (3), 273–5.

Rozic-Hristovski, A., Hristovski, D. and Todorovski, L. (2002) Users' Information Seeking Behavior on a Medical Library Website, *Journal of the Medical Library Association*, **90** (2), 210–17.

Shelford, T. J. and Remillard, G. A. (2002) *Real Web Project Management: case studies and best practices from the trenches*, Harlow, Addison Wesley Longman.

Shepperd, S., Charnock, D. and Cook, A. (2002) A 5-star System for Rating the Quality of Information Based on DISCERN, *Health Information and Libraries Journal*, **19** (4), 201–5.

Silberg, W. M., Lundberg, G. D. and Musacchio, R. A. (1997) Assessing, Controlling, and Assuring the Quality of Medical Information on the Internet: caveant lector et viewor – let the reader and viewer beware, *JAMA*, **277** (15), 1244–5.

Still, J. M. (2003) *The Accidental Webmaster*, Medford, NJ, Information Today Inc.

Strauss, R. and Hogan, P. (2001) *Developing Effective Websites: a project manager's guide*, Boston, MA, Focal Press.

Williams, P. et al. (2002a) Surfing for Health: user evaluation of a health information website. Part one: background and literature review, *Health Information and Libraries Journal*, **19**, 98–108.

Williams, P. et al. (2002b) Surfing for Health: user evaluation of a health information website. Part two: fieldwork, *Health Information and Libraries Journal*, **19**, 214–25.

20

Tapping into sources of research funding

Alison Winning

Introduction

Competition for external research funds is intense; even though many organizations advertise awards to support health research demand far exceeds availability. This imbalance creates an imperative for those seeking research funding to be aware of the range of funding opportunities available, the types of research funded by grant-giving organizations and the deadlines for key funding opportunities (Smith, 2000). Providing assistance to researchers in meeting these needs creates a prime opportunity for healthcare librarians to expand their role by utilizing existing skills, and indeed diversifying into new contexts, when retrieving, formatting and disseminating funding information.

Although provision of such services receives little coverage in the professional literature this is not to say that, within the UK, NHS and academic health librarians are not already providing funding-opportunity information to researchers, regularly or on an ad hoc basis. Evidence of librarians undertaking such initiatives internationally is also sparse. One paper has been published detailing the efforts of a US university to establish a dedicated joint research funding service between the health sciences library and the school of medicine (Means, 2000). This initiative is now flourishing, expanding beyond provision of funding information to incorporate support for grant writing and other functions.

Most librarians will not enjoy the luxury of developing a service dedicated solely to the provision of research-funding information. This chapter therefore seeks to support day-to-day practice by outlining practical areas for consideration when designing and delivering a funding-information service and highlighting the different types of funding available to health researchers. It also describes the main features of the major funding-information resources and illustrates various options for disseminating funding information. It concludes by presenting a case study of a librarian-led, funding-information service.

Designing and delivering a research-funding information service

The efficient and effective delivery of funding information depends on the answer to the following question: Is the right information reaching the right people at the right time?

An effective funding-information service must have clear aims and objectives defining the type of information to be delivered, the intended user group, the methods to be used and the frequency of the service. Table 20.1 highlights several considerations when planning the design and delivery of such a service. Ultimately all these factors require assessment against available individual library resources, particularly the availability of staff and time to source, format and deliver the funding information. It is also important to have funding to purchase access to fee-based funding databases, if needed.

Target audience and scope of information
Audience
Defining the intended audience is fundamental in determining the scope of a

Table 20.1   Service delivery considerations

Target audience	Will the service be intended for all or only specific healthcare professions?
Scope of information disseminated	Will the service: • disseminate opportunities from all or only specific funding organizations? • disseminate project-grant information or also educational opportunities such as postgraduate fellowships? • disseminate simply a list of grants with closing dates or also additional information such as a description of the award, etc.?
Identification of opportunities	Can you utilize information from other sources or will the information be original compilations?
Frequency and method of distribution	Electronic, print, weekly, monthly, etc.?

service and those tools that are to be utilized when collating information. The options are to provide a:

- multidisciplinary service
- profession-specific service
- subject-specific service.

There may be valid reasons for defining specific audiences but, in the current climate of NHS and academic collaboration in research, it may be prudent not to restrict the audience. Within certain NHS trusts and academic organizations, research and development (R&D) departments may provide funding information. These departments are aware of the research needs within their organizations and should be able to advise on appropriate audiences and suitable scope for the service. Librarians may be able to support organizations with tailored searches of funding-information resources. Such a *reactive* service is aimed at those researchers actively searching funding for a particular project or proposal. This is in contrast to *proactive* funding-information services that disseminate information as a prompt to researchers who create a proposal in response.

One determining factor in identifying a target audience is the anticipated workload. A subject-specific service is perhaps associated with the highest workload, because librarians need to search the resources using relevant keywords to identify opportunities relevant to the subject, then format and disseminate the information. Profession-specific services could be based on disseminating funding alerts produced by professional bodies and societies of that profession. For example, if providing a service particularly to nurses, a librarian might use funding information hosted by the Royal College of Nursing (RCN) at: www.man.ac.uk/rcn/ukwide/ukrfund.html (O'Carroll and McMahon, 1999). If the relevant body or society does not offer this service the librarian will have to search the resources for relevant opportunities, format and disseminate them.

Providing a multidisciplinary service may involve the librarian in sourcing original information from funding resources; however, organizations already exist which are sourcing and disseminating funding information on a much greater scale than many libraries can manage individually. One such organization is RDInfo which harnesses and disseminates multidisciplinary funding-opportunity information (Parker-Jones et al., 1998; Lester and Parker-Jones, 1999). The service is web based and information can be sourced by interrogation of the online database or by receiving funding alerts via e-mail. In supporting a multidisciplinary service the librarian could simply disseminate the weekly RDInfo alerts.

Scope

Requests for funding information typically have one of two purposes: service/practice development (e.g. funding to support a clinical trial) or professional/personal development (e.g. course bursaries). Tables 20.2 and 20.3 highlight key features of these types of funding.

Table 20.2 Service/practice-development funding

Programme grants	Support for long-term large-scale research investigating a set of interrelated questions, e.g. Research into Ageing www.ageing.org/research/index.html
Project grants	Support for discrete projects which are seeking to answer a single question. They are typically smaller in scale, time-frame and financial require-ments than programme grants, e.g. Alzheimer's Society Project Grants http://212.240.197.190/
Equipment grants	Support to purchase equipment which will aid the running of projects, e.g. Wellcome Trust Equipment Grants www.wellcome.ac.uk/en/1/biosfgunkfunequ.html
Pump-priming grants	Funding for preparatory work such as pilot studies, e.g. Yorkshire Cancer Research Pump Priming Grants www.ycr.org.uk

Table 20.3 Professional/personal-development funding

Fellowships	Support for individuals to undertake a period of concentrated research activity. They may be pre-doctoral or post-doctoral, clinical or non-clinical, e.g. Medical Research Council Clinical Training Fellowship www.mrc.ac.uk/index/funding/funding-personal_awards/funding-fellowships/funding-clinical_fellowships.htm

Continued on next page

Table 20.3 *Continued*

Studentships	Support for pre-doctoral researchers who undergo a research training programme leading to a PhD, e.g. Diabetes UK PhD Studentship www.diabetes.org.uk/research/grants/ types.htm#studentships
Postgraduate bursary/grant	Funding for one or both of the following: course fees and living costs, e.g. Arthritis Research Campaign Postgraduate Training Bursary www.arc.org.uk/research/forms/ postgradburs.htm
Seminar/conference attendance	Often difficult to obtain but professional bodies, royal colleges or societies may be likely sources of funding, e.g. British Geriatrics Society Nurses Study Grants www.bgs.org.uk/grants/annette/ granttest.htm#nurse
Travel awards/fellowships	Funding for travel to other areas to explore new initiatives relating to a field of work, e.g. Florence Nightingale Foundation Travel Scholarships www.florence-nightingale-foundation.org.uk/
Prizes	Acknowledgement of the work of an individual/team, e.g. Infection Control Nurses Association 3M HealthCare Awards www.icna.co.uk/awards/award_3m.asp

Regardless of your ultimate definition of the target audience and the scope of the service, it is important to be explicit and consistent so that users know what they can expect from the service. The value of providing a subject or profession specific service should be considered in the light of time and resource constraints. Unless specific inclusion criteria are used to ensure that relevant opportunities are not omitted it is perhaps wiser to include all funding opportunities relevant to your organization. Such an approach will increase the volume of information disseminated, requiring application of some method of organization and classification.

Depth of information

Unless you are providing a specialist service your likely role will be to disseminate key information which allows users to decide whether they are interested in the opportunity and provides them with a means of following this up for further information. Key information includes:

- funding organization
- title of award
- closing date
- URL of further information.

Dedicated services may provide supplementary information, which allows the researcher to screen the funding opportunities before accessing information only for those that are deemed relevant. Extra information includes:

- amount of money on offer
- exclusion and inclusion criteria
- duration of project.

Identifying opportunities

Resources

RDInfo is widely regarded as the premier resource for funding information within the NHS and would therefore be a key constituent for any healthcare librarian who wishes to provide a funding-information alert service. Librarians wishing to support on-demand comprehensive searching of funding resources may require additional access to several fee-based resources. Table 20.4 highlights the major resources which are generally accessible within the NHS and academia.

Comparison of the resources in Table 20.4 reveals much overlap in terms of the scope of the individual resources with respect to included organizations and the purpose of their funding. The Grant Register and organizations listed within the Association of Medical Research Charities (AMRC) have more idiosyncratic purposes. The AMRC lists solely funding from charities while the Grants Register lists only professional/personal-development funding opportunities. Another variation involves the cost of funding resources. RDInfo is probably the most widely used of the resources because of its comprehensive coverage and free availability. ResearchFortnight includes opportunities from other disciplines outside health and includes news and analysis of research policy in each issue. If these are irrelevant to your organization the additional cost

Table 20.4 Sources of funding information

	RDInfo	COS	AMRC	Research Fortnight	Grants register
Purpose of funding					
Service/practice development	•	•	•	•	○
Professional/personal development	•	•	•	•	•
Organizations					
Research councils	•	•	○	•	•
Industry	•	•	○	•	•
Charities	•	•	•	•	•
Government	•	•	○	•	•
EU	•	•	○	•	•
Access	Web 1	Web 2	Web 3	Web 4	Print
NHS	•	○	•	•	•
University	•	•	•	•	•
Cost	Free	Contact COS	Free	Paper edition £495 Online edition £895	£113
Features					
Browsing	•	○	•	•	•
Searching	•	•	■	•	○
Daily/weekly updating	Weekly	Daily	Unknown	Fortnightly in print	Annually
E-mail alerts	•	•	○	•	•

Key
• Available/Included
○ Not available/not included

1 www.rdinfo.org.uk
2 www.cos.com
3 www.amrc.org.uk
4 www.researchresearch.com

may not be justified. Community of Science (COS) has a range of associated features such as expert registers; however, it is available only within academic communities and, as it is typically purchased at an institutional level, its cost is not openly known. Coverage is international but there is a strong US bias. It is probably best to supplement this with specific UK-based resources when seeking UK opportunities.

Methods of identifying opportunities

E-mail alerts (Zimmerman et al., 2003), active searching and browsing resources are key methods of identification. As Table 20.4 demonstrates, RDInfo, COS and ResearchFortnight all offer e-mail alerting services. Librarians can receive these alerts, typically on a weekly basis, and then simply disseminate them within their own organization. Using this method all new opportunities and changes of detail can be identified. These are extremely useful yet some opportunities may not be identified within an appropriate timeframe if one relies solely on alert updates. Every year major funding organizations typically repeat funding schemes with closing dates falling in the same month each year, e.g the Medical Research Council. Sometimes the closing date is not confirmed until a few months before the actual deadline and, depending on the award, this may not leave enough time to develop and submit a proposal in the absence of prior knowledge of the expected date. Browsing resources for agreed key opportunities up to six months in advance allows such opportunities to be identified thus enabling researchers to plan their proposal submissions. In identifying such key opportunities it is useful for a librarian to work with researchers to collate a list of target organizations. These can then be placed in a reference calendar for consultation by researchers.

Frequency and method of dissemination

If a service is to remain current it is advisable to disseminate weekly alerts. Ultimately, however, the frequency will be determined by the resources available to provide the service. The quickest and easiest method of dissemination is e-mail. Alternatives include intranet postings, inclusion in organization-wide information bulletins, and print distribution via noticeboards, libraries, audit, R&D, clinical-effectiveness departments and individuals.

One highly visible method is for the librarian to attend research group or committee meetings to disseminate funding information verbally. Such a method is more demanding because the librarian is providing an 'expert' service and is thus expected to have in-depth knowledge of the funding opportunities, more so than where remote electronic dissemination is used. Regardless of the method used librarians can become valuable members of the research team. Seeking out funding opportunities is vital to sustain ongoing research within an organization. A comprehensive service that is dedicated to providing this information enables researchers to focus their time on developing proposals and submissions. Librarians who choose to develop their skills further and become expert on the intricacies of the application processes for various funding bodies will also be better able to support researchers with their applications.

Funding searches

Providing a search service differs from the alert service in that detailed information is required when matching a proposal to an appropriate source of funding. The librarian then interrogates the resources to identify possible sources of funding. Essentially the type of research to be performed and the sector/profession/speciality within which it will take place need to be clarified. Tables 20.2 and 20.3 (pages 228–9) summarize the different types while Table 20.5 highlights the sectors and specialities which may be involved.

Table 20.5 Sectors and specialities

Sector	Profession	Speciality
Primary care	Nursing	Specialities within all of the professions, e.g. respiratory
Secondary care	Allied health professions	
Pre-hospital/emergency care	Medicine	
Social services	Health services management	

Librarians may wish to elicit more information in order to further refine the search such as illustrated in Table 20.6.

Table 20.6 Refining your search

Methodology	Certain organizations restrict streams of funding for specific methods, e.g. funding for clinical trials only
Amount of money required	If a funding body is offering only £1000 and your client is seeking £10,000, is this opportunity relevant?
Duration of funding	What is the duration of the project and will the funding support this?
Professional bodies/societies	Certain pockets of funding are available to members of certain societies.

The following case study, taken from the author's personal experience, is used to exemplify issues relating to the provison of funding information as included within a specialist academic information resource.

Case study

Aim

To implement a health-research funding-information service within a UK academic school of health research.

Objectives

* Disseminate project and professional development funding opportunities electronically to academic and NHS researchers.
* Undertake focused searches of the funding opportunity resources on behalf of researchers.

Implementation

The project comprised three services:

* funding search service
* weekly/monthly funding alerts
* reference calendar of opportunities.

Funding search service

Users included both academic staff and NHS-based researchers. The academic staff seemed to have greater awareness of the funding organizations available to them and the types of research they funded, hence did not use the funding search service as regularly as the NHS users. When a funding search was requested a form was completed providing details of:

* The requester:
  — name, organization, address, etc.
  — membership of any professional body
  — date for when the results were required
  — preferred format of results, print or electronic.
* Project details:
  — title of project, methodology, amount of money required and duration of project, purpose of money (e.g. equipment).

Core resources, utilized during a search, comprised:
* RDInfo
* Refund (now replaced by Refund/Community of Science)

- Department of Health R&D pages
- AMRC
- Wisdom (now defunct)
- MRC website
- PPP Foundation (now Health Foundation).

The search results provided details of the funding body, the award name, closing date and contact details of the funder. These were returned within a timeframe as negotiated with the requester. Maximum turnaround time was two weeks.

To advertise the funding service, and raise awareness of the funding resources available, a promotional leaflet was produced and distributed within the school and throughout the NHS region.

Funding alerts

On a weekly basis core resources were scanned for opportunities relevant primarily to the school of health research in which the service was based, but also for other key opportunities relevant to the NHS. The alert service was not comprehensive because only major opportunities of relevance to the NHS were identified. Smaller more specialized opportunities were not detailed. Users were therefore directed to RDInfo for their other needs.

Alerts were posted on the school's website and an e-mail alert was distributed to notify members of a funding mailing list, created to support the service, that the pages had been updated. The website was an extremely basic text-based tool which linked the details of the awards to the relevant organizational website. Attitudes to the web pages varied because many users would have preferred to have all of the information about each opportunity available on these pages without having to follow links to other organizations' sites.

Weekly alerts were collated monthly and published on the website. Monthly alerts were distributed in a print format, detailing relevant URLs, to those users who wished to display them in their departments and disseminate them to interested parties who did not have access to e-mail. At monthly research committee and school board meetings, the librarian verbally presented monthly alerts to research leads and heads of section. This was to reinforce awareness of key opportunities identified via the weekly alerts rather than to present new information.

Reference calendar

As research proposals are often drafted months ahead, in anticipation of upcoming awards, a calendar detailing opportunities 12 months in advance was also available on the website. This contained 'guesstimated' closing dates of opportunities up to 12 months in advance. Key opportunities were identified through discussion with the research staff.

Conclusion

This chapter has identified an area for potential development of the librarian's role in exploiting the knowledge base to support health researchers. It has also illustrated how implementation of a health research funding information service can operate at many levels, from identifying key resources such as RDInfo and promoting their use to providing a multifaceted service as detailed in the case study. Detailed within the chapter are examples of funding information resources, and methods of delivering a funding service, to provide a reference source to support local developments in supporting research within your organization. This source can be further expanded, depending on your organization's needs and interests and information that you encounter as you implement your service.

Librarians should not underestimate the importance of a funding-information service to a research team or their potential to develop skills in this area. Provision of such services provides the librarian with an expert role which can be developed to varying degrees and which will come to be viewed as an expert resource by your organization and its researchers.

Key points

- Librarians have a great opportunity to support research within their organization by utilizing existing skills and developing new skills and expertise in this field.
- Discuss the needs of your organization with key figures involved in research; utilize these discussions to develop clear aims and objectives for your service.
- Collate a list of key funding-information resources to which you have access, for your own and your users' benefit.
- Reach the right people at the right time; implement a multi-method of dissemination throughout your organization; be consistent with the frequency of your bulletins.
- Promote and advertise the role of the library in identifying research funding.

References

Lester, N. and Parker-Jones, C. (1999) A Digest of Research Funding and Training Opportunities, *Nursing Standard*, **13** (26), 31–2.

Means, M. L. (2000) The Research Funding Service: a model for expanded library services, *Bulletin of the Medical Library Association*, **88** (2), 178–86.

O'Carroll, D. and McMahon, A. (1999) Research Funding, *Nursing Standard*, **14** (11), 31.

Parker-Jones, C. et al. (1998) RDInfo: a digest of medical research funding information – reveal the design of a new compendium, *British Journal of Healthcare Computing and Information Management*, **15** (10), 18–20.

Smith, M. (2000) Making the Most of Research Funding Opportunities, *Nurse Researcher*, **8** (1), 4–18.

Zimmerman, E. et al. (2003) KeyMail: select dissemination of information on research funding opportunities to university scientists, *Journal of Research Administration*, **34** (1), 3–7.

21

Supporting syntheses of the literature

Janette Boynton

Introduction

Systematic reviews, health-technology assessments and guidelines are central in the drive towards improving the quality of patient care. They support decision making in the health service, providing evidence about the effectiveness of treatments and about how the delivery and organization of services can be improved. This chapter outlines the major organizations involved in these activities before paying attention to the role of the information specialist in supporting research synthesis. Question formulation, recognizing the 'best' evidence to answer a question, identifying sources to search and searching information sources effectively are discussed and the necessity for teamwork emphasized. In conclusion, key challenges of the information specialist's role, and initiatives taken to address them, are discussed.

The NHS quality agenda

Quality is at the top of the NHS agenda (Great Britain. Department of Health, 2000a). Government policy in recent years indicates a commitment to modernizing the NHS and improving the quality of patient care (Great Britain. Department of Health, 1997, 1998a, 2000b; Scottish Office, 1997; Scottish Executive Health Department, 2000, 2003). Central to delivering this agenda is research evidence about the effectiveness of treatments and how the delivery and organization of services can improve patient care and ensure better outcomes (Great Britain. Department of Health, 1998b).

Systematic reviews, health-technology assessments and clinical guidelines (from now on referred to collectively as reviews) underpin evidence-based decision making. They reduce large quantities of primary information into 'palatable pieces for digestion' by decision makers (Mulrow, 1995). More importantly, they produce reliable results upon which to base decisions, by using robust processes to locate, appraise and synthesize research evidence (Song et al., 2000). Table 21.1 lists organizations that undertake reviews.

Systematic reviews

Systematic reviews differ from traditional narrative reviews in seeking to identify, appraise and synthesize all studies on a specific clinical question (Chalmers and Altman, 1995; Cook, Mulrow and Haynes, 1997). Systematic reviews can use quantitative (including meta-analysis) or qualitative methodologies to synthesize the results of individual studies.

The Cochrane Collaboration and the Campbell Collaboration are committed to preparing, maintaining and promoting access to systematic reviews. The Cochrane Collaboration was established in the UK in 1992 under the NHS R&D Programme and it is now a major international initiative (Clarke and Oxman, 2003). The Campbell Collaboration, launched in February 2000, and modelled on its sister organization, undertakes systematic reviews in social welfare, education and criminal justice (Schuerman et al., 2002). The NHS Centre for Reviews and Dissemination (NHS CRD) was established in 1994, also as part of the NHS R&D Programme. It specifically aims to provide information on the effectiveness of treatments and the delivery and organization of healthcare.

Health-technology assessment

Health-technology assessment (HTA) is a 'multidisciplinary field of policy analysis that studies the medical, social, ethical and economic implications of the development, diffusion and use of health technology' (INAHTA, 2000). 'Health technology' encompasses drugs, devices, techniques and procedures. HTAs may include systematic reviews or meta-analyses, but also consider the wider social and economic implications of the introduction of a new technology (www.nelh.nhs.uk/systematic.asp).

Both the National Institute for Clinical Excellence (NICE) and NHS Quality Improvement Scotland provide guidance for decision makers based on HTAs. Other countries have HTA bodies with most being members of the International Network of Agencies for Health Technology Assessment (INAHTA) and/or the European Collaboration for Health Technology Assessment (ECHTA). Health Technology Assessment international (HTAi), launched in June 2003, similarly serves the HTA community.

Clinical guidelines

Clinical guidelines provide appropriate treatment and care recommendations for patients with specific diseases and conditions. Historically, the royal colleges produced guidelines but in 1993 the Scottish colleges established the Scottish Intercollegiate Guidelines Network (SIGN) to take on this role. More recently NICE has created national collaborating centres to develop guidelines, most of which harness expertise based in the royal colleges. Both SIGN and NICE prepare evidence-based guidelines, developed from a systematic review of the scientific evidence, making them less susceptible to bias.

Table 21.1 Organizations undertaking systematic reviews, HTAs and guidelines

Organization	Web address (as at June 2003)
Campbell Collaboration	www.campbellcollaboration.org/
Cochrane Collaboration	www.cochrane.org/
ECHTA	www.ecahi.org/
HTAi	www.htai.org/
INAHTA	www.inahta.org/
NHS CRD	www.york.ac.uk/inst/crd/
NHS Quality Improvement Scotland	www.nhshealthquality.org/
NICE	www.nice.org.uk/
SIGN	www.sign.ac.uk/

The role of the information specialist

> A comprehensive, unbiased search is one of the key differences between a systematic review and a traditional review.
> (Clarke and Oxman, 2003)

Information specialists are integral to review teams, alongside health-service researchers, clinicians, statisticians and economists. They are central to the first step of the process: the comprehensive identification of studies to answer the review question(s). While other team members may have experience of searching, the skills required to provide information support for a review are highly specialized. Literature searches need to demonstrate an understanding of the 'bewildering array' of information sources to be used to answer clinical questions (Booth, 2000), and of their idiosyncratic indexing processes. A systematic literature search includes identification of previous reviews, scoping searches and retrieval of primary studies.

Identifying previous reviews

The decision to undertake a review is based, in part, on a preliminary evaluation of the evidence base. Has this question already been answered? If not, can an answerable question be formulated? Is there a reasonable evidence base? Can a clear answer be produced within a reasonable timeframe? (Health Technology Board for Scotland (HTBS), 2001). The information specialist supports this preliminary review by searching for previous systematic reviews, HTAs, guidelines and other evidence-based reports. Previous reviews may indicate whether an answerable question can be formulated and the nature of the evidence base.

Several resources disseminate information from completed and ongoing systematic reviews or HTAs. Systematic reviews prepared and maintained by the Cochrane Collaboration are accessible via the Cochrane Database of Systematic Reviews (CDSR), part of the Cochrane Library. NHS CRD maintains the Database of Abstracts of Reviews of Effects (DARE) containing records of quality-assessed reviews. The Health Technology Assessment (HTA) Database indexes HTAs produced by members of INAHTA. CDSR and DARE provide good starting points for identifying reviews, but gaps in their coverage relate to both subject and time period. Some subjects will require searches of relevant bibliographic databases, journals and websites. The TRIP database (TRIP), a meta-search engine providing hyper-linked access to high-quality medical information, may be useful in consolidating such information.

Ongoing review work is indexed in the CDSR and the HTA database. In addition, the National Research Register, which includes the NHS CRD Register of Reviews Database, covers ongoing research. The NHS Trusts Clinical Trials Register went live in Summer 2003. It will register all randomized controlled trials (RCTs) carried out in England where research costs have been met by the NHS.

The best source of information on 'quality evaluated' guidelines is the National Guideline Clearinghouse. This US-based database includes guidelines from most leading guideline organizations worldwide. UK guidelines can be identified through the National electronic Library for Health (NeLH) Guidelines Finder. Additional information on guidelines is found via the recently established Guidelines International Network (GIN).

If the review is to include an economic evaluation the NHS Economic Evaluation Database (NHS EED), a database of quality-assessed economic evaluations produced by NHS CRD, and the Health Economic Evaluations Database (HEED), produced by the Office of Health Economics, provide the best starting point.

Scoping searches

'Scoping searches establish the feasibility of a review question and investigate how searching and appraisal can be operationalised' (Booth and Fry-Smith, 2003). Focused searches across the Cochrane Central Register of Controlled Trials (CENTRAL), MEDLINE and EMBASE for general medical issues, CINAHL for nursing and allied health issues and PsycINFO for psychology and the psychological aspects of healthcare will assist in evaluating the evidence base (Glanville, 2001).

Scoping searches indicate the volume and quality of literature on a topic. They are used to develop the research protocol: in formulating the question(s), defining inclusion and exclusion criteria, planning the methodology and setting timelines. Scoping searches also indicate how much the review may cost in terms of database searches, interlibrary loans, translations and staff time (Booth and Fry-Smith, 2003).

Identifying primary studies

Once the feasibility of a review has been established the next stage, and the most time-consuming for the information specialist, is to identify primary studies. Aiming to identify all potentially relevant studies for inclusion in the review reduces biases known to influence their conclusions (Fry-Smith and Gold, 2000). Studies indicating that a treatment works are more likely to be published, more likely to be published in English and more likely to be indexed in a major bibliographic database (Song et al., 2000; Egger et al., 2003). Such 'dissemination' biases (Song et al., 2000) as publication bias, language bias and database bias suggest that reviews based only on studies that are easy to locate will overestimate the efficacy of treatment. See Figure 21.1.

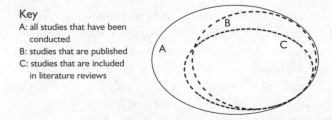

Key
A: all studies that have been conducted
B: studies that are published
C: studies that are included in literature reviews

Figure 21.1 Many completed studies may not be published and published studies may not be included in literature reviews
Reproduced from Song et al. (2000) with kind permission from the National Coordinating Centre for Health Technology Assessment

Snowball (2002) proposes a four-step framework to minimize bias in the search process:

- formulate clear search question(s)
- recognize the 'best' evidence to answer the question
- identify the most likely sources to search
- search information sources effectively.

Formulating clear search question(s)

Question formulation is fundamental to the review process. Well structured questions guide the review, defining the inclusion and exclusion criteria, the search strategy to identify primary studies, and data to be extracted from each study (Counsell, 1997). Typically, questions originally given for a review are poorly formulated. Counsell shows how a poorly formulated question, e.g. 'What are the best treatments for preventing relapse in alcohol dependence?', can be turned into a clearly formulated, well articulated question. This will contain all four parts of its 'anatomy' (Richardson et al., 1995) and might look like: 'In alcohol dependence (patient or problem being addressed), is acamprosate (intervention or exposure being considered) or naltrexone (comparison intervention or exposure) more effective for preventing relapse (outcomes of interest)?' Reviews with multiple questions similarly require that each question is broken down into its constituents to ensure comprehensive searching.

Recognizing the 'best' evidence to answer the question

Once questions are formulated the review team must agree on the study design(s) that provide the 'best' evidence to answer the questions. Most clinical questions involve therapy and prevention, diagnosis, aetiology and causation, prognosis and natural history, economics or qualitative research (McKibbon, 1999). Different clinical questions require different research methods, or study designs (Paisley, 2000). For reviews of therapeutic interventions, RCTs represent the highest level of evidence. For reviews of other areas, cohort studies or case-control studies may represent the 'best' evidence. To provide the least biased answer to a question, a review should include studies that use the 'strongest design which is possible, practical and ethical' (Sutherland, 2001).

Different questions that could be posed for alcohol dependence are provided in Table 21.2.

Table 21.2 Different types of clinical questions

Type of clinical question	Example question
Therapy	In alcohol dependence, is acamprosate or naltrexone more effective for preventing relapse?
Diagnosis	What is the accuracy of screening for alcohol problems in primary care?
Aetiology	What are the environmental risk factors associated with binge drinking in college students?
Prognosis	What is the long-term prognosis of patients with alcoholic cardiomyopathy following total abstinence?
Economics	Are brief interventions cost effective for problem drinkers?
Qualitative	What are adolescents' perceptions of parental alcoholism?

The information specialist needs to work closely with other members of the review team, to identify the type of question(s) to be addressed by the review and to identify those study designs that provide the 'best' evidence.

Identifying the most likely sources to search

Having formulated well-structured questions and reached consensus on study design, the following sources may be useful in identifying primary studies. Bibliographic databases detail the source, and often provide abstracts, of published material. While MEDLINE and EMBASE are the largest general medical databases, more specific health-related databases include CINAHL and the British Nursing Index (nursing), PsycINFO (psychology and psychological aspects of related disciplines) and AMED (allied and complementary medicine). If review question(s) can be answered by RCTs then CENTRAL is the best starting point. Directories of databases, such as the Gale Directory (http://library.dialog.com/bluesheets/html/bl0230.html), can help in selecting appropriate databases. Increasingly, publishers and database suppliers provide access to packages of e-journals, or full text 'databases'. Some databases, rather than being subject-specific, index a specific type of material; for example, conference proceedings in the Index to Conference Proceedings and Web of Science Proceedings and dissertations in the Digital Dissertations and Index to Theses.

Registers of research cover research funded by a particular body and/or research on a specific topic (e.g. the Medical Research Council's Funded Projects Database, the National Research Register, cancer.gov). Such registers prospectively register trials, making it possible to identify ongoing research or completed research that has never been published. The metaRegister of Controlled Trials (mRCT) provides a single interface to the major research registers.

If time permits it may be pertinent to handsearch key journals. This involves checking a journal from cover to cover, reading every article for relevance (Lefebvre and Clarke, 2001). Two recent studies suggest that handsearching, for RCTs, is not very effective (Helmer et al., 2001; Savoie et al., 2003). This testifies to the success of the Cochrane Collaboration, in improving the indexing of RCTs in MEDLINE and establishing CENTRAL.

Interested parties, such as experts in the field, researchers and manufacturers, should be contacted to identify unpublished clinical and cost-effectiveness information that is not in the public domain. They may also supply information about current service structure and emerging developments and about the experiences of users and patient-focused outcomes (HTBS, 2002a, 2002b, 2002c). OMNI (Organising Medical Networked Information) and NMAP (Nursing, Midwifery and Allied Health Professions) provide internet subject gateways to high-quality healthcare information. Searches of the internet using Google, AltaVista, etc. may identify additional leads. In addition, the websites of manufacturers, professional bodies, patient and voluntary organizations may be visited for information.

Searching information sources effectively

When constructing search strategies it is necessary to return to the anatomy of the question and to translate the natural language of the question(s) into terms that can be used to search databases and websites. Searches to identify primary studies often forfeit precision (the proportion of retrieved studies that are relevant) for sensitivity (the proportion of relevant studies that are identified), in attempting to minimize bias. Maximizing sensitivity will require the following:

* to allow for variance in natural language, all synonyms for search terms should be identified
* to overcome indexing errors, subject headings *and* free text terms should be used
* to allow for variant spellings and word-endings, truncation and wildcard facilities should be used
* proximity operators can be used to combine two or more free-text words to allow for intervening words.

For the review question: 'In alcohol dependence, is acamprosate or naltrexone more effective for preventing relapse?' the question would translate to terms listed in Table 21.3.

Table 21.3 Search terms for a review on alcohol dependence

Population	Intervention	Comparison	Outcome
Alcoholism/	Taurine	Naltrexone/	Temperance/
Alcohol drinking/	acamprosate.tw.	natrexone.tw.	temperance.tw.
alcoholic?.tw.	campral.tw.	trexan.tw.	sobriety.tw.
alcoholism.tw.			((control$ or reduc$
dipsomania$.tw.			or restrict$) adj2
			drink$).tw.

Search terms and syntax are for MEDLINE (Ovid interface)

Subject headings can be identified from indexing tools or by looking at how relevant papers are indexed. Most subject headings should also be searched as free text. Additional free-text terms may be identified from relevant papers or by consulting experts. Once subject headings and free-text terms are identified they can be combined using Boolean logic. A combined strategy is presented in Figure 21.2.

1	Alcoholism/	11	Naltrexone/
2	Alcohol drinking/	12	naltrexone.tw.
3	alcoholic?.tw.	13	trexan.tw.
4	alcoholism.tw.	14	or/11-13
5	dipsomania$.tw.	15	Temperance/
6	or/1-5	16	temperance.tw.
7	Taurine/	17	sobriety.tw.
8	acamprosate.tw.	18	((control$ or reduc$ or restrict$)
9	campral.tw.		adj2 drink$).tw.
10	or/7-9	19	or/15-18
		20	6 and 10 and 14 and 19

Figure 21.2 Search strategy for a review on alcohol dependence

It may be necessary to use different permutations of sets to ensure that maximum sensitivity is achieved. Some questions may have only two parts: there may be no comparator, or no single comparator, and all outcomes may be of interest.

When restricting a search by study design, methodological or quality filters can be used to retrieve 'best' evidence (Paisley, 2000). Filters combine search terms to 'filter' the literature for high-quality studies using either the study design (e.g. randomized controlled trial, cohort study) or methodological criteria (e.g. blinding, sensitivity and specificity) as indicators of study quality. Filters are combined with a subject search to limit results to high-quality studies.

Haynes et al. (1994) developed optimal search strategies for identifying clinically sound studies in MEDLINE. Other filters exist for RCTs (Dickersin, Scherer and Lefebvre, 1995), systematic reviews (White et al., 2001) and evidence-based medicine (Harrison, 1997). In addition, filters exist for economic evaluations (McKibbon, 1999; http://agatha.york.ac.uk/nfaq2.htm; www.sign.ac.uk/methodology/filters.html) and qualitative research (McKibbon, 1999; Grant, 2000, 2001).

Development of a search strategy is iterative. It requires trial searches, examination and discussion of the results with the review team and consultation with experts in the field (Glanville, 2001). Table 21.4 lists web addresses for some major databases and search engines.

Table 21.4 Web addresses for databases and search engines

Database/search engine	Web address (as at June 2003)
AltaVista	http://uk.altavista.com/
Cochrane Library (includes CDSR, CENTRAL, DARE, HTA database, NHS EED database)	www.nelh.nhs.uk/cochrane.asp
Google	www.google.com
Guidelines International Network	www.g-i-n.net/
MRC Funded Projects	http://fundedresearch.cos.com/MRC/
mRCT	www.controlled-trials.com/mrct/
National Guideline Clearinghouse	www.guideline.gov/
National Research Register	www.update-software.com/National/
NeLH Guidelines Finder	www.nelh.nhs.uk/guidelinesfinder/
NHS CRD website (includes DARE, HTA database, NHS EED database)	http://agatha.york.ac.uk/welcome.htm
NMAP	http://nmap.ac.uk/
OMNI	http://omni.ac.uk/
TRIP	www.tripdatabase.com/

All other databases discussed in this chapter are only available on subscription

Beyond searching

Information support extends beyond the literature search to include systematic handling of results to ensure that inclusion or exclusion of studies can be accounted for subsequently. Many organizations use bibliographic-management software, such as Reference Manager, EndNote or Procite, to manage this process. Search results are added to the bibliographic software and passed to members of the review team for selection. Once selection is complete full text is acquired from sources such as the British Library, the BMA library or, increasingly, from the internet.

Systematic searching requires that strategies are recorded and then detailed in the review report. This is a key responsibility of the information specialist. The validity of the review will be assessed on whether it includes all relevant studies, or at least an unbiased sample of relevant studies (Egger et al., 2003). The information specialist is often involved in reference checking and in compiling lists of included and excluded studies.

Challenges for the information specialist

Systematically and comprehensively identifying all studies raises several methodological challenges:

- *Publication bias* – a longstanding problem that continues to hinder the comprehensive identification of relevant studies. Proposed solutions include international registers of clinical trials and other types of studies (Dickersin et al., 1987; Song et al. 2000), but progress is slow.
- *Time versus quality trade-off* – as reviewers face increasing pressure to produce high-quality products in ever-shorter periods of time. Empirical research to identify those review components that particularly influence the bottom line is now urgently needed (Taylor, 2002). Given both time and costs involved, this applies equally to the identification of studies (Booth, 2003; Egger et al., 2003)
- *Complexity of review questions* – as reviews become more methodologically complex, they seek to answer multiple questions and use a variety of evidence. Honest, Bachmann and Kahn (2003) conclude that information support for a review with multiple questions, though complex, remains possible with concerted effort.
- *Widening perspectives* – as research focuses on users and providers of services (Hawker et al. 2002), questions about patient and practitioner perspectives, attitudes and beliefs are increasingly asked. The evidence required is qualitative in nature and difficult to locate (Dixon-Woods, Fitzpatrick and

Roberts, 2001; Evans, 2002; Hawker et al. 2002). Retrieval and indexing issues associated with qualitative research have not enjoyed similar scrutiny to quantitative information (Booth, 2001; Dixon-Woods, Fitzpatrick and Roberts, 2001) but this is being addressed.

Conclusion

'Systematic reviews [health-technology assessments and guidelines] have found an important role in health services research, and the growing interest in evidence based approaches to decision making make it likely that their use will increase' (Petticrew, 2001, 99). NICE and NHS Quality Improvement Scotland lead the way in providing evidence-based guidance and advice to improve patient care. The information specialist is central to such bodies: first, to avoid duplication of effort; second, to establish the feasibility of the review; and finally, to minimize the potential for bias. This final step is time consuming and involves question formulation, identification of 'best' evidence, identification of sources and effective searching of those sources.

Given the need for timeliness in producing reviews and the increasing complexity of review questions, the methodology of the review process needs to be revisited. Information specialists require resolution of issues about the most effective ways to deal with publication bias, about whether the benefits of comprehensive literature searches outweigh the costs and how searching can be optimized for reviews with multiple questions drawing on different types of evidence.

Key points

- The growth in importance of reviews, as an aid to decision making, has created considerable opportunities for information specialists.
- Information specialists are integral members of review teams alongside health-service researchers, clinicians, statisticians and economists.
- 'Identification of previous reviews' and 'scoping searches' are necessary to avoid duplication of effort and to establish the feasibility of a review.
- Searches for primary studies should be comprehensive and unbiased. Questions need to be clearly formulated and the 'best' evidence for answering the question agreed, prior to identifying the sources to search.
- Empirical research is needed to answer methodological questions, and to provide an evidence base for issues relating to information retrieval.

References

Booth, A. (2000) Selecting Appropriate Resources. In Booth, A. and Walton, G. (eds), *Managing Knowledge in Health Services*, London, Library Association Publishing.

Booth, A. (2001) *Cochrane or Cock-eyed: how should we conduct systematic reviews of qualitative research?*, presented at Qualitative Evidence-based Practice Conference, Coventry University, 14–16 May.

Booth, A. and Fry-Smith, A. (2003) Developing the Research Question, *Etext on Health Technology Assessment (HTA) information resources*, www.nlm.nih.gov/nichsr/ehta/chapter1.html.

Booth, A. (2003) In Search of the Evidence, *Health Information and Libraries Journal*, **20** (2), 116–18.

Chalmers, I. and Altman, D. G. (eds) (1995) *Systematic Reviews*, London, BMJ Publishing Group.

Clarke, M. and Oxman, A. D. (eds) (2003) *Cochrane Reviewers' Handbook 4.1.6*, www.cochrane.dk/cochrane/handbook/handbook.htm.

Cook, D. J., Mulrow, C. D. and Haynes, R. B. (1997) Systematic Reviews: synthesis of best evidence for clinical decisions, *Annals of Internal Medicine*, **126** (5), 376–80.

Counsell, C. (1997) Formulating Questions and Locating Primary Studies for Inclusion in Systematic Reviews, *Annals of Internal Medicine*, **127** (5), 380–7.

Dickersin, K. et al. (1987) Publication Bias and Clinical Trials, *Controlled Clinical Trials*, **8** (4), 343–53.

Dickersin, K., Scherer R. and Lefebvre C. (1995) Identifying Relevant Studies for Systematic Reviews. In Chalmers, I. and Altman, D. G. (eds), *Systematic Reviews*, London, BMJ Publishing Group.

Dixon-Woods, M., Fitzpatrick, R. and Roberts, K. (2001) Including Qualitative Research in Systematic Reviews: opportunities and problems, *Journal of Evaluation in Clinical Practice*, **7** (2), 125–33.

Egger, M. et al. (2003) How Important are Comprehensive Literature Searches and the Assessment of Trial Quality in Systematic Reviews?: empirical study, *Health Technology Assessment*, **7** (1).

Evans, D. (2002) Database Searches for Qualitative Research, *Journal of the Medical Library Association*, **90** (3), 290–3.

Fry-Smith, A. and Gold, L. (2000) Finding the Evidence. In Burls, A. et al. (eds), *West Midlands Development and Evaluation Service Handbook*, Version 2.2. Birmingham, West Midlands Development and Evaluation Service.

Glanville, J. (2001) Identification of Research. In NHS Centre for Reviews and Dissemination, *Undertaking Systematic Reviews of Research on Effectiveness: CRD's guidance for those carrying out and commissioning reviews*, CRD Report 4, 2nd edn, York, NHS CRD.

Grant, M. J. (2000) *Development of an Optimal Search Strategy for Qualitative Research*

Methodologies. Presented at Qualitative Evidence-based Practice Conference, Coventry University, 15–17 May.

Grant, M. J. (2001) *Searching for Qualitative Research Studies on the MEDLINE Database*. Presented at *Qualitative Evidence-based Practice Conference*, Coventry University, 14–16 May.

Great Britain. Department of Health (1997) *The New NHS: modern, dependable*, London, Stationery Office.

Great Britain. Department of Health (1998a) *A First Class Service: quality in the new NHS*, London, Stationery Office.

Great Britain. Department of Health (1998b) *Research and Development: towards an evidence-base for health services, public health and social care*, London, Stationery Office.

Great Britain. Department of Health (2000a) *Research and Development for a First Class Service: R&D funding in the new NHS*, London, Stationery Office.

Great Britain. Department of Health (2000b) *The NHS Plan: a plan for investment, a plan for reform*, London, Stationery Office.

Harrison, J. (1997) Designing a Search Strategy to Identify and Retrieve Articles on Evidence-based Health Care Using MEDLINE, *Health Libraries Review*, **14** (1), 33–42.

Hawker, S. et al. (2002) Appraising the Evidence: reviewing disparate data systematically, *Qualitative Health Research*, **12** (9), 1284–99.

Haynes, R. B. et al. (1994) Developing Optimal Search Strategies for Detecting Clinically Sound Studies in MEDLINE, *Journal of the American Medical Informatics Association*, **1** (6), 447–58.

Health Technology Board for Scotland (HTBS) (2001) *Criteria and Process for Selection of Topics to Undergo Health Technology Assessment*, Glasgow, HTBS.

Health Technology Board for Scotland (2002a) *Guidance for Manufacturers on Submission of Evidence Relating to Clinical and Cost Effectiveness in Health Technology Assessments*, Glasgow, HTBS.

Health Technology Board for Scotland (2002b) *Guidance for Patients, Carer and Voluntary Organisations on Submissions of Evidence to Health Technology Assessments*, Glasgow, HTBS.

Health Technology Board for Scotland (2002c) *Guidance for Professional Organisations on Submissions of Evidence to Health Technology Assessments*, Glasgow, HTBS.

Helmer, D. et al. (2001) Evidence-based Practice: extending the search to find material for the systematic review, *Bulletin of the Medical Library Association*, **89** (4), 346–52.

Honest, H., Bachmann, L. M. and Khan, K. (2003) Electronic Searching of the Literature for Systematic Reviews of Screening and Diagnostic Tests for Preterm Birth, *European Journal of Obstetrics Gynaecology and Reproductive Biology*, **107** (1), 19–23.

INAHTA (2000) INAHTA: *International Network of Agencies for Health Technology Assessment: global networking for effective healthcare*, Stockholm, INAHTA.

Lefebvre, C. and Clarke, M. J. (2001) Identifying Randomised Trials. In Egger, M., Davey Smith, G. and Altman, D. G. (eds), *Systematic Reviews in Health Care: meta-analysis in context*, London, BMJ Publishing.

McKibbon, A. (1999) *PDQ Evidence-based Principles and Practice*, London, BC Decker Inc.

Mulrow, C. (1995) Rationale for Systematic Reviews. In Chalmers, I. and Altman, D. G. (eds), *Systematic Reviews*, London, BMJ Publishing.

Paisley, S. (2000) Filtering and Evaluating the Knowledge Base. In Booth, A. and Walton, G. (eds), *Managing Knowledge in Health Services*, London, Library Association Publishing.

Petticrew, M. (2001) Systematic Reviews from Astronomy to Zoology: myths and misconceptions, *British Medical Journal*, **322** (7278), 98–101.

Richardson, W. S. et al. (1995) The Well-built Clinical Question: a key to evidence-based decisions, *ACP Journal Club*, **123** (3), A12–A13.

Savoie, I. et al. (2003) Beyond MEDLINE: reducing bias through extended systematic review search, *International Journal of Technology Assessment in Health Care*, **19** (1), 168–78.

Schuerman, J. et al. (2002) The Campbell Collaboration, *Research on Social Work Practice*, **12** (2), 309–17.

Scottish Executive Health Department (2000) *Our National Health: a plan for action, a plan for change*, Edinburgh, Scottish Executive.

Scottish Executive Health Department (2003) *Partnership for Care: Scotland's health white paper*, Edinburgh, Scottish Executive.

Scottish Office (1997) *Designed to Care: renewing the National Health Service in Scotland, presented to Parliament by the Secretary of State for Scotland by command of Her Majesty*, December 1997, Edinburgh, Stationery Office.

Snowball, R. (2002) 'Find the Evidence': reflections on an information skills course for community-based clinical health-care staff at the Cairns Library, Oxford, *Health Information and Libraries Journal*, **19** (2), 109–12.

Song, F. et al. (2000) Publication and Related Bias, *Health Technology Assessment*, **4** (10).

Sutherland, S. E. (2001) Evidence-based Dentistry: Part IV, research design and levels of evidence, *Journal of the Canadian Dental Association*, **67** (7), 375–8.

Taylor, R. (2002) National Institute for Clinical Excellence (NICE): HTA rhyme or reason? *International Journal of Health Technology Assessment*, **18** (2), 166–70.

White, V. J. et al. (2001) A Statistical Approach to Designing Search Filters to Find Systematic Reviews: objectivity enhances accuracy, *Journal of Information Science*, **27** (6), 357–70.

Conclusion: new roles and new challenges

Graham Walton and Andrew Booth

Introduction

The health sector never remains static. New drugs are developed; new illnesses appear; and governments tinker with health-service delivery to meet their political agendas. The information needs of health consumers, health professionals and health students evolve and modify. As some library and information services no longer meet users' needs new services appear to meet emerging new demands. This chapter revisits those areas (health service, technologies, user needs, information-provider roles and consumer requirements) explored in a corresponding chapter in this book's companion volume (Booth and Walton, 2000) and proposes how these may develop. The chapter concludes with a prospective glance at the likely impact of evidence-based information practice on the domains covered by this book.

Health services

Health library and information services will have to demonstrate increasing flexibility in coping with pressures from the perpetually changing health service. The dire implications of failing to do this have been explored in the context of the higher education hybrid library service (Walton and Edwards, 2001). In the UK, the NHS has experienced 20 years of being reformed and restructured on what appears an annual basis (Harris and Wood, 1999). This is unlikely to cease so NHS librarians cannot anticipate any permanence with regard to structures, policies or direction. The creation of the NHS Library and Knowledge Development Network (LKDN) exemplifies such pressures. In 1999, regional health authorities were deconstructed and Workforce

Development Confederations were created. The LKDN was established to take on the work previously undertaken by the Regional Librarians Group. Already the LKDN itself is unclear about the way forward as Workforce Development Confederations have been aligned closely with Strategic Health Authorities.

The level of private funding going into health will likely increase, evidenced by more public–private partnerships. Governments cannot sustain the necessary level of new hospital building and maintenance without relying on financial alternatives to central taxation. The introduction of private financing into health requires libraries to demonstrate that they are an asset rather than a cost. The NHS LKDN is undertaking an impact study of the library in healthcare. Impact studies and cost-benefit analyses are vital to assist librarians in justifying their services. More evidence will be required as emphases are placed on monitoring and standards (NHS Library and Knowledge Development Network, 2003). Libraries will be increasingly expected to demonstrate the quality and value placed on services they deliver.

Health services will continue to move towards supporting 'good health' or 'wellness' rather than treating diseases. Increasing numbers of 'wellness centres' will be set up such as that established near Wolverhampton (Roche, 2000) where a multidisciplinary team has a 'holistic approach in treating mind, body and soul' and provides a range of alternative therapies. Libraries will be expected to provide access to knowledge bases around good health and alternative therapies.

The impact of an ageing population is inescapable. Andrews (2001) has explored what is required to ensure the health and well-being of growing proportions of older people during the opening decades of this new century. Many health services will have to modify and develop to accommodate increasing numbers of elderly users. Librarians will have to address human-resource issues as health and library workforces become older.

Technologies

Predicting those technologies that will significantly impact on healthcare is not straightforward. Within the library and information context, it is highly likely that the technology will demonstrate features of integration, personalization and portability. It will be fascinating to observe how world wide web technology influences library and information services and healthcare in general.

The past few years have witnessed major integration between technologies. Mobile phone users can now use their phone to take digital pictures, listen to MP3s and maintain an electronic diary. A networked personal computer can be used for similar functions. The possibilities and opportunities for 'library information' to become increasingly integrated with the electronic patient record

(EPR) lie within our grasp. Curry and Sawyer (1999) argue persuasively for the value of bringing together the disparate information that impacts and informs patient care. They question the benefits that will accrue if information is interfaced as opposed to integrated. The integration of the clinical librarian into the clinical team illustrates the possibilities where an EPR brings together different categories of information. Another rationale for integrating clinical information (patient information and reference information) is that it provides an effective tool to support evidence-based practice (Goncalves et al., 1999). Such integration provides real opportunities for the health librarian to work with clinicians and IMandT staff to increase access to their services.

In the 1960s, an advert for an alcoholic drink used the memorable slogan 'Any time, any place, anywhere'. This 'Martini culture' is even more evident 30 years later as people expect to be able to access services where they want them and when they want them. Within health, wireless technologies, personal digital assistants (PDA) and tablets can help to achieve this vision. The potential of these technologies for libraries is amusingly described by Williams (2003). Much uncertainty clouds the implications and potential for these developments and more clarity will emerge over the next few years. Projects are starting to explore how PDAs can be used in the clinical setting. Anderson, Hamilton and Oliver (2002) claim that the PDA can be used by the clinician for personal knowledge and time management, patient information, hospital information, clinical guidelines and drug prescription, research and audit and reference information. All these applications will require much further work if their potential is to be realized. The PDA also has a role within the domain of education and training of health professionals (Doran, 2003). Various education providers have started to experiment with the PDA to enable students to utilize more flexible learning.

World wide web technology has been used within a health context for ten years but it could be applied much more widely than it is currently. De Lusignan (2003) reviews the literature on the internet and the NHS and concludes that 'patients and clinicians use the Internet in inconsistent and suboptimal ways, but the lack of outcomes based studies hampers identification of ideal strategies'. Notwithstanding the considerable scope of the internet for creativity and experimentation its potential is hamstrung by this lack of research on its impact on health (Powell, Darvell and Gray, 2003). Health librarians must therefore seek to ensure that they continue at the centre of web-based developments. The paucity of research on the impact of the world wide web constrains the evidence-based practitioner roles explored later in this chapter.

User needs

Such changes in the wider world impact on the needs and expectations of library users as they evolve and respond to resultant demands. Only by having an in-depth understanding of their users will librarians ensure a close correspondence between users' needs and provision of library services. The past year has seen the potentially crucial concept of personalization start to emerge. This is the 'process of gathering user-information during interaction with the user, which is then used to deliver appropriate content and services, tailor-made to the user's needs' (Bonnet, 2001). This phenomenon was pioneered by the online bookshop, Amazon. Through patterns of use, it was able to develop services that respond proactively to individuals' likely future needs. Various world wide web search engines similarly offer increasing sophistication and extensive customization (Notess, 2001). Libraries are beginning to explore how more services can be customized to specific user needs. The rationale is to reduce information overload by allowing users to select as little or as much information as they need from their personal pages (Reade, 2001).

Personalization will likely provide a better service to users by anticipating their needs, thereby facilitating efficient interactions to satisfy both parties. It should help to build up a relationship which will encourage users to return for subsequent visits. Issues attached to such opportunities include user identification, differentiation and interaction (Hafner, Keating and Lin, 2000). As clinicians encounter customized services in other aspects of their lives, they will expect the same provision from their library services. Koutrika (2002) provides a fascinating projection of digital library services with personalized services at their centre.

Information-provider roles

Recent years have witnessed considerable changes that have impacted upon the information-provider role:

> In the last decade of the 20th century the role of the health librarian has altered remarkably from that of custodian of a relatively passive collection of printed materials to one of intermediary in the provision of access to the world's healthcare knowledge base.
> (Lancaster, 2000)

Indeed, the concept of information provision has itself been challenged. Just as consumer health has witnessed developments in 'self care', information provision has seen the popularity of 'end-user' approaches. No longer is the literature search the exclusive and jealously guarded province of the intermediary.

First CD-ROM searching and, even more so, direct access to the internet offer a wealth of information not previously envisaged (Marfleet and Kelly, 1999). Notable among developments is the universal availability of the PubMed MEDLINE database. Of comparable impact, however, is a plethora of 'core content' deals on a regional or national basis whereby, upon authentication of user status, health professionals are able to enjoy free searching of commercial databases (Hernando and Gibbens, 2003). Which librarian of the late 1980s and early 1990s could have envisaged national access to such evidence-based products as the Cochrane Library and Clinical Evidence?

At the same time great strides have been made in providing access to the content, not merely bibliographical details, of printed journals. The BMJ Publishing Group has been a high-profile opinion leader in pioneering this revolutionary model of information provision and the content of core electronic journals is now purchased as a national resource (Hernando and Gibbens, 2003). While wholesale packaging of content by electronic publishers has significantly improved the availability of certain journals it has been challenged by competing 'free-range' models as stimulated by the BioMed Central (Anonymous, 2002; Fletcher, 2002) and PubMed Central initiatives (Delamothe and Smith, 2001). While preprint services have yet to enjoy the same popularity within medicine as they undoubtedly experience within physics they reflect a broadened recognition that knowledge is a free-flowing commodity.

Ironically neither increased bibliographical control nor widespread availability of publications has undermined the credibility or importance of the local information provider. In fact developments in evidence-based healthcare in particular have had a profound effect:

> Librarians are no longer seen as just providing a support service. It's brought us centre stage, as evidence-based practice requires real expertise in handling information and knowledge. And it's focused attention on the skills that people need in order to formulate questions, locate, find, judge and appraise evidence.   (Chalmers, 2000)

Just as lawyers have faced do-it-yourself will-making and doctors have encountered over-the-counter medication, this challenge has increased awareness of the more transparent areas of professional practice while placing a premium on less accessible areas of expertise and experience. In contrast to the experience of the early pioneers of the LATCH programmes (Winning and Beverley, 2003), clinical librarians today find themselves not only providing information but also delivering training and specialist support (Marfleet and Kelly, 1999). This 'holding on while letting go' approach is fundamental to several information provider roles – for example, consumer health information providers who offer web access to self-care resources and yet also act as guardians and arbiters of quality.

A related development is the growth in specialist centres and, increasingly, specialist roles within those centres (Beverley, Booth and Bath, 2003). Whereas a decade ago specialist information resources for systematic reviews were located at one or two nationally supported centres (Glanville, 1994; Lefebvre, 1994) nowadays many university departments either possess or can negotiate access to dedicated searching expertise. Such a critical mass has led to the development of the National Institute for Clinical Excellence Information Specialists Group and its international counterpart, the HTAi Information Group (formerly the Specialist Interest Group for Information Retrieval within the International Society for Technology Assessment in Health Care).

While the impact of new information provider roles such as the primary-care knowledge manager, the clinical librarian and the information-skills trainer should not be underplayed it would be misleading to imply that new skills are concentrated exclusively in such roles. The NHS has witnessed a fundamental and pervasive broadening of its skills base and health librarians are by no means exempt from this trend. The library manager of today requires not only the technical and professional skills of their 1980s counterparts, enhanced to a significant degree, but also a variety of specialist skills in marketing, project management, evaluation and knowledge management, to name but a few. This extensive training agenda emphasizes the challenges faced, within our profession alone, by the NHS University as well as such targeted initiatives as the National electronic Library for Health's Librarian Development Programme (Fraser, 1999). Hence the Librarian Development Programme (Toth et al., 2000; Turner et al., 2002) aims to support librarians moving into new roles, focusing on:

- supporting the development of digital skills in health librarians
- providing opportunities for librarians to develop the skills and experience to take on knowledge management roles
- encouraging the development of evidence-based librarianship
- promoting an understanding of the processes involved in clinical decision making.

Consumer health developments

Similar technological and cultural drivers are at work within consumer health. Consumer health information services handle a wide range of health-related enquiries from patients and the public. Traditionally, such enquiries involve providing understandable information about health problems, healthcare processes, local services and self-help groups. Increasingly, however, funders and enquirers expect information providers to supply information about the effectiveness of healthcare interventions to inform participation in treatment decisions (Entwistle, Watt and Herring, 1996). This, in turn, requires consumer health information professionals to prove that information that they provide is effective. Self-care information is assumed to reduce the inappropriate utilization of medical care (Carney et al, 2000). In actuality the evidence is equivocal (Moore, LoGerfo and Inui, 1980; Kemper, 1982; Lorig et al., 1999; Piette et al., 2000). There is almost a complete dearth of evidence of the effects that widespread use of the internet may have on actual health outcomes (Bessell et al., 2002). As internet access increases (Brodie et al., 2000), and user-driven demand grows, the need for evidence about whether online health information causes more harm than good becomes increasingly urgent.

Consumer-health providers have increasingly harnessed the tremendous power of the internet to complement locally sensitive solutions (Jones, 2000). They thus refer consumer enquirers to appropriate sites on the internet as well as to their own locally packaged information materials. Consumer-health-information professionals have had to acquire the skills or resources required to provide good-quality research-based information about healthcare effectiveness in formats that are appropriate for their enquirers (Entwistle, Watt and Herring, 1996). They also need to be familiar with initiatives to develop quality and ethical standards for health information on the internet (Risk and Dzenowagis, 2001)

The 'resourceful patient' is now better informed than ever about their health, perhaps even more so than their doctor (Muir Gray, 2002), and increasingly expects doctors to make decisions *with* and not *for* them (Nash, Hicks and Dillner, 2003). Advocates for such an approach include the Institute of Medicine in the USA (Committee on Quality of Health Care in America, 2001) and the UK National Health Service (Great Britain. Department of Health, 2001). In addition, the distinction between information designed for consumers and information targeted at health professionals is increasingly blurred (Nash, Hicks and Dillner, 2003). The provision of free access to MEDLINE from 1997 onwards in effect made that considerable resource available to millions of health consumers worldwide. In launching the PubMed service Vice-President Gore said:

This development, by itself, may do more to reform and improve the quality of health care in the United States than anything else we have done in a long time.
(Modlin, 1997)

To illustrate this fact the Vice-President searched for references to a condition he had once suffered, comparing treatments recommended in the results with the treatment his doctor had offered. Recognizing that: 'Doctors and patients need the same evidence based information, served up in parallel, drawn from the same sources' (Nash, Hicks and Dillner, 2003), the BMJ Publishing Group has announced a website called BestTreatments (www.besttreatments.org), based on *Clinical Evidence* and categorizing treatments according to their effectiveness. An underlying principle is that 'users can drill down from the top level statements on effectiveness to the evidence summaries in *Clinical Evidence*, (Nash, Hicks and Dillner, 2003). Patients not only require such information to answer their cognitive need (to know more about their condition) and to support their affective need (to cope with the effects of the condition) but also use information in modifying their future behaviour (Sweetland, 2000).

While the National Library of Medicine continues to provide free access to MEDLINE, including its specially tailored consumer interface, MEDLINEplus (Booth, 2002a), consumer health information has become increasingly digitized and available on the internet (Wagner and Jimison, 2003). e-health is big business (DeNelsky, 2000) and major players, such as the American Medical Association and Kaiser Permanente, have invested heavily in proprietary consumer health information systems. Facilities available via the world wide web include everything from risk-assessment tools to interactive health advice through to news of latest medical developments.

Of course provision of increasing amounts of information to health consumers is not only a positive development. It may lead to worsening outcomes as a result of 'information overload' (Hibbard, Slovik and Jewett, 1997). Not to be underestimated is the considerable time and cognitive effort that searching, obtaining and processing such materials may involve (Fast, Vosburgh and Frisbee, 1989). While this is true of healthy individuals this is particularly the case for those who are ill and typically under time constraints and emotionally stressed, making it more difficult for them to understand what they have retrieved. This situation is aggravated by the variability, and indeed inaccuracy, of much patient-oriented information available via the internet (Jadad and Gagliardi, 1998). At worst, misinformation may put patients in danger, at best health professionals may spend much time refuting inaccurate statements (Welsh, 1998).

Two complementary characteristics are the diversity of applications for which consumers may access information and the variety of channels by which information providers might choose to deliver it. Consumers may access internet-based information to shape their treatment preferences and to select healthcare providers (Eysenbach and Diepgen, 1999). They may seek online consultations, support, self-management and screening tools, and buy medicines online (Bessell et al., 2002; Rose et al., 2002). Healthcare services may be delivered across national boundaries (Coiera, 1998) with direct-to-consumer marketing of pharmaceuticals (Menon et al., 2002) becoming a growing phenomenon. The multichannel approach is best illustrated by NHS Direct which has developed from three pilot call centres in 1998 to a fully multichannel service utilizing telephone call centres, the internet, touchscreen kiosks and digital interactive TV (Jenkins and Gann, 2002). Such varied approaches, aiming to reach as many different audiences as possible, are complemented by the increasing personalization of the service.

Finally, notwithstanding tremendous strides in relation to the content, delivery and indeed philosophy of consumer health information provision, major challenges remain to be overcome. Lancaster (2003) investigated 'demand for detailed [as opposed to basic] health information from public library users' and concludes that there remains low usage, difficulty in accessing information at the right level of difficulty, and a distinct knowledge gap.

Towards evidence-based information practice

This volume has made substantial reference to the published literature, albeit within a traditional context of overview. Increasingly the impact of evidence-based librarianship/information practice is being felt within the health information domain (Eldredge, 2000; Booth, 2002b). While efforts to produce a considerable body of evidence for our profession will inevitably require significant investment (Booth, 1998; Booth and Haines, 1998) a far more immediately realizable objective is the development of a profession of evidence-based information practitioners. Two conferences for teachers and developers of evidence-based healthcare, held in Sicily in 2001 and 2003, have identified six generic characteristics of an evidence-based practitioner (Hopayian and Hooper, 2003):

- constantly questioning
- sceptical of current practice
- listens to and values other people's perspectives
- aware of the validity and limitations of their own knowledge
- possesses a level of knowledge of evidence-based practice appropriate to their own situation
- continuously learning.

Such characteristics, developed within the context of the 'reflective practitioner' (Schon, 1983, 1987) and the 'learning organization' (Senge, 1993) can go a long way towards creating roles that not only respond to but also anticipate the future information needs of users, staff and commissioners alike:

Evidence-based practice is about best practice and reflective practice, where the process of planning, action, feedback and reflection contributes to the cyclic process of purposeful decision making and action, and renewal and development.

(Todd, 2003)

If health-information professionals are to manage and exploit knowledge for health services to the benefit of their users, and to further their own professional status, they will actively pursue current and rigorous information on the effectiveness and efficiency of information interventions:

Health librarians will need to engage with this culture, supporting the evolution of a research-based profession – in particular developing a better understanding of the information seeking behaviours of health professionals and engaging in regular horizon scanning in order to respond to the needs of library users. Essentially, health librarians will need to demonstrate in their own practice, the evidence-based approach that they advocate to others.   (Lancaster, 2000)

While this book and even more so its predecessor have focused on the information professional's role in supporting evidence-based practice it is to be hoped that future offerings, by ourselves and our contributors, will see an increased emphasis on initiating and developing evidence-based information practice.

References

Anderson, S. D., Hamilton, P. and Oliver, C. (2002) Personal Digital Assistants for Doctors, *Health Information on the Internet*, **27**, 4–6.

Andrews, G. R. (2001) Promoting Health and Function in an Ageing Population: care of older people, *British Medical Journal*, **322** (7288), 728–9.

Anonymous (2002) BioMed Central Offers Free Research Articles Online, *Medicine on the Net*, **8** (11), 8.

Bessell, T. L. et al. (2002) Do Internet Interventions for Consumers Cause More Harm than Good?: a systematic review, *Health Expectations*, **5** (1), 28–37.

Beverley, C. A., Booth, A. and Bath, P. A. (2003) The Role of the Information Specialist in the Systematic Review Process: a health information case study, *Health Information and Libraries Journal*, **20** (2), 65–74.

Bonnet, M. (2001) Personalization of Web Services: opportunities and challenges, *Ariadne*, **28**, www.ariadne.ac.uk/issue28/personalization/.

Booth, A. (1998) Testing the LORE of Research, *Library Association Record*, **100** (12), 654.

Booth, A. (2002a) MEDLINEplus: a golden gateway to health information resources, *Evidence Based Medicine*, **7**, 136, www.nlm.nih.gov/medlineplus.

Booth, A (2002b) From EBM to EBL: two steps forward or one step back?, *Med Ref Serv Q*, **21**, 51–64.

Booth, A. and Haines, M. (1998) Room for a Review?, *Library Association Record*, **100** (8), 411–12.

Booth, A. and Walton, G. (2000) Some Concluding Trends and Themes. In Booth, A. and Walton, G. (eds) *Managing Knowledge in Health Services*, London, Library Association Publishing.

Brodie M. et al. (2000) Health Information, the Internet, and the Digital Divide, *Health Affairs*, **19**, 255–65.

Carney, N. et al. (2000). *Assessment of Self-care Manuals*, Portland, OR, Oregon Health Sciences University.

Chalmers, F. (2000) NHS Librarians Take Centre Stage: profession at cutting edge of clinical support, *Guardian*, (9 November).

Coiera, E. (1998) Information Epidemics, and Immunity on the Internet, *British Medical Journal*, **317**, 1469–70.

Committee on Quality of Health Care in America, Institute of Medicine (2001) *Crossing the Quality Chasm*: a new health system for the 21st century, Washington DC, National Academy Press.

Curry, P. and Sawyer, M. (1999) Working with the Electronic Patient Record and Making It Work for Us: a case for data integration, *British Journal of Healthcare Computing*, **16** (3), 17–18, 20.

Delamothe, T. and Smith, R. (2001) PubMed Central: creating an Aladdin's cave of ideas: we have seen the future, and it works, *British Medical Journal*, **322** (7277), 1–2.

de Lusignan, S. (2003) The NHS and the Internet, *Journal of the Royal Society of Medicine*, **96** (10), 490–3.

DeNelsky, S. J. (2000) *The History of e-Health*. Paper presented at e-Health Connections. Health in the Digital Age, 7–9 May, Stanford University, CA.

Doran, B. (2003) Learning and Teaching, *Health Information and Libraries Journal*, **20** (2), 119–23.

Eldredge, J. D. (2000) Evidence-based Librarianship: an overview, *Bulletin of the Medical Library Association*, **88**, 289–302.

Entwistle, V. A,, Watt, I. S. and Herring, J. E. (1996) *Information about Health Care Effectiveness: readings for consumer health information providers*, London, King's Fund.

Eysenbach, G. and Diepgen, T. L. (1999) Patients Looking for Information on the Internet and Seeking Teleadvice: motivation, expectations, and misconceptions as expressed in e-mails sent to physicians, *Archives of Dermatology*, **135**, 151–6.

Fast, J., Vosburgh, R. E. and Frisbee, W. R. (1989) The Effects of Consumer Education on Consumer Search, *Journal of Consumer Affairs*, **23**, 65–90.

Fletcher, G. (2002) Averting the Crisis in Medical Publishing: open access journals, *Health Information on the Internet*, **30**, 6–7.

Fraser, V. (1999) Continuing Professional Development in the NHS: what is to be done?, *Health Libraries Review*, **16** (4), 268–70.

Glanville, J. (1994) Evidence-based Practice: the role of the NHS Centre for Reviews and Dissemination, *Health Libraries Review*, **11**, 243–51.

Goncalves, S. et al. (1999) Integration of all Information Sources in a Clinical Environment, *Health Informatics Journal*, **5** (4), 193–9.

Great Britain. Department of Health (2001) *The Expert Patient: a new approach to chronic disease management for the 21st century*, London, Department of Health.

Hafner, A. W., Keating, J. J. and Lin, Z.-Y. (2000) One to One Customization of Library Patron Relationships, *Journal of Library and Information Science*, **26** (2), 19–29.

Harris, S. and Wood, B. (1999) Large Scale Organisational and Managerial Change in the UK, 1968–1998: from blueprint to bright idea and 'manipulated emergence', *Public Administration*, **77**, 751–68.

Hernando, S. and Gibbens, S. (2003) Guest editorial. *Health Information and Libraries Journal*, **20** (3), 129–33.

Hibbard, J. H., Slovic, P. and Jewett, J. J. (1997) Informing Consumer Decisions in Health Care: implications from decision making research, *Milbank Quarterly*, **75**, 395–414.

Hopayian, K. and Hooper, L. (2003) *Steps Towards a Matrix for Levels and Methods of Assessment of the Evidence Based Practitioner*, Sign Posting the Future in EBHC: 2nd International Conference of Evidence-Based Health Care Teachers and Developers, Utveggio Castle, Palermo, Italy, 10–14 September, 2003.

Jadad, A. R. and Gagliardi, A. (1998) Rating Health Information on the Internet: navigating to knowledge or to Babel?, *JAMA*, **279**, 611–14.

Jenkins, P. and Gann, B. (2002) Developing NHS Direct as a Multichannel Information Service, *British Journal of Healthcare Computing and Information Management*, **19** (4), 20–1.

Jones, R. (2000) Developments in Consumer Health Informatics in the Next Decade. *Health Libraries Review*, **17** (1), 26–31.

Kemper, D. W. (1982) Self-care Education: impact on HMO costs, *Medical Care*, **20**, 710–18.

Koutrika, G. (2002) *A Personalised Perspective on Personalisation*, Personalisation and Digital Libraries Seminar, 18 October, http://library.open.ac.uk/aboutus/myolib/ seminar_presentations.htm.

Lancaster, J. (2000) Planning the Future by the Present: a personal view, *Health Libraries Review*, **17** (1), 2–6.

Lancaster, K. (2003) Patient Empowerment: how can the NHS help people take more responsibility for their own health?, *Library & Information Update*, 2 (3), 36–7.

Lefebvre, C. (1994) The Cochrane Collaboration: the role of the UK Cochrane Centre in identifying the evidence, *Health Libraries Review*, 11, 235–42.

Lorig, K. R. et al. (1999) Evidence Suggesting that a Chronic Disease Self-management Program can Improve Health Status while Reducing Hospitalization: a randomized trial, *Medical Care*, 37, 5–14.

Marfleet, J. and Kelly, C. (1999) Leading the Field: the role of the information professional in the next century, *Electronic Library*, 17 (6), 359–64.

Menon, A. M. et al. (2002) Trust in Online Prescription Drug Information among Internet Users: the impact on information search behavior after exposure to direct-to-consumer advertising, *Health Marketing Quarterly*, 20 (1), 17–35.

Modlin, M. (1997) Vice President Gore Launches Free MEDLINE, *NLM Newsline*, (March–August), 52, 2–4.

Moore, S. H., LoGerfo, J. and Inui, T. S. (1980) Effect of a Self-care Book on Physician Visits: a randomized trial, *JAMA*, 243, 2317–20.

Muir Gray, J. A. (2002) *The Resourceful Patient*, Oxford, eRosetta Press.

Nash, B., Hicks, C. and Dillner, L. (2003) Connecting Doctors, Patients, and the Evidence, *British Medical Journal*, 326, 674.

NHS Library and Knowledge Development Network (2003) *Quality and Statistics Working Group*, www.lkdn.nhs.uk/quality.htm.

Notess, G. R. (2001) Customization Options for Web Searching, *Online*, 25 (1), 55–6, 58.

Pictte, J. D. et al. (2000) Do Automated Calls with Nurse Follow-up Improve Self-care and Glycemic Control among Vulnerable Patients with Diabetes?, *American Journal of Medicine*, 108, 20–7.

Powell, J. A., Darvell, M. and Gray, J. A. M. (2003) The Doctor, the Patient and the World Wide Web: how the internet is changing healthcare, *Journal of the Royal Society of Medicine*, 96 (2), 74–6.

Reade, T. (2001) Unpacking the Trunk: customization and MyLibrary@NCState, *Computers in Libraries*, 21 (2), 30–4.

Risk, A. and Dzenowagis, J. (2001) Review of Internet Health Information Quality Initiatives, *Journal of Medical Internet Research*, 3 (4), e28.

Roche, K. (2000) UK's First 'Wellness Centre' Takes Preventive Action, *Nursing Times*, 96 (39), 44–5.

Rose, P. W. et al. (2002) Doctors' and Patients' Use of the Internet for Healthcare: a study from one general practice, *Health Information and Libraries Journal*, 19 (4), 233–5.

Schon, D. (1983) *The Reflective Practitioner: how professionals think in action*, New York, Basic Books.

Schon, D. (1987) *Educating the Reflective Practitioner: towards a new design for teaching and learning in the professions*, San Francisco, CA, Jossey Bass.

Senge, P. M. (1993) *The Fifth Discipline: the art and practice of the learning organization*, London, Random House.

Sweetland, J. (2000) Users' Perceptions of the Impact of Information Provided by a Consumer Health Information Service: an in-depth study of six users, *Health Libraries Review*, **17** (2), 77–82.

Todd, R. (2003) *Learning in the Information Age School: opportunities, outcomes and options*, International Association of School Librarianship (IASL) 2003 Annual Conference, Durban, South Africa, 7–11 July 2003.

Toth, B. et al. (2000) National electronic Library for Health: progress and prospects, *Health Libraries Review*, **17** (1), 46–50.

Turner, A. et al. (2002) A First Class Knowledge Service: developing the National electronic Library for Health, *Health Information and Libraries Journal*, **19** (3), 133–45.

Wagner, T. H. and Jimison, H. B. (2003) Computerized Health Information and the Demand for Medical Care, *Value in Health*, **6** (1), 29–39.

Walton, G. and Edwards, C. (2001) Flexibility in Higher Education Libraries: exploring the implications and producing a model of practice, *Journal of Librarianship and Information Science*, **33** (4), 199–208.

Welsh, S. (1998) A Guide to Consumer Health Information on the 'Net, *Free Pint*, (15 October), Issue 24, www.freepint.co.uk/issues/151098.htm.

Williams, J. (2003) Taming the Wireless Frontier: PDAs, tablets, and laptops at home on the range, *Computers in Libraries*, **23** (3), 10–16.

Winning, M. A. and Beverley, C. A. (2003) Clinical Librarianship: a systematic review of the literature, *Health Information Libraries Journal*, **20** (Suppl. 1), 10–21.

Index